A Garden Catechism

A Garden Catechism

100 Plants in Christian Tradition and How to Grow Them

Margaret Rose Realy, Obl OSB

Illustrated by Mary Sprague • Foreword by Sherry Weddell

Our Sunday Visitor
Huntington, Indiana

Nihil Obstat
Msgr. Michael Heintz, Ph.D.
Censor Librorum

Imprimatur
✠ Kevin C. Rhoades
Bishop of Fort Wayne-South Bend
November 8, 2021

The *Nihil Obstat* and *Imprimatur* are official declarations that a book is free from doctrinal or moral error. It is not implied that those who have granted the *Nihil Obstat* and *Imprimatur* agree with the contents, opinions, or statements expressed.

28 27 26 25 24 23 2 3 4 5 6 7 8 9

Our Sunday Visitor Publishing Division
Our Sunday Visitor, Inc.
200 Noll Plaza
Huntington, IN 46750
1-800-348-2440

ISBN: 978-1-68192-556-1 (Inventory No. T2437)
1. GARDENING—General.
2. REFERENCE—Personal & Practical Guides.
3. RELIGION—Christianity—Catholic.

eISBN: 978-1-68192-557-8
LCCN: 2021952983

Cover and interior design: Amanda Falk
Cover and interior art: Mary Sprague

Printed in the United States of America

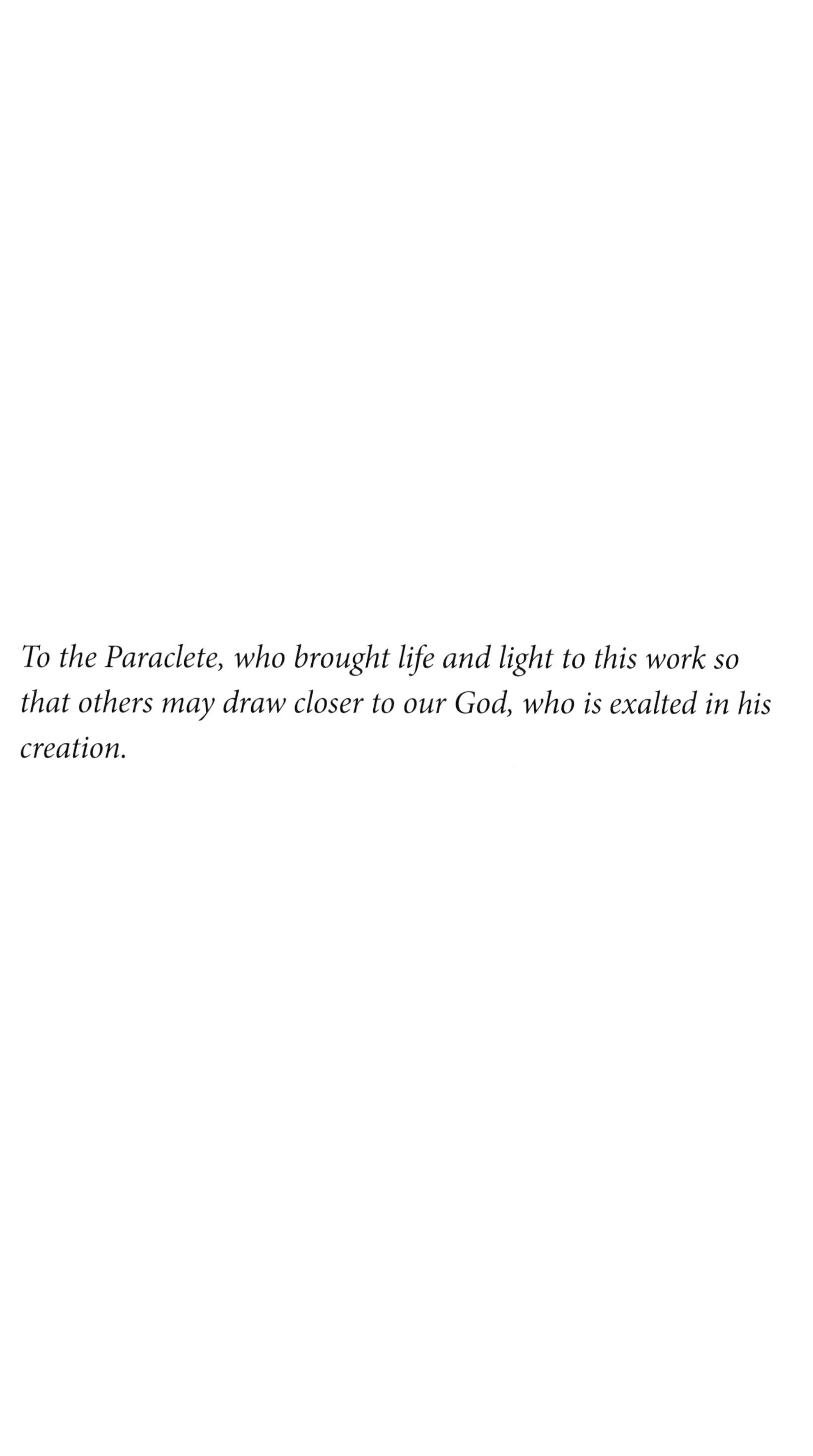

To the Paraclete, who brought life and light to this work so that others may draw closer to our God, who is exalted in his creation.

Once more I will set forth my theme
to shine like the moon in its fullness!
Listen to me, my faithful children: open up your petals,
like roses planted near running waters;
Send up the sweet odor of incense,
break forth in blossoms like the lily.
Raise your voices in a chorus of praise;
bless the Lord for all his works!
Proclaim the greatness of his name,
loudly sing his praises,
With music on the harp and all stringed instruments;
sing out with joy as you proclaim:
The works of God are all of them good;
he supplies for every need in its own time.

— Sirach 39:12–16

Contents

Foreword

Stop me if you've heard this before: Everything I know about gardening, I learned the hard way.

Years ago, I moved to Colorado Springs and bought a heavily discounted one-third-acre fixer-upper bordering a neighborhood park, with a wonderful view of the Rockies — 6,700 feet high and dry. My property was filled with potential and dead lawn, yucca, and railroad ties, but I dreamed of somehow making it an enchanted place. After watering for a year and producing a harvest of giant Scotch thistles, I brought in a savvy landscape designer. She took one look and summed up my situation with brisk precision: "There's nothing here to save." When I asked her how long it would take for a new garden to reach maturity, she answered: "Eight years."

So it began. I took her design plan and double-dug flower beds, hauled in good soil, planted, fertilized, and watered. I pruned and mulched, and replanted when things failed. I bribed male relatives, friends, and seminarians to tackle some of the toughest tasks — like the paths, stone wall, and pondless waterfall — and hired skilled help when I could afford it. Together, the garden and I survived blizzards and hail bombs. Eight years, fourteen water-wise trees, sixty-five hardy shrubs, and hundreds of tough-as-nails perennials later, I found out that my landscape designer was right. A lush, green, and undaunted garden with a view of Pikes Peak now completely fills what was once the neighborhood eyesore.

My garden has a profound, ever fresh spiritual meaning for me personally and even for my work. When I speak, I often use before-and-after pictures of the garden to illustrate the parable of the sower and our mission of evangelization. It is a living year-round testimony to the grace of God at work in redemption that is available to all of us in and through Jesus Christ, bringing life and beauty out of our individual and communal brokenness. My garden is also a place from which I pray for (and sometimes chat with) all the locals walking their dogs or their babies in strollers, as well as for the larger community in which we all live.

So you will understand when I admit that while I was reading Margaret Rose Realy's *A Garden Catechism*, I kept wishing I'd had access to her wisdom when I was creating my garden! Margaret is an Advanced Master Gardener, and her mastery of the practical art of designing and planting a new garden is evident throughout! I kept stopping as I read to take notes and look up recommended flowers that I had once considered but have not yet planted.

Margaret writes in her preface that when she rededicated her life to God as an adult, she wondered how she could evangelize, as she was "only a gardener and a supplicant." What a wonderful question, to which her book is a uniquely valuable answer! *A Garden Catechism* is a one-of-a-kind guide to envisioning and deliberately creating gardens of prayer and healing that can touch many people, and that are profoundly rooted in our Catholic faith and horticultural history. I have quite a collection of gardening books myself and have never come across anything like it.

And so timely. I was fascinated recently to learn that the Pew Forum found that there are huge numbers of Americans who reject conventional Christian faith in God, but find a great deal of spiritual meaning and fulfillment from being outdoors and experiencing nature.[1] The eleven-thousand-member community of Catholics who talk evangelization twenty-four seven in the Forming Intentional Disciples Forum on Facebook have discussed how the surprising spiritual impact of nature — including access to natural beauty in a garden — can be another bridge to faith in Jesus Christ for the unchurched and unbelieving, which most of us have never explored before!

May many thousands of gardeners be as blessed and inspired as I have been by Margaret's brilliant work of love in *A Garden Catechism*.

Sherry Weddell

Author's Preface

"The earth shall be filled with knowledge of the Lord."

— Isaiah 11:9

When I chose to begin an eremitic life — one of solitude and prayer — I planned to make a rededication to the Church as an adult, since my confirmation as a teenager had been cultural rather than personal. While I was on a silent retreat at St. Francis Retreat Center in DeWitt, Michigan, my spiritual director, Fr. Larry Delaney, encouraged me as part of that rededication to speak an oblation of service to God's people. I wondered how I could evangelize; I was only a gardener and a supplicant.

While I was on that retreat, contemplating what Father had asked and walking about the ninety-five-acre property, the Holy Spirit touched my heart. The beautiful land was all woodlands and expanses of groomed lawn. It offered an opportunity for outdoor spaces where retreatants could sit and quiet their mind, allowing the inflow of grace.

With that thought, and a few months after my rededication to the Church, I began my ministry of creating gardens of prayer and memorial.

It all started simply enough. I met once a week with Tim Simon, the groundskeeper. From there I would proceed onto the property and into solitude and silence, recalling a line from a poem, "God, I can push the grass apart / And lay my finger on Thy Heart."[1]

Kneeling on the soil, laboring in a garden, can be a deep and unifying prayer with the Creator. That work became a comforting and familiar movement in my spiritual life. During those first two summers working the grounds, I began to imagine gardens dedicated to the Holy Spirit, the Blessed Mother, Saint Francis — it was, after all, the St. Francis Retreat Center — to angels, and saints.

I wrote a proposal for a garden society, like an altar society, and presented it to Father Delaney. Little did I know how that simple proposal would affect my calling to silence and prayer! Through the years, the Holy Spirit touched the hearts and hands of many gardeners as together we created gardens and woodland paths.

Flowers had been part of my childhood. The family business was greenhouses; I loved being beside my maternal grandmother as she worked in her yard; I began college with classes in horticulture. Plants and nature defined who I was and brought me the greatest happiness. In time, I brought that love of all things green into my designs for the outdoor prayer spaces.

What I had not anticipated, besides coordinating a group of boisterous and jolly gardeners, was the curiosity from retreatants about the new outdoor spaces. The questions were not so much about landscape design and horticulture, but about *why* had I chosen this plant or that for the gardens.

I soon realized there was a need to instruct the faithful in how to connect with the Creator through his creation and historiated Christian symbolism. A retreat I offered, titled "God in the Garden," resulted in my first book, *A Garden of Visible Prayer.* The material focused on how to create a personal sacred space outdoors, one step at a time. Some of that material is included here.

That retreat and book guided folks to determine what garden elements led them into contemplation and prayer.

It was not enough.

The questions continued: "Why did you choose *this* shrub?" "Why *those* flowers for *that* garden?" "Why is (whatever plant) symbolic of (whatever saint)?" The historiated aspects of paintings, architecture, and manuscripts all offer a visual narrative of the symbolisms of nature, but these were new to nearly all of the retreatants. They had questions — many questions. I found myself discussing how the plants are represented in our Christian history, and debunking the negative pagan symbolisms of plants.

This book, dear reader, addresses those questions. It is an array of plants, from herbs to trees, associated through art, the doctrine of signatures, history, or pious legends with the sentiments of Christian Faith.

A *catechism* is a way of teaching the Faith that strengthens the bonds of unity in our Church and, as the *Catechism of the Catholic Church* says, "enlivens the faith of the People of God."[2] This book, I pray, will help you create a garden that is more than just a landscape. You will receive the tools to create a faith-based garden that symbolically expresses the teachings of Sacred Scripture and the *Catechism* in a fresh new light, matched to your own spiritual life in a way that draws you into a deeper personal relationship with Our Lord.

The array of regionally based and culturally significant plants and symbolisms are more diverse than what could be included in this single volume. I've gathered plants with the broadest range of application in a garden that are familiar representations in Christian art and architecture, referred to in metaphors and parables, or mentioned in folklore through traditions and fanciful tales.

The material is also intended, like my previous book *A Catholic Gardener's Spiritual Almanac*, to offset and debunk neopagan notions of ritualistic plant uses, and reestablish Christian plant symbolism.

While studying how to develop gardens of visual prayer, you will be drawn deeper into our faith. Whether you choose to craft a themed garden — such as Stations of the Cross, divine mercy, Bible, or Marian — you will learn the stories behind the plants you choose, and be able to share that symbolism with the friends, family, and children who visit your garden.

Don't let the ascribed symbolism limit your application of a plant for your garden. Like a word in *Lectio Divina*, a plant may speak to you in a unique way and find a place in your heart beyond what is written here. For me to say to you "here is how you should meditate within your garden" seems condescending; what I hope is to offer a direction, and you will find *your* way to focus and pray within nature.

In nature, we see an earth embroidered with prayer. We can see how God has organized his creation, and understand it in such a way as to continue our mission of prayer and stewardship. The Bible teaches us of God's ways as it reaches through thousands of springtimes, from Eden to Gethsemane and through the eschaton. Throughout Holy Scripture, farmlands, fields, and gardens are rich in metaphor and symbol, through which our faith is developed.

We as gardeners can further this awareness of our God, not only personally through our experience of *ora et labora* — to pray within our work — but also as a means of evangelization. We can share with others the stories and symbolisms of the plants we've chosen. In the simplicity of the daily and ordinary, we offer a gentle and loving invitation to be opened to the Holy Spirit — who will take it from there.

Spiritually dedicated gardens are those that attend to the interior need of our heart, mind, and soul, offering a place where both people and plants can grow. They are places where we allow our spirit such openness to our God that our interior landscape is rejuvenated.

In creating gardens of prayer, we not only draw closer to the Creator through his creation, but we can also express our Christian faith symbolically, and follow many a pope's lead to draw closer to the environment in order to act responsibly toward it. We all agree that we will not protect that which we do not cherish, and rhetoric alone will not change a person's life, whereas experience often does.[3] And the experience of a garden opens us in a way few other experiences can.

As you look to a faith-filled garden as a way to draw closer to Our Lord, remember the quote about the interior garden from St. Teresa of Ávila: "A beginner must think of herself as one setting out to make a garden in which her Beloved Lord is to take his delight."[4]

Let us begin!

Getting Started

"The family needs a home, a fit environment in which to develop its proper relationships. For the human family, this home is the earth, *the environment that God the Creator has given us to inhabit with creativity and responsibility."*

— Pope Benedict XVI, World Day of Peace, 2008

As you read about the Christian symbolism of the one hundred plants listed here, designate those that touch your heart. This book is meant to be worked through, written in, dog-eared, and smudged with the soil on your hands. Don't be afraid to thoroughly make this book a personal statement of your endeavors — press flowers between its pages, attach plant tags or garden pictures. You can also create a garden journal to keep track of your garden's development and your spiritual growth.

This book presents vintage-style botanical illustrations of each plant, with easy-to-understand culture information for growing it in your garden. The four plant sections — Flowers, Herbs and Edibles, Grasses and More, and Trees and Shrubs — introduce you to the faith-filled symbolisms of each plant within our Church's history. You can select just one or two plants to add to an existing landscape, such as a tree or a group of shrub roses to surround a grotto, or you can develop a completely new garden with a dedicated theme.

You can create a white garden dedicated to the Holy Spirit, or a monochromatic garden in reds for the Sacred and Immaculate Hearts. A path or circle for a home Stations of the Cross can be accomplished not only with designated plants, but also by making stepping stones for each Station (see An Introduction to Prayer Gardens). There is an abundance of possible plants for a Bible, Marian, or Rosary garden.

The plant entries are sorted by their most common name, and included with each is its symbolism in Christianity, and the culture information on how to grow a suitable variety or cultivar that coincides with the historical species.

Catechetical information includes how the plant connects to our faith and the story behind its moniker or use in art. Horticultural information — a refresher for those with some gardening experience and easy enough for the beginner — will address:

1. The characteristics of the plant (ground cover, size in imperial/metric, flowering season, etc.)
2. Habitat for growing the plant (light, water, soil, Hardiness Zone, etc.)
3. Landscaping attributes such as fragrance, deer resistance, seasonal color, or pollinator attractant

You will find at the side of each entry a quick visual key of symbols, one set for prayer gardens and another for landscape and culture. With this you can, for example, quickly flip through the pages looking for the little blue book that represents the Bible, and find the plants that will work best for this theme in a shady location or on a sunny hillside. (Look at the end of this section for a key to each of the symbols.) In the back of the book you will also find a chart of all the plants neatly organized by their prayer garden and culture attributes (p.288–305).

The Basics of Floriography

The symbolisms and meanings I have gathered here include a variety of moral and religious themes, sentimentalities, and legends. Plants carry different meanings to the writer and poet, to the horticulturalist and herbalist, or to the religious. The interpretation may also vary if the focus is on spiritual versus temporal concerns.

Meanings of plants and their usage can be found as early as the iconography in Egyptian tombs. The doctrine of signatures also applied particular attributes to plants; "In the 1st Century AD, the Greek physician and author of *Materia Medica*, Pedanius Dioscorides, described medicinal plants according to a divine intention. His belief was that God marked objects with signs, or 'signatures,' of their purpose. This notion of divine design persisted as a central aspect of medical doctrine throughout the middle ages."[1]

In a relatively illiterate medieval society, messages were often conveyed by images; in illustrated illuminated prayer books and manuscripts, as well as church decorations in stone or paint, flora and fauna frequently conveyed information as well as beauty. The Renaissance artists used plants in their work in much the same way, as a language to tell a story.

Floriography, the language of flowers, was developing as early as the seventeenth century in Turkey; the Victorian era then sentimentalized much of the symbolism.

Ultimately, there was and is no set dictionary of the sentimentality of plant meanings and symbolisms;[2] but the most authoritative perspective, which I have relied on here, comes from art history throughout Christianity. A single plant often has various, though similar and sometimes conflicting, meanings ascribed to it. Don't overthink it. Focus on the plants that you enjoy and are drawn to, and let yourself delight in their colorful stories and histories.

HOW TO BEGIN

To start the journey of a dedicated outdoor prayer space, begin by establishing what elements are important to you. If you have decided to create a Rosary garden, or maybe a Stations of the Cross garden, it is as simple as laying out the theme in the landscape and plugging in some of the plants listed in this book suited to your region.

I anticipate that some of you who sincerely want a prayer garden are possibly overwhelmed reading about all the different plants in this book, and wondering where to even start! In the paragraphs that follow is a simple guide on how to begin. For those of you wanting to personalize a prayer garden, jump to An Introduction to Prayer Gardens, at the back of the book (p. 276) and do the written work in the Development of Intent section first. There you will learn what spiritual elements are important to you, and how to apply this knowledge in a personal or traditionally Catholic-themed prayer garden.

As for your black thumb? Take heart: There is also a section on Gardening Basics (p. 231); though not exhaustive about horticulture, it is extensive enough for the new gardener to lay a solid foundation on which to grow. Also included is a section on Supplemental Catholicism (p. 259) which includes some essential basics such as liturgical and Rosary garden colors, how to create a shrine, traditional daily and monthly dedications, and more.

THE THREE Ds OF CREATING A GARDEN

A simplified way to begin creating a prayer garden is with the three Ds:

1. **Discern**
    a. the environment of your existing or new garden, and
    b. what elements lead you into a prayerful state.
2. **Design** your space based on what you've discerned.
3. **Develop** the space.

Discerning Environment

Begin by discerning the environment for its location and growing conditions. Walk around the property and look for a small space that offers some privacy. Keep in mind that you will want to sit in the shade — this can be from trees or buildings, or created with an arbor, shade sail, or patio umbrella.

You may already have a section of garden that needs only the addition of spiritual elements — statues, icons, and such — and a few symbolic plants. If not, look for less-visited areas beside structures, or at the edge of a woodlot or open range. Keep in mind that your journey to the area will allow you to shift gears from your daily demands to a prayerful retreat.

Once you have determined the area for your prayer garden, evaluate its growing conditions. You'll need to know what Hardiness Zone you live in (there are maps for North America, Europe, and Australia). Determine the type of soil, ease of watering, exposure to wind, and the amount of sunlight or shade. There is a saying among gardeners: right plant, right place. Follow this rule always! The environment will guide you in successful plant selection for the next stage of your discernment process: choosing vegetation that holds personal meaning and leads you into a sense of prayerfulness. Again, the chapter on Development of Intent will assist you in selecting ornamental elements, colors, and a focal point (which is often a Christian component.)

Design

The next phase is design, and you don't have to be a landscape architect to create a beautiful garden space. Follow the three-by-three rule: three heights, three textures, three colors. During the process keep in mind the four seasons: forms and shapes in winter, flowering and budding in spring, the succession of blooms in summer, and the colors of autumn.

To lessen the chance of becoming overwhelmed in this step, focus on one group of threes at a time.

Start with heights. This seems intuitive, but bears reminding: You want the shortest plants in the front nearest you, mid-height plants behind those, and tallest ones in the center or at the back of your viewing area. Read the plant tag for mature size. Too often a sweet little shrub in a pot is a bully in the garden! The creamy pastel and pink dappled willow, for instance, grows 2–3′ / 61–91 cm high and nearly as wide per year until it matures at 10–12′ / 3–3.7 m — it makes a beautifully large and dense hedge to enclose a garden area.

When considering textures, *fine* is thread-like and up to the width of a finger, as in grasses; *medium* is an average of one to two fingers wide; and *broad* leaves are the greatest in width. Keep in mind that leaves have textures and can be puckered, coarse, or smooth and shiny. Degree of difference and visual diversity in textures make for an interesting garden area.

For color selection, have a color wheel at hand, and recall what harmonious, monochromatic, and complementary mean — see the section on Color

Theory (p. 280) for a refresher. Early in the discerning process, you probably chose a color that had relevance for your theme. Locate that color on the wheel and then decide on the other colors using a color theory combination. Remember that greens are diverse in color too, and different shades of greens — such as variegated, blue-green, or chartreuse — can be strikingly beautiful in their simplicity.

Deeper color tones should be placed to the front and brighter tones towards the back. This isn't a hard and fast rule, but if you are working with a small space, brighter colors draw the eye up and out, making the space feel larger.

The last step in the design process is framing the garden space. If the location is beside a structure, a sense of enclosure may already exist. Otherwise, to enhance a sense of separateness, use a low fence or an arbor, a line of tall narrow shrubs, or even tall ornamental grasses. To divide off a portion of a porch or large deck, use a line of identical containers with coordinating plants.

Development

The last of the three Ds is development: planning out installation of the plants you've selected. Draw a rough outline of the garden space — see Creating a Base Map in Gardening Basics (p. 234) — and try not to get obsessed about accuracy-to-the-inch.

Start with where you will enter or sit in the garden, and decide where you will place the religious focal element you chose. This could be a cross, statue, or shrine.

Now draw where you want the plants you've selected to be placed using a coding system designating each plant — such as letters or colored shapes like triangles and squares. Be sure to check your notes for the plants' mature size and ideal color placement. (Gardening Basics includes a formula for calculating the number of plants for your space on page 249.)

After you've purchased the plants, head outdoors and begin the installation of your prayer garden. Follow the layout you created as you place your focal element and plants in their designated spots. You will find some plants will need to be moved to get a visually appealing space. Now and then sit where you will pray and step back to look at your placement — rearrange as needed, walk away, come back, and sit and pray again. Look at your arrangement, imagine the plants matured, and make adjustments as needed.

You're now ready to begin planting. Work from one side to the other, from back to front, planting your way around the garden. Ask Our Lord to help you grow in faith, pray to the Holy Spirit to plant seeds in your soul so that you may be fruitful, and petition the saints to help guide you along the path to holiness.

Always include a second chair in your prayer garden in case someone joins you, and to help you imagine that Jesus, Mother Mary, or a saint is sitting with you as you pray.

Let us continue to draw closer to Our Lord and his Church, and draw others into desiring to be closer to all that is holy, through the gentle revelations of creation.

PRAYER GARDEN SYMBOL KEY

 Jesus, Sacred Heart, Divine Mercy, Stations of the Cross

 Holy Spirit, Fruits of the Spirit, Virtues

 Marian, Immaculate Heart, Rosary

 Bible

 Saints, Saint Joseph

 Angels

LANDSCAPE SYMBOL KEY

 Pollinator attractant

 Wildlife desirable

 Deer resistant

 Cut flowers

 Fragrant

 Edible fruit

 Autumn interest

 Part shade

 Full shade

 Bog garden

 Drought tolerant

 Clay tolerant

 Black walnut tolerant

Flowers

Anemone

Anemone coronaria

CHRISTIAN REFERENCE

The *Anemone coronaria* is one of the Middle East's most striking flowers. It is among the flowers described as "the lilies of the field" in the Bible (see Mt 6:28–30; Lk 12:27). The anemone grows in such abundance in the Holy Land that in the spring, the ground in some locations is carpeted for weeks by a mass of scarlet.

This flower caused quite a stir when a twelfth-century Bishop of Pisa ordered earth from the Holy Land to be spread on the city's Camposanto ("holy ground," or cemetery). The following Easter, the whole city was astonished to see a miraculous carpet of red anemones appear, the legendary blood-red significant of the passion.[1]

Anemone coronaria 'Hollandia'

The anemone's association with death comes not only from Christ's passion, but also because of its ephemeral nature. The naturalizing red species goes dormant shortly after it flowers, and for this reason is rarely used in domestic gardens. Other more suitable red varieties listed below are Harmony Double Scarlet, The Governor, and Hollandia. Most anemones make excellent cut flowers for the home or altar, with some blooms lasting two to three weeks.

The genus name *Anemone* is Greek for wind — the wind was thought to help open the new buds and pull away dead petals. The species name comes from the Greek word *coronaria* indicating its use during festivals, and for its central crown-like structure of anthers and pistils.

In its native environment, this wildflower grown in full sun is drought tolerant, and "A single anemone flower blooms for more than a week. During the course of bloom the flower gradually grows in size and its stem further elongates; additionally the flower … is constantly facing the sun."[2]

Following the sun is called heliotropism, and the action of folding together when sunlight is low is termed nyctinasty. The genus *Anemone* exhibits both movements. Because of its sensitivity to light, it was considered a predictor of an approaching rainstorm.

Anemone coronaria is the national flower of the state of Israel and grows wild over most countries in the Middle East.

Symbolism:
- grief
- death
- Christ's passion

Prayer Garden Theme:
- Sacred Heart
- Stations of the Cross
- Bible
- saints

CULTURE

The Hardiness Zones of anemones are cultivar specific. The plant requires full sun to light afternoon shade, and average watering during its growing season; it tolerates drought once dormant. Soil is average and needs to be well drained. Size and bloom period is cultivar specific; size averages 6–10″ / 15–25 cm spread by 8–24″ / 20–61 cm height, and flowering can begin from early to late spring and continue for weeks.

The garden varieties of *Anemone coronaria* cultivars are planted in spring in colder climates, with some being suitable for open woodland gardens.

Soak anemone tubers in water for twelve hours the night before planting. Because the tubers can be small ellipsoids and hard to tell top from bottom, set them on their sides when planting.

***Anemone coronaria* 'St. Brigid'** was developed in Ireland in the early nineteenth century and is a colorful mix of double, slightly ruffled blooms in red, purple, magenta, and white that open in late spring. It is hardy in Zones 7–10, requires full sun, and prefers light afternoon shade. Water regularly during blooming period and run dry during dormancy. It needs well-drained soil.

There are many beautiful anemones to choose from. Listed here are the red cultivars, in keeping with the theme of the passion of Christ:

***Anemone coronaria* 'Harmony Double Scarlet'**: Zones 5–9, part sun preferring afternoon shade, average well-drained, evenly moist soil, 6″ / 15 cm spread by 8–10″ / 20–25 cm height, spring blooming.

***Anemone coronaria* 'The Governor'**: Zones 7–10, full sun, average watering, well-drained soil, 6–9″ / 15–23 cm spread by 8–12″ / 20–30 cm height, blooms for up to four weeks mid- to late spring.

***Anemone coronaria* 'Hollandia'**: Zones 7–10, full sun preferring afternoon shade in warmer climates, average watering, well-drained soil, 6–9″ / 15–23 cm spread by 10–24″ / 25–61 cm height, excellent cut flower, blooms mid- to late spring.

Begonia, Angel Wing

Begonia* spp., *Begonia coccinea

CHRISTIAN REFERENCE

Begoniaceae is a large family of flowering plants having, at the time of this writing, around 1,800 species and at least ten thousand cultivars, some of which are used medicinally or culinarily.

Begonia coccinea

The begonia was discovered by explorer and botanist-monk Charles Plumier during expeditions to the New World in the seventeenth century. Because of the difficulty in bringing specimens back to Europe, Plumier recorded the details and instead brought drawings of plants previously unknown to Europeans. The first begonias didn't arrive in Europe until the mid- to late eighteenth century.[3]

The religious symbolism of the red-flowering begonia as the Sacred Heart of Jesus, or pink-flowering as the Immaculate Heart of Mary, was ascribed because of its blooms — specific to the fibrous root species. Buds and portions of the opened flower are shaped like a heart, and the pendant-clustered red cluster of flowers appears to be dripping blood. The four petals that make up the flower recall the cross, and the gold stamens the crown. In Spanish the red begonia is called *corazon-de-jesus*.

There are several cultivars suitable for prayer gardens and for indoor prayer spaces. You only need to select those you find endearing … notice I didn't say just one!

The angel wing begonia, *Begonia coccinea*, is named for the shape and arrangement of its leaves. A fibrous root begonia, it is considered a cane type; this plant has relatively straight and brittle stems that arch slightly. It is popular for its beautiful leaves and prolific flowers that bloom throughout the year.

The starleaf begonia, *Begonia heracleifolia*, is also known as Mary's Fringe or Star of Mary. A moisture-loving plant with rhizomatous roots, it is grown for its interesting asymmetrical palmate (star-shaped) leaves. The flower has the familiar heart shape as a bud, opening with only two petals.

In a Rosary garden, plant the begonia at the Second Joyful Mystery, The Visitation.* Here reflect on the heart of Mary, her nature of charity.

*See Supplemental Catholicism (p. 259) for a list of the mysteries of the Rosary, as well as the Stations of the Cross, for easy reference.

Symbolism:
- Sacred Heart of Jesus
- Immaculate Heart of Mary
- enduring love

Prayer Garden Theme:
- Stations of the Cross
- divine mercy
- Marian
- Rosary
- angels

For the Stations of the Cross garden, this flower is appropriate at most any station, though the significance of the Blood of Christ would be represented best at the Eleventh or Twelfth Station, or at the Thirteenth Station, Jesus' Body Is Taken Down from the Cross, planting a red for Jesus and a pink for Mary.

CULTURE

The Angel Wing begonia, *Begonia coccinea*, is a tender annual, hardy in Zones 9–11, growing best in bright indirect sun (part shade). It will tolerate full shade, but will become leggier and produce fewer blooms. Watering needs are average — I've not found it to be drought tolerant as some references indicate. Grow in rich, evenly moist, and well-drained soil.

Size is cultivar specific. In general, this begonia will grow 18–24″ / 46–61 cm spread by 12–24″ / 30–61 cm height, with many cultivars having arching stems. The pendulant clusters of terminal flowers will bloom all season, and in the right indoor conditions will bloom continually with regular feeding.

Bleeding Heart

***Lamprocapnos spectabilis* cvs. (formerly *Dicentra spectabilis*)**

CHRISTIAN REFERENCE

Here is another plant indicative of the Sacred and Immaculate Hearts: *Lamprocapnos spectabilis*, bleeding heart.

The stories associated with this plant vary widely among cultures; all have the same connection to the flower shape — a heart — and love. Some legends are of tragedy, others fairy tales, and most prominent among western culture is the sense of unconditional love and compassion.

Among Catholics, this unconditional love and compassion for the sufferings of others — a connection that goes beyond death — is found most vividly in the devotion to the Sacred Heart of Jesus. The month of June is dedicated to his Sacred Heart and is about God's love for us. Love is the only gift we can give to God who needs nothing, and it's the only gift he desires from our own hearts.

Here is a sweet poem from a prayer card devoted to the Sacred Heart of Jesus:

When your dreams but disintegrate,
Slipping through your hands as a sieve,
Let me be the one to hold you,
Let me be the one to give.
When your heart is dark
And you've nothing left to say,
Let me be the one to guide you,
Let me light your way.
When you feel your life drifting,
Your days short of time,
No longer must you weary,

Lamprocapnos spectabilis

Gently lay your bleeding heart
next to mine.[4]

This spring-flowering plant is an excellent choice for a wide range of liturgical gardens.

Use a red bleeding heart at the Thirteenth Station of the Cross, Jesus' Body Is Taken Down from the Cross. The red and white of the heart-shaped flower remind us of the mixture of blood and water from Our Lord's pierced side.

A pink bleeding heart is symbolic of Mary's heart. In Luke 2:35 we read, "(and you yourself a sword will pierce) so that the thoughts of many hearts may be revealed." We are not to be discouraged by Mary's perfect, sinless heart; how she loved is a model for how we should strive to love God.

The feast day of the Immaculate Heart of Mary is August 22, her Immaculate Conception is December 8, and the Presentation of the Lord is February 2. In all of these holy days Mary's Immaculate Heart is revealed. Consider planting a pink bleeding heart at the Fourth Joyful Mystery, the Presentation in the Temple.

Symbolism:

- Jesus' heart
- Mary's heart
- compassion
- unconditional love,
- sacrificial love

Prayer Garden Theme:

- Sacred Heart,
- divine mercy
- Stations of the Cross
- virtues
- Marian, Rosary

CULTURE

Lamprocapnos spectabilis cultivars are generally hardy in Zones 3–9 and require part to full shade. They need a moist environment, so keep the ground damp and the leaves dry; a high level of organic material allowing for well-drained conditions is important, and if provided, this plant will grow in areas with a higher composition of clay. Additional watering may be required if planted among trees with extensive surface roots.

Bleeding heart will grow to an average 18–24″ / 46–61 cm width by 24–26″ / 61–66 cm height. Its flowers bloom in late spring, often above emerging leaves, and are desired by hummingbirds.

Though not a true ephemeral plant, its foliage will go dormant with summer's heat. Locate this bleeding heart among later-developing perennials such as ferns and hostas.

Keep children and pets — especially dogs — away from this plant; it is toxic if eaten in large enough quantities, causing seizures and liver damage.

Bluebells

Scilla bifolia

CHRISTIAN REFERENCE

Bluebells, which includes any of the *Scilla* species (as well as *Hyacinthoides italica*) are commonly called Squill or Harebell, and are found widespread in Asia Minor and in central and southern Europe.

Scilla bifolia

Its flowers — which can be a deep rich blue to pale lavender — are associated with our holy mother Mary. The six stamens[5] surrounding the central pistil together with the pistil represent the seven sorrows of Mary; the pistil signifies her greatest sorrow, her Son's crucifixion. The flower is also associated with her constancy to God, and the humility she showed in that constancy.

Because of this plant's prolific nature, I would add that it reflects an earlier translation of the Canticle of Mary, "My soul proclaims the greatness of the Lord" (Lk 1:46), and her gratitude in the next verse, "my spirit rejoices in God my savior."

In a Rosary garden, place this flower within the Joyful Mysteries, particularly The Annunciation. Bluebells represent humility, constancy, and gratitude; you could also use the spring-blooming and less prolific Virginia bluebells, *Mertensia virginica*.

We associate Saint George with bravery (and killing dragons!). Due to his chivalrous behavior — protection of women, dependence on faith and might of arms in fighting evil, and generosity to the poor —

devotion to Saint George became popular in Europe during the tenth century, and in the fifteenth century his feast day was as popular and as important as Christmas.[6] Bluebells are associated with this mighty saint because they were in bloom on his feast day of April 23. On that date churches were decorated and people wore the flower in his honor.[7]

Symbolism:

- humility
- constancy
- gratitude

Prayer Garden Theme:

- fruits of the Holy Spirit
- Marian
- Rosary
- Saint George

CULTURE

Scilla species in general are hardy in Zones 3–8, requiring full sun to light shade. They will grow well among trees, where they'll receive sufficient sunlight in spring before trees leaf out. Not truly drought-tolerant, they will endure occasional dry periods, though they prefer average watering. They grow best in organically rich, sandy loam — this being the fertile well-drained soil typical of many deciduous woodlands.

A single diminutive plant, growing from a tiny bulb, has a 3″ / 8 cm spread by 3–6″ / 8–15 cm height; it naturalizes (grows wild in a region to which it is not native) and develops large colonies, forming impressive drifts of color.

The blooms are deep blue to light lavender and will flower for weeks in early spring (some cultivars rebloom in summer or autumn). It is one of only a few plants whose buds show color while breaking ground. They provide early food for bees.

The grass-like leaves disappear in summer with only the racemes — spikes of flowers which bloom from the bottom up — remaining to dry and spread the seeds.

Hyacinthoides italica has a nearly identical culture, though different floral array and leaf arrangement.

Butterfly Weed

Asclepias tuberosa

CHRISTIAN REFERENCE

Many of us are familiar with the spiritually reflective nature of butterflies; their journey through life reflects the process of spiritual transformation to rebirth. The caterpillar's metamorphosis has long been used as an image of Our Lord's resurrection.

Butterflies also live only a few weeks to a few months, reminding us that life is short. When we think of death — *memento mori* is Latin for the spiritual practice "remember your death" — we are reminded again of metamorphosis, letting go of a previous life on earth for the freedom of a life in eternity with God.

In the modern language of flowers, the butterfly weed is indicative of letting go. For a Stations of the Cross garden, plant it at the Eighth Station, Jesus Meets the Women of Jerusalem, where he encourages them to focus not on him — to let him go — and instead focus on their children's lives. Parents know all too well that they rear their children only to let them go.

Butterfly weed could also be used in a garden dedicated to St. Mary Magdalene. We read in John 20:15–17 that St. Mary Magdalene had gone to the tomb and found Jesus' body missing. When a man spoke to her, "she thought it was the gardener and said to him, 'Sir, if you carried him away, tell me where you laid him, and I will take him.' Jesus said to her, 'Mary! …

Asclepias tuberosa

Stop holding on to me, for I have not yet ascended to the Father.'"

In a Rosary garden this plant's symbolism of letting go to do God's will would be appropriate within any of the mysteries: in the Joyful Mysteries, The Annunciation; in the Luminous Mysteries, at The Transfiguration; in the Sorrowful Mysteries, at The Agony in the Garden. It is especially appropriate in the Glorious Mysteries, because of the color, particularly at the third mystery of Pentecost where The Descent of the Holy Spirit enflames the apostles to let go of their fears and teach the way of Christ.

Symbolism:

- letting go
- remembrance
- freedom

Prayer Garden Theme:

- Stations of the Cross
- Marian
- Rosary
- saints

CULTURE

The *Asclepias tuberosa* cultivars are hardy in Zones 3–9, some to Zone 11, and require full sun to light shade in afternoon.

They require average to light watering, being drought tolerant. They will grow in most any soil — clay, shallow rocky, sandy, loam — as long as it meets the requirement of being well drained, otherwise crown rot will be an issue. They are also salt tolerant. Similar to daylilies, butterfly weeds hold their ground and help prevent erosion because of their deep taproot. Also because of their deep taproot, they do not transplant well.

Depending on cultivar, most butterfly weeds grow 12–18″ / 30–46 cm spread by 18–24″ / 46–61 cm height. They are slow to break ground until late spring to early summer, so mark well where you've planted them to prevent damage, thinking there is a bare spot in the garden that needs to be filled.

These long-blooming perennials begin to blossom in midsummer and continue through to autumn. The native species often found along ditch lines is a bright yellow-orange, though there are cultivars that are yellow, orange, and red, or entirely a vivid red. Whatever the color, the flowers attract pollinators and are a host for certain butterflies.

My experience has been that butterfly weed hosts aphids — which are like candy to ladybugs — and in my mind, can be classified as a trap-crop. (A trap-crop is a form of companion planting where a specific plant attracts agricultural pests away from nearby preferred plants.) If possible, plant the butterfly weed in its own colony downwind in the garden to help reduce aphids migrating to other plants.

Calla Lily

***Zantedeschia* spp., *Zantedeschia aethiopica* 'Flamingo'**

CHRISTIAN REFERENCE

Calla, or arum, lilies, which grew abundantly in damp, low-lying regions of South Africa, were highly desired plants in the eighteenth century. These plants were treasured by Dutch botanist and artist Jan Commelin. Their Latin name, *Zantedeschia*, was given in honor of Italian botanist Giovanni Zantedeschi. Decades later they were prized by the Duchess of Beaufort, Mary Somerset, who was one of the earliest women botanists in Britain. In America, a similar looking wild arum was called *Calla palustris*.[8]

Zantedeschia aethiopica 'Flamingo'

Though similar in appearance, the calla lily, *Zantedeschia*, and peace lily, *Spathiphyllum*, are two very different members of the *Araceae* family.

The symbolisms of the calla lily point toward Easter and the Resurrection, representing rebirth. Some consider the flower, in the shape of a trumpet, to herald Jesus' victory over death. For this reason it would do well at the end of a Stations of the Cross garden or in a Sacred Heart of Jesus garden.

It is easy for Christians to understand why this same flower, used at Easter and for weddings, would also be part of funerals. The flower's prominent symbolism of new birth, hope, and promise are all part of our faith in life after death.

In a Rosary garden, include

it at the First Glorious Mystery, The Resurrection, or the Fourth Glorious Mystery, The Assumption of Mary into Heaven.

In a white garden dedicated to the Holy Spirit, consider planting the white calla lily if the area is damp. If the area is dry, it will do well in a container when frequently watered.

In art depicting the annunciation, artists often use the calla lily in the same manner as the white lily, *Lilium candidum*. This is because both flowers carry the symbolisms of purity, holiness, and faith. With its attribute of rebirth, the calla lily also signifies youth and innocence, both qualities of the Virgin Mary at the time the Archangel Gabriel appeared.

Use of the calla lily in wedding ceremonies — and for final professions of consecrated religious — follows the theme of purity, promise, and hope in a new life together. It is also the flower that marks a sixth wedding anniversary.

Symbolism:

- hope
- watchfulness
- promise
- rebirth

Prayer Garden Theme:

- Sacred Heart
- Stations of the Cross
- Holy Spirit
- Rosary

CULTURE

Zantedeschia aethiopica "Flamingo," like most calla lilies, is hardy in Zones 8–10, requiring full sun and afternoon shade in hotter climates; planting on the east side of a structure works well.

Its water needs are high and specific: medium to wet environments where there is not standing water. The soil should be rich, cool, evenly moist, and well drained. These plants love to grow next to a pond or at the edge of bog or rain gardens.

These are stemless plants with flowers and leaves that rise from the rhizomatous root. They grow 18–20″ / 46–51 cm spread by 20–32″ / 51–81 cm height, blooming in midsummer. They make excellent container plants as long as any companion plants also require the same evenly moist soil.

Be mindful of where you locate *Zantedeschia* species — all parts of the plant contain calcium oxalate and are mildly poisonous to cats, dogs, and horses.

Canterbury Bells

Campanula rotundifolia, Campanula medium cvs.

CHRISTIAN REFERENCE

There are Christian references to plants that seem silly, but they brought a sense of sharing something in common with the holy. In parts of Europe there are many plants associated with Mary through folklore and legends that do just this: bring a sense of unity with our Holy Mother. One such folktale is associated with Canterbury bells, which are also known as bell flowers and distinctly different from *Scilla bifolia*. The flowers look like a lady's night cap, and the tale was told that it was the color and shape of the one our Holy Mother used to keep her curls in place.

Campanula rotundifolia has also been associated with grief since the Middle Ages, and was often planted on or near a grave. Because this plant symbolizes everlasting love, it carries well the sense of the eternal love of God, and blue represents eternity. Another reference to death is that bells often pealed at funerals, especially those of royalty.

"Canterbury bells … are also styled 'Bells of St. Paulinus' because he is the reputed inventor of bells … of which the flowers of the Campanula remind us. Bells soon after the time of St. Paulinus certainly came to be used in churches and abbeys … and consequently clock bells, came into general use in the monasteries of Europe in the eleventh century."[9]

Campanula medium

There are other saints associated with this flower, and bells. Pilgrims who journeyed to St. Thomas of Canterbury's shrine would do so with bells on poles and on their horses' harnesses. The flower *Campanula rotundifolia* grew along the roadside and looked like the celebratory bells of the pilgrims.

As for Saint George, these plants, much like the *Scilla*, were in bloom on his feast day in Europe — April 23. Saint George holds a unique place among the saints because he is known and revered by both Muslims and Christians.[10]

For a Stations of the Cross garden, use Canterbury bells at the Fourth Station, Jesus Meets His Mother. Mary, in all humility and through great suffering, trusted in God's plan for her Son.

Interestingly, about 50 percent of the world's "bluebells" occur throughout the United Kingdom in woodlands, fields, and roadsides. There is a lot of confusion with the vernacular name, and in folklore or legends it could refer to *Campanula rotundifolia*, *Hyacinthoides non-scripta*, or *Scilla nutans*.

Symbolism

- constancy
- everlasting love
- grieving
- humility

Prayer Garden Theme:

- Stations of the Cross
- Marian
- saints

CULTURE

Campanula medium cultivars are biennial, hardy in Zones 5–8 and require full sun to light afternoon shade in warmer climates. They can be a bit fussy; watering needs are average, but soils must be cool — these plants do not like their roots getting hot, and though striking, make a poor choice for containers. The soil also needs to be evenly moist and well drained. Site in an area that has low humidity — good air movement seems essential.

Depending on cultivar the plant will grow to 12–16″ / 30–41 cm spread by 24–36″ / 61–91 cm height. Its tall stalks of flowers begin to bloom in late spring and continue on until midsummer. Staking may be required, and hoop or grid supports work well considering that these plants reseed and form small colonies.

Carnation

Dianthus spp., *Dianthus barbatus*

CHRISTIAN REFERENCE

The botanical name *Dianthus* is the Latin form of a Greek word meaning "God's flower," and as such bears the loveliest of symbolisms: the pledge of love. For this reason, any of the *Dianthus* species can be used in any spiritual garden.

Dianthus barbatus

The carnation is strongly associated with the passion of Christ. The single-petal red *Dianthus* represents a pure love and would be appropriate planted within Stations of the Cross. With many cultivars being low and somewhat mounding, they would make a lovely edging along the Way.

Another reference to the passion comes from author Lucia Impelluso in the book *Nature and Its Symbols,* where she writes: "According to medieval legend, the tears shed by the Virgin Mary when she saw her son crucified fell to the ground and turned into carnations. The flower, moreover, was commonly called *chiodino* ('little nail') because of the shape of its buds, and here too became associated with the Passion of Christ."[11]

Again, any *Dianthus* species would work well in a Rosary garden. For more specific plantings consider the Joyful Mysteries, especially The Nativity of Our Lord, or the Glorious Mysteries, particularly The Coronation of Mary as Queen of Heaven and Earth. Of course, as with the Stations of the Cross, use this plant also within the

Sorrowful Mysteries.

Carthusian pinks, *Dianthus carthusianorum*, is a bushy sub-alpine native wildflower growing in grassy dry habitats throughout much of Europe. This small flower was named in honor of the monks of the Carthusian order, founded in the eleventh century in the Chartreuse Valley in the French Alps.[12] The flower was colloquially called Our Lady's Bedstraw, for its tiny but sturdy floral stems look like a delicate straw, and its mounded basal foliage appears soft and cushy.

Similarly, these typical foliage mounds of the *Dianthus barbatus* were called Our Lady's Tufts and were said in folktales to grow where she walked.

Symbolism:

- flower of God
- pledge of love
- love

Prayer Garden Theme:

- Sacred Heart
- divine mercy
- Stations of the Cross
- Marian, Rosary
- saints

CULTURE

The *Dianthus* is a diverse genus of plants that includes annuals, perennials, and biennials in native species and cultivated varieties. I have selected from garden varieties the *Dianthus barbatus* cultivar commonly called sweet William.

Sweet William is hardy in Zones 3–9 requiring full sun to light afternoon shade. Water is average, and organically rich soil must be well drained; these plants are prone to crown rot if too wet and won't tolerate wet soil in winter.

Dianthus barbatus cultivars range in size from 5–12″ / 13–30 cm spread by 4–18″ / 10–46 cm height.

Sweet William flowers have a spicy fragrance, as do the leaves, and bloom from late spring to autumn frost. Though a biennial, the plant will reseed and seem to flower yearly; established beds are known to endure for years. Blooms can be in shades of red, magenta, pink, lavender, white, and often picotee (petals edged with a second color), with some having fringed petals, and nearly all a distinct contrasting "eye."

Reblooming can be encouraged by removing spent flowers. To allow the biennial to reseed, stop deadheading in midsummer for flowers the next season.

Columbine

Aquilegia spp., *Aquilegia* × *hybrida* 'Songbird Cardinal'

CHRISTIAN REFERENCE

The columbine is one of the more familiar plants in Christian symbolism. Its common name indicates a bird, from the Greek *kolymbos* for "small bird," in Latin *columba* or dove. This refers to the inverted flower, which resembles a circle of five small birds, with the white blooming variety appearing as doves. (Several of the modern cultivars have lost much of this resemblance, with the spur of the flower — formerly curved inward like the neck of a dove — now modified and elongated.) Referred to as dove flower, it is symbolic of the Holy Spirit.

Aquilegia × *hybrida* 'Songbird Cardinal'

The botanical name *Aquilegia* comes from Latin for "water collecting," because of the way water beads up on the leaves, collecting at the junction and flowing down the stem to the roots.[13] Here, the leaves allude to the Holy Trinity and, to take this a step further, the water of baptism and the development of solid roots in faith. All four Gospel writers, when describing the baptism of Jesus, speak of the Holy Spirit descending "like a dove."

There are often seven blooms per flowering stem, which allude to many elements of the Catholic Faith: the seven sacraments, the seven gifts of the Holy Spirit, the seven sorrows of Mary, and the seven last words of Jesus. The number seven is associated with completion and fulfillment.

In art, the purple columbine when painted with Jesus represents victory. Plant this columbine at the end of the Stations of the Cross. A red columbine is said to represent the state of being anxious and trembling, and could be planted at the Eighth Station, Jesus Meets the Women of Jerusalem.

The purple columbine is also appropriate for a Rosary garden, at the Fifth Sorrowful Mystery, The Crucifixion. Plant a white columbine at the First Luminous Mystery, The Baptism in the Jordan.

The white flowering cultivars work well in a Holy Spirit garden — also known as a night garden because, being all white, flowers seem to glow even in the dark. The red and white flowering varieties are a lovely addition to a divine mercy garden.

Symbolism:

- suffering
- victory
- peace

Prayer Garden Theme:

- divine mercy
- Stations of the Cross
- Holy Spirit
- Rosary

CULTURE

The *Aquilegia* species have similar culture requirements within a range of varieties, some cultivated and others through habitat.[14] The native species develops similar but somewhat differently shaped and colored flowers, different positions for presenting its flowers, and different spur shapes in response to its primary pollinator.[15]

The *Aquilegia* × *hybrida* 'Songbird' cultivars are hardy in Zones 3–9, and tolerate full sun if properly mulched but prefer light shade, especially in afternoon. Watering needs are average, and the soil needs to be organically rich, evenly moist, and well drained. This plant strongly dislikes wet feet. Culture information indicates this cultivar will tolerate clay soils; this has not been my experience with others in the species.

"Songbird" cultivars grow 18–24″ / 46–61 cm spread by 20–28″ / 51–71 cm height. The flowers, typical of the species, appear inverted as they bud, and reverse the nod to face upwards when fully bloomed. The large 3″ / 8 cm bicolor flower appears in late spring and the plant continues to flower through early summer. Remove spent flowers to prolong bloom period.

Cornflower and Chicory

Centaurea cyanus* and *Cichorium intybus, Centaurea montana

CHRISTIAN REFERENCE

These two genera share the same symbolisms because of their similarity in flower and growth habits.

The chicory is one tough little plant! This flower is pretty much able to withstand whatever is thrown at it, whether drought, salts, poor soils, intense heat, or being cut down — it resurrects and grows anew. Sounds like perseverance in our faith, doesn't it? For this reason it has several associations with Christ.

Centaurea montana

Both chicory and cornflower have long been associated with agriculture. They were usually found — and in some places still are — growing among grain fields, commonly wheat. Here is one of the symbolisms associated with Jesus: Christ, the grain of wheat, and the cornflower signifying the blue of heaven.

The *Centaurea cyanus* species name, *cyanus*, means blue, and for both cornflower and chicory, is symbolic of eternity and new life. Recalling those who have passed away, the cornflower is worn in France as a *le bleuet* for remembrance, much like the red poppy in the United Kingdom, Canada, Australia, and United States.

The chicory and cornflower are both symbols of endurance (in faith) and courage, upon which one relies when entering the afterlife. This association began, for the cornflower, before the Bronze Age. "In ancient Egypt, reproductions of cornflowers have been found [in tombs] dating back to the first half of the 4th millennium BC. … Florists used cornflower heads for grave decorations. … Plants were given to the deceased to accompany him on his way."[16]

All parts of *Centaurea cyanus* were used medicinally and thought to be a cure for snake bites. Here again is the cornflower's association with Jesus. In Christianity the snake is one of the symbols of the devil, and the "cure" against the devil is Christ, who triumphed over sin.

The flowers of both plants are also shaped like a crown, and because of their color and association with heaven, are regionally referred to as Mary's crown. Use the garden variety of these plants in a Rosary garden at the Fifth Glorious Mystery, The Coronation of Mary as Queen of Heaven and Earth.

Symbolism:
- heaven
- Mary's crown
- endurance

Prayer Garden Theme:
- Jesus
- Marian
- Rosary

CULTURE

The garden-variety cornflowers, *Centaurea montana* cultivars, have similar culture requirements with size and color variations.

This perennial is hardy in Zones 3–8, requiring full sun. Watering needs are low, and it is fairly drought tolerant. Cornflowers grow in average to poor soils, as long as the soil is light and well drained.

Centaurea montana sizes average 18–24″ / 46–61 cm spread by 12–24″ / 30–61 cm height. They spread by stolons — creeping horizontal stems, like strawberry plants — so tend to naturalize and form dense colonies. Plan on dividing plants every three years.

These are long-blooming perennials of purples, magentas, blues, or whites that begin setting buds in early summer. The tight scalelike buds look like mini pineapples whose tops open to form 1½–2½″ / 3.8–6.3 cm feathery flowers, with the center often a contrasting color.

Deadheading encourages a longer bloom period, and for larger naturalized colonies, cut back plants by two-thirds. My experience has been that the leaves often become dried out and unsightly after flowering. Shearing back will allow for fresh leaves, which improves the overall appearance of the garden.

Crown Imperial

Fritillaria imperialis, Fritillaria imperialis* var. *rubra-maxima

CHRISTIAN REFERENCE

There is a legend about the Garden of Gethsemane and the crown imperial plant, *Fritillaria imperialis*. As Jesus walked into the garden for the last time, all the flowers bowed their heads, except for the flowering crown imperial that held its stiff white blooms high. Our Lord gently placed his hands on the flower and said, "Lily, be not so proud." At that the plant hung its flowering head and blushed with shame. Its tears lingered on its petals. On that day it lost its color of innocence, white, and when you find it growing in its native land, you'll see it is red (although some species are also yellow). If you look inside the drooping flower cups, you can still see the pearl-like tears attached to the top.[17]

Fritillaria imperialis* var. *rubra-maxima

Because of this legend, include this flower at the entrance to the Stations of the Cross, or in a Rosary garden at the First Sorrowful Mystery, The Agony in the Garden. It can also be planted at any of the Joyful Mysteries with the symbolism of honoring God, or at the Fifth Glorious Mystery, The Coronation of Mary as Queen of Heaven and Earth.

The plant's botanical name comes from the shape of the flowers. Its genus name, *Fritillaria*, comes from Latin *fritilus* meaning "dice cup"; and again from Latin, the species name *imperialis* comes from *imperium* for empire, and so a king's crown. Here we recall the soldiers who rolled dice for Jesus' garments (see Mt 27:35), and his title as King of Kings (see 1 Tm 6:15; and Rv 17:14; 19:11–16).

Another *Fritillaria* that is associated with saints is the diminutive *Fritillaria meleagris,* checkered fritillary. In the language of flowers, the checkered fritillary represents persecution, and can represent in your garden those who were martyred.

Symbolism

- honor
- glory

Prayer Garden Theme:

- Stations of the Cross
- Marian
- Rosary

CULTURE

The crown imperial is hardy in Zones 5–8, though there are claims that specific cultivars are hardy to Zone 4. They require full sun and will tolerate light afternoon shade. Watering is average, though soil requirements regarding water are specific. The soil must be deeply organically rich; evenly moist; and, most importantly, well drained. These bulbs are prone to rot if the soil is too wet. The bulbs need to be planted on their side; they have a hollow crown (an opening at the top of the bulb) that will collect water and rot the bulb if planted vertically.

Fritillaria imperialis var. *rubra-maxima* has a mature size of 8–10″ / 20–25 cm spread by 2–3′ / 61–91 cm height, making it a striking plant at the back of a border bed. Placing the crown imperial behind other plants is important; like most spring bulbs the foliage dies back, going dormant in summer.

Though the bulbs are large, site them well and plant properly; they are fragile and best left undisturbed.

Cyclamen

Cyclamen persicum, Cyclamen hederifolium

CHRISTIAN REFERENCE

The Persian cyclamen is a native plant in the Holy Lands, growing wild throughout most of the Middle East and south central Europe. The native species, *Cyclamen persicum,* are long-lived perennials that grow in woodlands, shrublands, and hillsides. They begin to bloom in large drifts in early November and, in some locations, continue into May. They go dormant during the long Mediterranean summer, then rejuvenate with the winter rains.

Cyclamen hederifolium

Often referred to as the florist cyclamen, the red or white cultivars are a popular plant at Christmas. Like the poinsettia, they represent in Christian color symbolisms white for holiness, red for suffering, and green for new life.

Though not mentioned in the Bible by name, they are considered one of the "flowers of the field" mentioned in Matthew 6:28, which also recalls the splendor of King Solomon. Because of the recurved petals that shape the flower, one of its common names is Solomon's crown.

This flower is associated with the Blessed Mother for a variety of reasons. The cyclamen bows in a manner indicative of humility, as the Virgin Mary would have done at the annunciation. The white cyclamen often has red at the base of the petals where they form the chamber and attach to the stem; the white and red representing the

Immaculate and Sorrowful Heart of Mary.

The cyclamen, much like the chrysanthemum, is associated with funerals and cemeteries. This association may come from its flowering in early November, and its traditional use in the decoration of tombs and churches on All Saints Day.

Symbolism:
- acceptance
- resignation
- diffidence
- Mary's sorrows

Prayer Garden Theme:
- Marian
- Rosary
- Bible

CULTURE

Listed below are two winter-hardy species of cyclamen; one blooms in autumn, and the other in late winter to early spring. Both prefer a sheltered area. Plant either species in groups to create drifts of color; they will colonize as a ground cover, making them a wonderful selection for woodland gardens or naturalizing areas. Both go dormant in summer heat.

Easy to grow, *Cyclamen hederifolium* cultivars are hardy in Zones 5–9, requiring part to full shade but being a bit more tolerant of morning sun. Watering needs are average to low. Average soils are tolerated, but for the best showy blooms, the soil should be organically rich and deep, evenly moist, and well drained; the bulbs will rot if too wet. This cyclamen grows 6–12″ / 15–30 cm spread by 4–6″ / 10–15 cm height, and naturalizes. It bears fragrant flowers in mid- to late autumn.

Cyclamen coum cultivars are hardy in Zones 4–9, also requiring part to full shade. Watering needs are low in summer, and average in early autumn to "waken" the bulbs. It has the same soil requirements: organically rich and deep, evenly moist, and well drained. Again, the bulbs will rot if too wet. A spreading ground cover growing to a 4″ / 10 cm height, its fragrant flowers appear in late winter to early spring and grow well with the early flowering snowdrop (*Galanthus nivalis*). Foliage appears in late autumn. It too self-sows and will colonize an area, creating the familiar drifts known to this genus.

A special consideration: Do not plant these species together with the goal of a colorful display in both spring and autumn. The fall-blooming *Cyclamen hederifolium* is the more dominant species and will crowd out the finer and more delicate winter-blooming *Cyclamen coum* cultivars.

Delphinium

Delphinium spp. *(Delphinium × cultorum), Delphinium grandiflorum*

CHRISTIAN REFERENCE

The metaphors associated with delphiniums are also attributed to larkspurs and sometimes monkshood. Originating in northern Africa, southern Europe, and central Asia, the *Delphinium* species is not the same as its cousin, larkspur (*Consolida* spp.). "Despite being frequently mislabeled and confused for each other — even by experts — the two plants do have differences; enough difference that larkspur (*Consolida ajacis*) was recently reclassified out of the *Delphinium* genus into its own species. … Larkspur is also an annual while *Delphinium* is a perennial. … There are about 40 species of larkspur and 300 of *Delphinium*."[18] Their similarity in appearance has historically led to coalescing symbolisms throughout the Middle East and Europe.

Delphinium grandiflorum

The Delphinium received its botanical name from the Greek for dolphin, which the shape of the flower's bud resembles. The dolphin was perceived by fishermen as a guide to safe harbor, often bringing joy to sailors long at sea — hence the *ichthys*, the familiar simple two-line fish symbol that was a marking along the way for pilgrims to find safe haven on their journeys. Here the symbolism of levity and lightness was transferred to the delphinium and its visually similar cousins.

In Christian art this "fish" is portrayed more than any other aquatic animal. The dolphin symbolizes resurrection and salvation, and in some paintings is seen bearing souls across earthly waters to the eternal world. When the dolphin is depicted with an anchor or a boat, the fish represents the human soul, and the anchor or boat represents Christ. The *ichthys* became a sort of "secret password" among early Christians and is now a popular symbol for Christianity.

The association of the blue delphinium with the Virgin Mary — besides its color — is through Mary's tears and comes from the symbolism of a strong bond of love; and that maternal bond is none greater than hers for her son. The strength of that bond was ever apparent, to both the Father's will and Jesus' mission, as she tearfully journeyed with her Son through his passion.

Symbolism:

- lightness
- levity
- ichthys
- strong bond of love

Prayer Garden Theme:

- Bible
- Marian

CULTURE

The *Delphinium × cultorum* cultivars,[19] which include 'Pacific Giant', 'New Millennium', and 'Magic Fountain', are tall and singular in flowering habit. The *Delphinium grandiflorum* var. *chinensis* sometimes referred to as Chinese delphinium is generally branched and shorter, and tolerant of slightly dryer conditions. Both are perennials hardy in Zones 3–8 and 4–9, respectively. Keep in mind that in regions with high humidity and wet winters or summers, crown rot will be an issue.

They require full sun and appreciate dappled afternoon shade in warmer climates. Water requirements are average, though regular. *Delphinium grandiflorum* are a bit more tolerant of dryer conditions, though not drought tolerant. Soils should be evenly moist, organically rich, and very well drained.

Delphinium × cultorum are large, averaging 18–24″ / 46–61 cm spread by 3–5′ / 91cm–1.5 m height. They need to be planted in a sheltered area and often require support for their heavily bloomed stalks.

Delphinium grandiflorum are generally shorter and well branched at 8–12″ / 20–30 cm spread by 12–18″ / 30–46 cm height.

Both species bloom early to midsummer in shades of blues, purples, pinks or white. Removing spent flowers is recommended; they rarely reseed well or true to cultivar. These are short-lived perennials and should be divided every other year.

Feed with low-level soluble or slow-release granular fertilizer; broadcast an alkaline supplement in the spring before plants emerge.

For a similar look, grow the larkspur, *Consolida* spp., a sturdy annual that will reseed and are less finicky than delphiniums. Hardy in Zones 2–11, lark spurs need full sun, average water, and evenly moist, well-drained soils. They will grow 12–18″ / 30–46 cm spread by 2–3′ / 61–91 cm height, blooming early to midsummer and dying back in heat. Site so that other late-season flowers will fill in the bare spots.

English Daisy

***Bellis perennis, Bellis perennis* 'Pomponette'**

CHRISTIAN REFERENCE

The English daisy of lore is the low-growing species with abundant white flowers that children would weave into daisy chains for crowns. In *Hamlet*, Shakespeare used a daisy chain to represent Ophelia's innocence.

Though there are about a hundred "daisies" in the world, in the beginning there was only the little white *Bellis perennis*, first appearing in eleventh-century writing as "Day's eye."[20] The common name, daisy, is an abstraction of that phrase and references the manner in which the white petals fold up at night — termed nyctinasty — then reopen in the morning to reveal the yellow eye. The expression "fresh as a daisy" comes from this flower.

The buds of the English daisy are tight round "pearls" of white, and for this reason in some areas of Europe it is called Marguerite daisy; the etymology of both daisy and the name Margaret means pearl.[21] This flower became a symbol for St. Margaret of Antioch because of its name and its nature to open with the light and always face heavenward.

***Bellis perennis* 'Pomponette'**

A Christian legend tells how the prolific daisy is said to have sprung from the copious tears shed by St. Mary Magdalene; for the sorrow of her sins and the redemption of her soul, during the passion of her beloved Jesus, and on her way to the tomb to anoint Our Lord. Use this flower at the Eighth Station of the Cross, Jesus Meets the Women of Jerusalem, or at the Fourteenth Station, Jesus Is Laid in the Tomb.

The genus name *Bellis* comes from the Latin *bellus* meaning pretty or charming; *perennis* for everlasting (perennial). The association with innocence, purity, and rebirth comes from a Celtic story that says for every unborn child lost in miscarriage, a flower with a golden disc surrounded by silver petals grows.[22] When imagining the prolific waves of the daisy in the fields, we can only imagine the number of children in Ireland, whose death preceded birth.

Symbolism:
- innocence
- purity
- rebirth
- new beginnings
- St. Margaret of Antioch,
- St. Mary Magdalene

Prayer Garden Theme:
- Stations of the Cross
- saints

CULTURE

The English daisy, *Bellis perennis*, has a motley reputation ranging from "attractive low-spreading ornamental flower" to "common weed of fields and abandoned areas."

The *Bellis perennis* 'Pomponette' is the cultivar most grown in home gardens. Though listed as a biennial, in most of the United States and Canada it grows as an annual because of its cold and heat sensitivity. The cultivar name 'Pomponette' was given to describe the small, tightly clustered petals reminiscent of the woolen balls or pom-poms attached to garments for decoration.

Said to be hardy in Zones 4–8, it requires full sun to afternoon shade, water is average, and it is not drought tolerant. Soil should be well drained and consistently evenly moist but not soggy.

This cultivar grows 5–7″ / 13–18 cm spread by 4–6″ / 10–15 cm height, slightly taller when it blooms in early summer. The flowers in pinks, reds, whites, or lavenders are an impressive 1″ / 2.5 cm across and fully doubled with an often nearly hidden yellow center. To encourage prolonged blooming, remove spent flowers.

Because it often declines in the heat of summer, plant in small groupings to avoid large bare spots in the garden. Consider planting it in front of late-summer blooming perennials.

Fritillaria

Checkered lily, *Fritillaria meleagris*

CHRISTIAN REFERENCE

The checkered lily is native to the flood plains of Europe. This dainty perennial can be seen flowering in the spring, growing in large colonies.

Fritillaria meleagris

In the language of flowers, the checkered fritillary represents persecution, and when you see the nodding, dark blood-red flower, its name seems well suited. It can represent in your garden the many men and women martyred for our faith.

Fritillaria meleagris "in still life paintings often featured its chequered purple flowers drooping beneath gaudy tulips in a sinister little allegory of life and death. Local names include death bell, Lazarus bell, and leper's lily. A sense of chance, if not doom, was also reflected in the name fritillary, likening the shape of the flowers to a dice box — *fritillus* in Latin."[23]

The casting of dice (or lots) for Our Lord's cloak is mentioned in all four Gospels; a confirmation of the prophecy in Psalm 22:19. If the area is consistently damp around the Ninth Station, Jesus Is Nailed to the Cross, this plant is a somber reminder of Our Lord's suffering.

In a Rosary garden this spring-flowering bulb is appropriate planted within the Sorrowful Mysteries at any of the five mysteries, but especially so at the Crucifixion and Death.

A familiar legend, similar to a story of its proud cousin the crown imperial, *Fritillaria imperialis,* is found in several writings (the origin of which has been difficult to pinpoint). The story is that before the crucifixion the checkered lily was pure white and the cupped flowers erect. It stood upright during the suffering of Our Lord until darkness shrouded the earth at his death, and it saw that all of nature but itself was grieving. Then it bent low its head and donned the dark garments of mourning, and in grief began to weep for the death of Christ. It still hangs its head in the somber attire, and each petal bears what looks like a tear at the tip.

The species name, *meleagris,* comes from Greek and means "guinea fowl" or "turkey." It is commonly called guinea-hen flower because the dark-colored tessellated flower resembles the mottling of the bird's feathers.

Symbolism:

- persecution
- martyrdom

Prayer Garden Theme:

- Stations of the Cross
- Rosary
- saints

CULTURE

Fritillaria meleagris is hardy in Zones 3–8, requiring dappled to part shade. It may tolerate more sun in cooler Hardiness Zones with adequate moisture.

It requires consistently moist soil — even when dormant — that is organically rich and well drained; it is not a bog plant and will not withstand being submerged or constantly wet.

A delicate plant in appearance, it grows 3–6″ / 8–15 cm spread by 10–15″ / 25–38 cm height. In the right environment it will naturalize, spreading by seed, and is long lived.

The tessellated flowers are a striking 2″ / 5 cm long, blooming in early to mid-spring in burgundy and mauve or white and gray. There are several cultivars including pure white with green at petal base (*Fritillaria meleagris* 'Alba'), a nearly solid wine with deep yellow underside and edges (*Fritillaria uva-vulpis*), and pale yellow (*Fritillaria pallidiflora*) with broader leaves and multiple flowers per stem.

Geranium, Zonal

***Pelargonium* spp., *Pelargonium* × *hortorum* cvs.**

CHRISTIAN REFERENCE

I'll begin by clearing up confusion about the name of this plant. The bedding geranium we are familiar with, and the one presented here, is the *Pelargonium* genus and includes numerous cultivars. It was brought to Europe from South Africa in the seventeenth century, where it was found to be easily propagated and grown indoors.

Pelargonium × hortorum

The plant we call "wild geranium" is the *Geranium* genus, and it also has several species that can be found growing throughout the world. Both *Pelargonium* spp. and *Geranium* spp. are called storksbills and cranesbills, respectively, adding to the confusion for those not in the green industry.

The name *Pelargonium* comes from the Greek *pelargos*, which means "stork." *Geranium*, also from Greek, means "crane"; and for both genera, the reference is to the shape of the seed case. The common use of *zonal* is from the attribute of many *Pelargonium* varieties to form a dark circular band within the leaf zone.

The zonal geranium (*Pelargonium* spp.) offers a broad range of symbolisms — with regional attributes seeming to conflict — depending on species, cultivar, color, fragrance, or shape of leaf.

The white geranium, like most white flowers, symbolizes purity as well as a spiritual life, and is used at weddings signifying conjugal happiness and fruitfulness. One of the monikers for the white-flowering geranium is beautiful lady, which fits well when this flower is used in a bride's bouquet.

I like how the symbolism of bridal favor relates to Mary, chosen as the bride of the Holy Spirit. As Catholics we make several assumptions about the married life of Mary. We know from Scripture that Saint Joseph listened attentively for God's word so as to love and protect Mary and their Son. In our own marriages we can focus on the holy family's relationship — always placing God at the center — in our own striving for domestic tranquility.

Irrelevant of the color, whether grown in the garden or indoors on a sunny windowsill, geraniums are iconic of a happy domestic life.

Symbolism:

- domestic happiness
- protection of home,
- kindness
- gentility
- bridal favor
- Beautiful Lady

Prayer Garden Theme:

- Marian

CULTURE

The species are divided into four groups: zonal (one of the most popular summer bedding plants, *Pelargonium × hortorum* cvs.), ivy-leaved (*Pelargonium × peltatum* cvs.), regal geraniums (*Pelargonium × domesticum* cvs.), and scented-leaf geraniums (various species, often lacking showy flowers). Although they are classified as perennials, they do not grow well in extreme cold or heat.

The zonal geranium, *Pelargonium × hortorum*, is hardy in Zones 9–11 and requires full sun, appreciating light afternoon shade in warmer regions. In climates with high humidity and rain, leaf molds and root rot are an issue.

This species requires average watering on a regular basis and prefers to dry slightly in between; it is intolerant of drought. The soil should be organically rich, evenly moist, and well drained. Supplementing with fertilizer is recommended.

Size varies by cultivar and ranges between 10–15″ / 25–38 cm spread by 6–24″ / 15–61 cm height. The flowers bloom all summer until frost, and range in color from white to corals, pinks, reds, or lavenders with petals solid or bicolored, single or doubled. The number of cultivars is dizzying!

The F_1 hybrids, known as seed geraniums, tend to be smaller in size and much more floriferous, having single florets. These are usually sold in flats or small pots.

The vegetative or cutting geraniums are larger and less floriferous plants, which have fuller, showier blooms with semi-double to fully doubled florets.

An early pinching back of the stem encourages a sturdier, bushier plant, whether grown in ground or containers. Deadhead the flowering stalk from the side of the stem to encourage blooming.

Gladiolus

Gladiolus spp., *Gladiolus* × *hortulanus* Grandiflora hybrids

CHRISTIAN REFERENCE

The Latin name for sword is *gladius* (e.g., "gladiator") and because of the shape of its leaves a common name for this plant is sword lily. The iris shares a similar symbolism in Marian devotion. In art, the spiked reed held by the Christ Child is thought to be the sword lily, indicating his Incarnation and place as King and Savior.

In a Rosary garden, plant the gladioli within the Joyful Mysteries, which offer meditations on the young life of the newborn King. On a more somber note, it can be planted at the Twelfth Station of the Cross as a reminder of the lance that pierced Our Lord's side.

I like to use this plant in a garden dedicated to St. Michael the Archangel, who is often depicted with a spear or sword, defending and protecting. The colors gold or orange are often used to symbolize Saint Michael, so select gladioli within that palette.

Gladioli can be used in any gardens dedicated to a warrior saint such as the apostle Saint Paul — who encouraged Christians to put on the "armor of God" (see Eph 6:10–17) and was martyred by the sword — or a garden dedicated to St. Joan of Arc. There are several patron saints who fought for the Church and are depicted with a sword, whether for bravery in defending the Church or for martyrdom by its use.

Gladiolus × *hortulanus*
Grandiflora hybrid

Symbolism:

- sword
- faithfulness
- moral integrity
- generosity

Prayer Garden Theme:

- Jesus
- fruits of the Holy Spirit
- Rosary
- saints
- angels

CULTURE

The bold *Gladiolus* × *hortulanus* Grandiflora hybrids are the most recognizable of the gladioli. Corms — large roots similar to bulbs — are hardy in Zones 8–11, require full sun, and appreciate light dappled shade during the afternoon in warmer regions.

Watering is average, though must be consistent especially during the growing season. Soil needs to be evenly moist, well drained, and organically rich. The size of the plant varies by cultivar; the Grandiflora group (which includes a dwarf with the same culture needs) grow 8–18″ / 20–46 cm wide by 3–5′ / 91 cm–1.5 m height when in bloom.

The fragrant blooms — particularly loved by hummingbirds and butterflies — can be solid or bicolor, smooth or ruffled, and grow predominantly along one side of a 1–4′ / 30 cm–1.2 m stem. The flowers open from the bottom up, and the scape can bear eighteen to twenty-six blooms. In cooler climates, they flower midsummer through early autumn, or until frost if the corms are planted in succession every two weeks starting in spring. Remove spent flowers from the stem for appearance; these plants are not rebloomers, so remove the stalk once flowering is completed.

If you desire to cut a few stems to bring indoors, do so in the early morning. Bring a sharp knife and a lukewarm bucket of water. Select stems with two to three open blooms, and cut diagonally upwards, immediately placing the stem in water. In zones where gladioli are hardy, be sure to leave at least four leaves on the plant so the corm will continue to develop for next season. Place the bucket of gladiolus in a cool dark area for a couple of hours before bringing it into the house, allowing any hidden bugs to move along. Every few days, remove spent flowers from stalk, cut an inch off the bottom of the stem, and refresh the water in the vase.

Because of this cultivar's growth habit — tall and slender, bearing a heavy load up top — they need protection from wind. A best practice for additional support is to dig deep when planting gladioli bulbs in the spring. Dig a trench 6″ / 15 cm deep and cover the corms with 2″ / 5 cm of soil. As plants begin to grow, add another 2″ / 5 cm of soil, and repeat a third time as they continue to develop. A heavy layer of mulch is advised since gladioli do not like to run dry.

Globe Amaranth

Gomphrena globosa

CHRISTIAN REFERENCE

The globe amaranth, along with several other genera, is classified as one of the *Immortelles* or "everlasting" flowers — being different from funerary flowers. The everlastings are plants that keep for an extended period when dried. Funerary flowers, for the most part, are those that accompany the deceased through to burial or, in some cultures, are planted around the grave.

Gomphrena globosa

The group of flowers that make up the *Immortelles* were used to decorate churches on the feast of the Ascension — which usually falls in mid- to late May when several of these plants are in bloom — and were associated with the joys of eternal life.

In the late nineteenth century a new custom began; it was common to see garlands of *Immortelles* decking graves in the countryside, and also in metropolitan areas — though the "folksy custom" was often viewed as uncultured. One author from that period noted that numerous shops near cemeteries in neighborhoods not far outside Paris were filled with garlands of *Immortelles,*[24] which were purchased on anniversaries, feast days, or any day of remembrance for the dearly departed. Often fresh-cut flowers were woven within the immortelle garlands to add temporary color.

Because of its symbolisms associated with eternal life, the globe amaranth has many applications in the Catholic garden. In a Rosary garden, plant it within any of the Luminous Mysteries, or at the Second Glorious Mystery, The Ascension. For a Stations of the Cross garden, anywhere along the path is suitable, for each station calls us to remember what Jesus suffered so that we may have eternal life.

The globe amaranth, though in the same family, is not from the genus *Amaranthus*, of which several species are used herbally and culinarily. Several *Amaranthus* species are grown as ornamentals in the garden. Two with Christian symbolisms — though not fully discussed in this book — are Joseph's coat (*Amaranthus tricolor*), a substantial plant with striking, vividly colored leaves, and love-lies-bleeding (*Amaranthus caudatus*), which has long, trailing, blood-red blooms.

Symbolism:

- everlasting or eternal love
- immortality
- unchangeability
- mercy

Prayer Garden Theme:

- Jesus
- Stations of the Cross
- divine mercy
- Rosary

CULTURE

Gomphrena globosa cultivars are hardy in Zones 9–11, and as such are grown as an annual from seed in most regions. They require full sun all day. Watering needs are average, and mature plants will tolerate drought conditions.

They need average soil and will grow in light clay — well, they'll grow most anywhere as long as the soil is well drained. They do not tolerate wet feet.

Average size is 6–12″ / 15–31 cm spread by 12–24″ / 30–61 cm height. Pinch back young plants to encourage bushiness and, because they are terminus bloomers, to increase flowering.

The clover-like flowers range in color from white to red, purple, pink, violet, lilac, and (in new species) orange or bicolored. Globe amaranth is an excellent annual that is a reliable bloomer all summer until frost, and can be cut for the vase or dried.

Germination rates are notoriously low, so if you are collecting seed heads (or buying packets) keep in mind that you will need to over-seed the area. Buying in cell packs is a better guarantee of their spot in a garden.

To dry the globe amaranth, or most any of the everlastings, begin by harvesting in late morning or early afternoon when the plant is dry. Cut flowering stalks and remove the leaves; if collecting several stems, arrange them in layered rows so as not to crush the flowers. Gather into small bunches, bundle together with string — rubber bands are often too strong for their delicate stems — and hang them upside-down in a dry, dark (to preserve color), and well-ventilated area. When using dried in arrangements keep them, and all everlastings, out of direct sunlight to help preserve color.

Hosta, *Assumption Lily*

Hosta plantaginea, Hosta sieboldiana 'Frances Williams'

CHRISTIAN REFERENCE

Did you know the assumption lily is not a lily but a hosta? This plant has a singular association in Christian symbolism: the Virgin Mary.

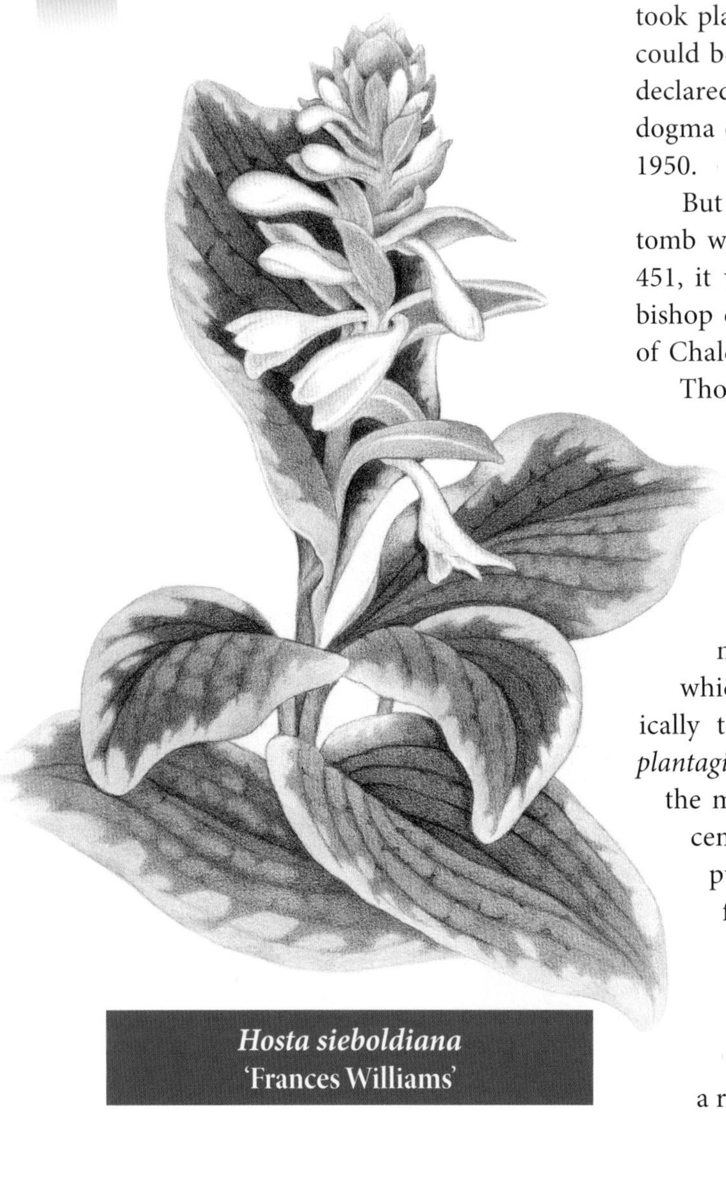

We honor the Virgin Mary's Assumption into heaven on August 15, with a holy day of obligation. This solemnity commemorates Mary's entrance into eternal life, body and soul, through her Son, Jesus, which took place before her physical body could begin to decay. Pope Pius XII declared the Assumption of Mary a dogma of our faith on November 1, 1950.

But did you know that Mary's tomb was not found empty? In AD 451, it was noted by Saint Juvenal, bishop of Jerusalem, at the Council of Chalcedon, that the apostle Saint Thomas was said to have found beautiful roses and lilies where Our Lady's body once lay.

So what does the hosta have to do with all this? One of its common names is the assumption lily, which seems to be tied specifically to the native species *Hosta plantaginea*. This hosta flowers near the middle of August, and its raceme — often up to 4' tall — of pure white trumpet flowers fills the air with fragrance from what smell and look like miniature Easter or Madonna lilies!

Plant any of the hosta in a rosary garden within the Glo-

Hosta sieboldiana 'Frances Williams'

rious Mysteries at the Fourth Mystery, the Assumption of Mary.

Symbolism:
- devotion

Prayer Garden Theme:
- Marian
- Rosary

CULTURE

With about seventy species and more than three thousand cultivars to choose from, these well-loved shade plants vary in size from the diminutive 5″ / 13 cm tall 'Blue Mouse Ears' to the nearly 4′ / 1.2 m tall 'Gentle Giant.' The leaves can be smooth or dimpled, solid chartreuse to a rich blue-green, as well as variegated, with nearly white to deep blue-green patterning. With such a wide assortment, and several cultivars that will tolerate full sun in northern zones, choosing a hosta for a Marian or Rosary garden will be easy. Choosing just one is what's difficult!

A sturdy and reliable variegated cultivar is *Hosta sieboldiana* 'Frances Williams'. Its culture is given below.

Hosta sieboldiana 'Frances Williams' is hardy in Zones 3–8 and requires full to partial shade, being somewhat tolerant of morning sun in northern climates. Having an average water requirement, it — like most hostas — prefers to be evenly moist and well drained.

A woodland soil that is organically rich is ideal, but it will grow in most any soil, including clay, as long as it is not constantly wet — again, the soil must be well drained. This hosta is mildly drought tolerant at maturity.

Mature size is 4–5′ / 1.2–1.5 m spread by 18–24″ / 46–61 cm height, with the flowering scape reaching up to 30″ / 76 cm tall.

White (sometimes pale lavender) flowers bloom along the raceme from early to midsummer. This cultivar is not fragrant. Remove spent stalks after flowering is completed.

The impressive colorful leaves are wide, puckered, with distinctive veination. The leaves can grow to 12″ / 30 cm long by 11″ / 28 cm wide, and are green-blue with uniquely patterned yellowish margins.

Like most *Hosta* spp., they can be planted singly as a specimen or grouped for a more dramatic presence in the garden. The hosta is considered by deer to be a delicacy and will be eagerly consumed!

Iris

Iris spp., *Iris* × *germanica* 'Lovely Senorita'

CHRISTIAN REFERENCE

Did you know you can grow a rainbow in your Marian garden?

The word *iris* comes to us from Greek and means "rainbow," indicating the array of colors of this genus. This flower's colors may express a rainbow — a covenant symbol first seen by Noah — but Mary fulfilled that promise of God. Beginning with her Immaculate Conception, she cooperates in the covenant of redemption through a divine-human relationship.

In Dutch art the iris is interchangeable with the lily as "Mary's flower," and is often depicted replacing the lily in renderings of the Annunciation.[25] The evolution of this symbolism came about because of the shape of its leaves — it is called sword lily, a name it shares with gladiolus. The association built on Mary's prophesied grief that, "you yourself a sword will pierce" (Lk 2:35). Simeon's prophecy developed into the Catholic devotion of the seven sorrows of Mary.

Later, Spanish painters also adopted the iris as an attribute of Mary, the Queen of Heaven, as a symbol of faith, hope, divine protection, wisdom, and light.[26]

Most of us are familiar with the stylized sword lily, *Iris persica*, as the emblem of French royalty. Originally called fleur de Louis, after King Louis VII's victory in a field covered in this compact little flower, the name later evolved into fleur-de-lys.[27]

The yellow iris, *Iris pseudacorus*, is native to the Holy Lands, where it

Iris × *germanica* 'Lovely Senorita'

grows along waterways, and is thought to be the reed-grass growing with the papyrus in Job 8:11. A common name is Jacob's sword; this iris is often called segg — a corruption of the word *sedge* — derived from an Anglo-Saxon word meaning a small sword.[28]

For a Stations of the Cross garden, place the iris at the Fourth Station of the Cross, Jesus Meets His Mother, recalling Simeon's prophecy. In a Rosary garden, grow at the Fifth Sorrowful Mystery, The Crucifixion, recalling Mary's greatest sorrow; the Fourth Joyful Mystery, The Presentation in the Temple; and the Fifth Glorious Mystery, The Coronation of Mary as Queen of Heaven and Earth. If you can grow the water-loving *Iris pseudacorus* in your Marian garden, it would represent her role as Queen of Heaven, given its gold crown.

Symbolism:

- Mary's sword
- Mary's grief
- Immaculate Conception

Prayer Garden Theme:

- Stations of the Cross
- Marian
- Rosary
- Bible

CULTURE

The easily grown bearded iris, *Iris × germanica* cvs., is a favorite among gardeners. It is hardy in Zones 3–10, requiring full sun and average watering, though it will tolerate an occasional drought.

The soil needs to be organically rich and well drained. This plant is intolerant of clay soils; the rhizomes (horizontal underground stems) do not like to be kept wet and will rot. Their rooting structures need some air and light, so do not place mulch on the growing tip.

There are hundreds of cultivars of the bearded iris; sizes vary, but average 1–2′ / 30–61 cm spread by 2–3′ / 61–91 cm height.

Fragrant flowers bloom along a thick stalk from late spring to early summer. Deadhead spent flowers for appearance and to prevent seed set, which takes energy away from the rhizome.

Irises will sometimes fail to set blooms. According to the Missouri Botanical Garden, "The most frequent causes of failure to flower or sparse flowering are (1) rhizomes are planted too deep, (2) plants are located in too much shade, (3) plants were given too much fertilizer or (4) plants have become overcrowded and need division."[29]

The iris has specific planting needs: in mid- to late summer, plant rhizomes shallowly with no more than 0.5″ / 1.3 cm of soil, 12–18″ / 30–46 cm apart, with the vegetative tip slightly exposed. The nature of the rhizome is to spread from the vegetative end. Orient the rhizome so the growing end faces into the garden and not toward the edge of a bed. Divide plants every three to four years, immediately after flowering.

Jerusalem Cross, Maltese cross

Silene chalcedonica (Lychnis chalcedonica)

CHRISTIAN REFERENCE

A consuming fire, burning with the love and devotion of both the lover and the beloved — what an amazing symbolism for this flame-red flower! The sacrifice and love of Jesus, Mary's love and courage to stay with her son, the wisdom of the Holy Spirit burning in us to continue God's mission on earth; all this can be contemplated through the blooms of the Jerusalem (Maltese) cross.

Silene chalcedonica

This species' flowers, which form an umbel,[30] will usually have five but sometimes four red petals. It was the four-petal that inspired the design of the Maltese cross.

The Sovereign Military Hospitaller Order of Saint John of Jerusalem (the Order of Malta) is a lay monastic order originally founded in 1048 by Amalfi merchants in Jerusalem, who developed hospitals to care for Christian pilgrims living in or visiting the Holy Lands. Later, Rome assigned the order the responsibility of a military to defend Christians from attacks in the region.[31]

According to tradition, it was the Knights of Malta who brought the *Silene chalcedonica* plant to Europe in their journeys home from the Holy Land.[32] The eight points on the Maltese cross — a symbol adopted by the Knights of Malta in 1126 — were said to reflect the knights' eight obligations or aspirations. The Maltese cross flower structure resembles this historical graphic, which is now a common firefighter symbol.

The five-petal blossom is shaped like a star and is compared with God's burning love shining down on his people, a light through our journey. His love for us is embodied by Jesus and his Sacred Heart, and shared in the Holy Spirit's indwelling in our hearts.

The strength of this plant's symbolism affords its use at any of the Stations of the Cross, or within the Sorrowful Mysteries of the Rosary. As for a Marian garden, there was never a love on earth that burned truer than that of Our Lady's Immaculate Heart!

Symbolism:
- burning love
- courage

Prayer Garden Theme:
- Sacred Heart of Jesus
- Stations of the Cross
- Holy Spirit
- virtue
- Marian
- Immaculate Heart of Mary
- Rosary

CULTURE

Silene chalcedonica is a perennial hardy in Zones 3–8, needs full sun and will tolerate light afternoon shade. This plant requires average watering in evenly moist, well-drained soils. Its deep tap root allows it to be somewhat drought tolerant.

Plants grow 10–12″ / 25–30 cm spread by 2–4′ / 61 cm–1.2 m height, and individual plants are short lived. They will form rejuvenating colonies through reseeding or rhizomes.

The intensely red flowers bloom all summer and can form striking dense 4″ / 10 cm umbels. Because they are terminal bloomers (the flower form at the end of the stem on which it grows), you will want to increase flowering stems by pinching back young plants in spring to promote additional branching. Deadhead by trimming back the flowering stem by one-third when flowers fade, to encourage further blooming and, if desired, prevent reseeding.

Because of their height they need protection from strong winds; pinching back in spring also makes for a sturdier plant, and one less prone to wind damage.

This perennial will grow in seaside or coastal gardens and along ditch lines or walkways, being fairly salt tolerant.

Lamb's Ear

Stachys byzantina

CHRISTIAN REFERENCE

Meekness does not mean timidness or cowardice, which would oppose the cardinal virtues as laid out in the *Catechism*; it actually reinforces them. The word comes to us from the training of a good war horse.

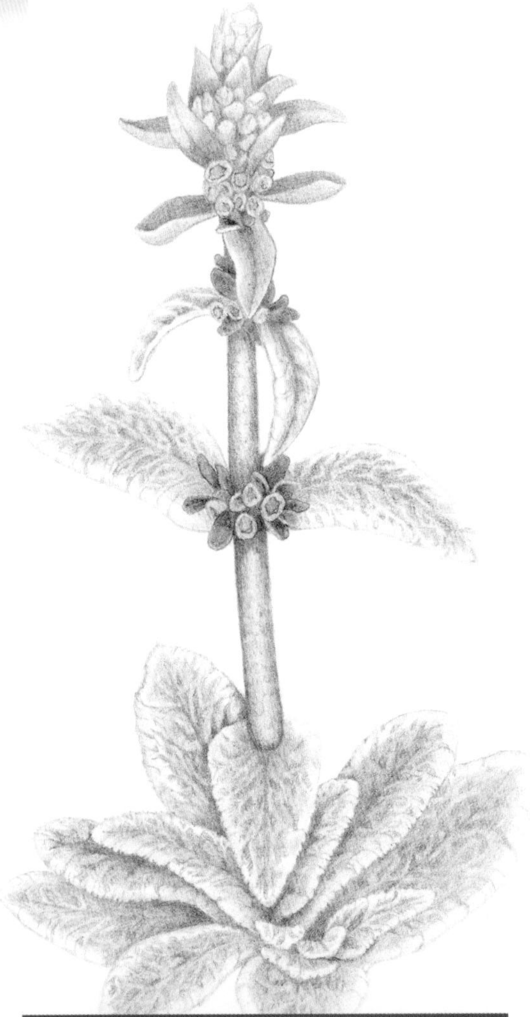

Incorporating the definition and etymology of *meek*, the word relates a sense of submissive obedience, being confidently docile or forbearing under threat. War horses in ancient Greece were trained to be meek, that is, to be powerful and obedient, under control of the warrior on their back during battle.

Somehow, though, the image of a lamb's fuzzy ear doesn't conjure up a connection with this warlike definition of meekness, until it is associated with Jesus, the Lamb of God.

Meekness is the perfect description of Jesus battling Satan during the time he walked on earth, and our Christian calling to continue fighting evil in our world. To be meek and humble of heart is to submit to God in full and steady confidence through the battle. And what is the battle? Living God's word in such a way as to evangelize by our actions, despite Satan's relentless attacks.

A person who is meek doesn't shy away from taking a stand; he or she takes a stand at the right time and in the right way. To be yoked with Jesus, to be "meek and humble of heart" (Mt 11:29), is to surrender to his working with us to bring glory to God.

Stachys byzantina

Mary was the ultimate model of humility, and meditating on her meekness to God in all things can help instill in us the same confidence of trusting God through whatever we face.

In a Rosary garden, the lamb's ear is appropriate at the First Joyful Mystery, The Annunciation, or at the First Sorrowful Mystery, The Agony in the Garden.

For a garden dedicated to the Stations of the Cross, place this plant in abundance at the entrance to the Way, or at the First Station, Jesus Is Condemned to Death.

Symbolism:

- meekness
- humility

Prayer Garden Theme:

- Stations of the Cross
- virtues
- Marian
- Rosary

CULTURE

Stachys byzantina, as the species name indicates, comes to us from the area once known as Byzantium, near present-day Istanbul. It is hardy in Zones 4–8 and requires full sun to light afternoon shade in warmer and dry climates. Its watering need is low. Keep this plant on the dry side, especially its leaves, which are prone to rot if too wet; avoid overhead watering. Good air movement is essential if high humidity is an issue in your area.

Poor soils must be well drained and stable for this shallow-rooted groundcover to thrive and spread by creeping stems. In organically rich soils it may become aggressive.

A single plant averages 1–2′ / 30–61 cm spread by 4–8″ / 10–20 cm height, with flowering scape (a leafless stalk) reaching up to 12–18″ / 30–46 cm. It will naturalize easily.

Lamb's ear is known more for its beautiful, thick silvery leaves than its small magenta flowers, which bloom in early summer atop a small-leaved fuzzy stalk. The genus name, *Stachys*, means "ear of corn" and aptly describes the terminal spike of blooms.

Expect some die-out if rain and humidity are high during the summer.

Lenten Rose, Christmas rose

Helleborus spp., *Helleborus* × *hybridus* 'Grape Galaxy'

CHRISTIAN REFERENCE

The Archangel Gabriel was quite busy during the Nativity of Our Lord, helping to honor Jesus with flowers; the pure white Christmas rose is historically called "The Christ's Herb."

Helleborus* × *hybridus
'Grape Galaxy'

A pious legend is told that at the time of the birth of Jesus, a young shepherd girl followed the Magi and wept outside the stable because she was poor and had nothing to give the baby. She sobbed, saying that she would have brought flowers if it hadn't been winter and the ground hard with frost; the only thing she could give the Child was her love. Suddenly the Archangel Gabriel appeared and asked the young shepherdess to follow him as he led her away into the cold, dark night. Stopping a short distance from the stable, he struck the frosty earth, and at once a small patch of the *Helleborus niger* sprang up and bloomed. The shepherdess was filled with joy and, drying her tears, plucked the beautiful white flowers and ran back to the manger to give them to the Holy Child.

From this legend, plant the Lenten rose at the Third Joyful Mystery, The Nativity of Our Lord. It can also be used at the First Joyful Mystery, The Annunciation. It is appropriate in any Marian garden, really.

The *Helleborus niger* also carries the common name of flower of Saint Agnes because of its symbolism of purity. St. Agnes of Rome was a thirteen-year-old virgin who was martyred in the third century in late January —

her feast day is January 21 — when this flower blooms. In the Holy Virgin Procession depicted in the great procession mosaics at the Basilica di Sant'Apollinare Nuovo, Ravenna, Agnes is one of the white-robed virgins, holding a red crown. A tiny lamb walks at her feet, looking up to her face; the white lamb is also part of her emblem of purity.

The genus name of this plant tells explicitly of its nature: All parts of the plant are poisonous to human and animals. *Helleborus* comes from Greek *hele-* to "take away," or possibly *helein-* meaning "to injure/destroy," and *bora* for "food."

Symbolism:
- purity
- humility

Prayer Garden Theme:
- Marian
- Rosary
- saints

CULTURE

There are several species of *Helleborus* to choose from, all with similar culture requirements. The most common and easiest Lenten roses to grow are the *Helleborus orientalis*. Hardy in Zones 4–9, this perennial requires full shade and will tolerate dappled partial shade. It does not grow well in direct sun, where even a few hours can cause leaves to splotch and crisp from sun scald.

Watering needs are average; it needs organically rich, evenly moist soil that is well drained. Do not allow plants to dry out in summer.

Individual plants average 12–18″ / 30–46 cm spread by 12–18″ / 30–46 cm height, forming larger clumps up to 24″ / 61 cm spread.

The nodding flowers — which can be 3-4″ / 8–10 cm in diameter and have large contrasting stamens and pistil — carry two to five blossoms per stem, and bloom in early spring. The *Helleborus orientalis* cultivars are the earliest to flower. The color of the blooms varies from white, chartreuse, and pinks to dark wine. Some species are doubled, speckled or mottled, and two-toned.

These are a true woodland perennial that appreciate the mulch naturally formed by leaves, and cool soils that are moist but not wet. The large, nearly evergreen leaves make for a lovely ground cover through summer when planted in drifts among trees.

Removing spent flowering stalks is advised, and be sure to remove old leaves in early spring before new growth becomes too advanced.

Depicted here is one of my favorites, *Helleborus* × *hybridus* 'Grape Galaxy'. A taller species at 18–22″ / 46–56 cm height, it blooms a week or two later than *Helleborus orientalis* cultivars with flowers bearing a "constellation" of stamens, and dark, speckled petals.

Lily of the Valley

Convallaria majalis, Convallaria majalis* var. *rosea

CHRISTIAN REFERENCE

The delicate lily of the valley — which isn't even in the *Liliaceae* family, but *Asparagaceae* — has a history associated with sorrow, going all the way back to Genesis and beginning with Eve. When being expelled from Eden, Eve cried with remorse, and her tears fell along the path of her departure. It is told that a trail of these flowers sprung up where her copious tears watered the earth.

The Virgin Mary, as the new Eve, also left a trail of tears. As Mary wept at the sentencing and passion of Jesus, her tears also fell to the ground, and the lily of the valley is said to have sprouted where they landed. The symbolism of this plant, also called Our Lady's tears, makes it appropriate to be planted anywhere along the path of a Stations of the Cross garden. If you want to use it in small groupings, place it at the First Station, Jesus Is Condemned to Death, or at the Fourth Station, Jesus Meets His Mother.

Convallaria majalis* var. *rosea

In mild to coastal climates, the lily of the valley flowers in early spring, near the date of the Annunciation. It is also considered a symbol of the Savior's advent, and associated with the Incarnation. For your Rosary garden, plant it among the Joyful Mysteries, or particularly at the first or third mystery.

Convallaria majalis has a similar symbolism to the white lily, and is often depicted in art indicating Mary's purity, chastity, and humility. These same sentiments have led to the lily of the valley being a desired flower in a bride's bouquet, especially among European royalty.

The lily of the valley is also associated with a fanciful story taking place in a Sussex forest between a hermit — Saint Leonard, whose feast day is November 6 — and a dragon. "The first recorded dragon was slain by St. Leonard in the 6th century. This was of course contemporary with the dawn of the Christianization of the native 'pagan' religion in [England]. … By tradition this saint was wounded during the battle with the dragon and wherever his blood fell, lilies-of-the-valley grew. Today, we can see an area known as the Lily Beds in this forest, where these lilies grow wild in abundance."[33]

Symbolism:

- chastity
- purity
- Annunciation/ Incarnation

Prayer Garden Theme:

- Stations of the Cross
- Marian
- Rosary
- saints

CULTURE

Convallaria majalis is a forest wildflower native to the northern hemisphere and grows in temperate climates; it does not like it hot. Hardy in Zones 3–7, preferring partial to full shade in organically rich woodland soils that are evenly moist and well drained, it appreciates a good layer of leaf mulch. It will grow in most any soil, including clay, and for this reason is considered an invasive species in some regions. Watering needs are average, and it will die back if kept too dry.

As a ground cover, it spreads exponentially by rhizomes — called pips — and averages 6–8″ / 15–20 cm height. It is an excellent plant for erosion control on shaded slopes.

Convallaria majalis is highly fragrant, blooming in spring with nodding, usually white, bell-shaped flowers along one side of a sturdy singular stalk that rises clasped between the leaves. It is an excellent long-lasting cut flower; lightly pinch near the base of the stalk and pull straight up, and immediately place the stem in tepid water.

Cultivars can bear flowers of a single bell or doubled petals, in white, pink, or rose with white edges as presented here. Variegated leaf varieties are said to be less invasive.

In autumn in a shady garden, the lily of the valley creates a carpet of gold leaves, with distinct inedible deep-orange berries.

Lily, Madonna, Saint Joseph, or Annunciation lily

Lilium candidum, Lilium longiflorum

CHRISTIAN REFERENCE

The Virgin Mary has no more iconic or recognizable flower than the lily. And let's not forget about Saint Joseph and the Archangel Gabriel! *Lilium candidum* is a symbol of both confirmation from God, and the purity of a soul.

Lilium longiflorum

In the Old Testament there are several verses that develop the symbolism of the lily; the qualities of beauty, fertility, spiritual flourishing, and purity of soul. In the Gospels of Matthew and Luke, the lily with its beauty is used to teach of dependence on God.

There are three legends associated with this flower's symbolism: the Annunciation, and two others that belong to Saint Joseph and his staff. The first was when the top of his staff burst into bloom, revealing God's choice of him to be the husband of the temple virgin, Mary. And again, at the Nativity, the lily confirmed his status as the foster father of the Christ.

Both Joseph and Mary had purity of heart, a single-mindedness to follow the will of God.

We are all familiar with the image of Archangel Gabriel presenting this flower to Mary at the Annunciation. Interestingly, the Annunciation is a solemnity for both Roman and Eastern Catholics.

In art the lily not only appears in scenes of the Nativity, but also in paintings of Madonna and Child. In images of the saints, it often represents virginity or the virtue of purity.

When the lily was painted or used on an altar, the pollen-loaded stamens were eliminated so as not to defile the "virgin chastity" of the bloom.[34]

Lilium candidum is known as the meadow lily throughout Europe and the Mediterranean. It grows on a long, slender 3–4' / 91 cm–1.2 m stalk with small leaves and delicate terminal blooms, which open in succession in early summer. The Easter lily, *Lilium longiflorum*, whose culture information is included below, has larger trumpet flowers arrayed at the top, opening randomly in late summer, and broader leaves along a 2–3' / 61–91 cm stem; it is a native plant of Japan and Taiwan. Really, any white lily would be appropriate in a prayer garden.

Symbolism:

- chastity
- purity
- innocence

Prayer Garden Theme:

- Marian
- Rosary
- Saint Joseph
- archangel

CULTURE

Lilium longiflorum cultivars are hardy in Zones 4–8, require full sun on their leaves, and appreciate having their roots kept cool by mulch or shade, especially in warmer climates. Average watering is needed, and the plant is not drought tolerant. Well-drained, evenly moist, organically rich soil to 6" / 15 cm deep is best, though the lily will tolerate most any garden soil that doesn't run dry.

The Easter lily is often forced to bloom in early spring and sold in pots. For the garden, plant bulbs in groupings of three or more in a wind-protected area. This plant grows 9–12" / 23–30 cm spread by 2–3' / 61–91 cm height, with large, white, fragrant flowers appearing in late summer. Remove spent flowers individually to prevent seed set — the chemical change in a plant that stops flower production while producing seeds — and cut off the top of the stem when the bloom cycle is completed.

If you choose to use it as a cut flower, leave at least half the green stalk to produce food for the bulb and next year's growth, which will be smaller and bear fewer blooms. Because of the excessive pollen load, remove the stamens before bringing indoors and as each blossom opens, to prevent the pollen from staining surfaces, clothes, and skin. To remove pollen grains that have dislodged and landed, gently place tape over pollen and lift. Do not try to brush off the grains — this smears and sets the pollen, staining even worse.

In Zones 4–5, a good layer of mulch will help protect the bulbs from winter kill.

Lilies, like hostas, are considered deer dessert.

Love-in-a-Mist, Black cumin

Nigella arvensis, Nigella damascena

CHRISTIAN REFERENCE

These little black seeds have the power to cure every sickness, except death? That is the legacy of the ancient and delicate black cumin, *Nigella arvensis.* "Nigella has been traced back more than 3,000 years to the kingdom of the Assyrians and ancient Egyptians and used since antiquity by Asian herbalists and pharmacists. A bottle of black cumin oil was found in the tomb of King Tutankhamen. The Romans used it for culinary purposes; in the Middle East nigella is added to bread dough."[35]

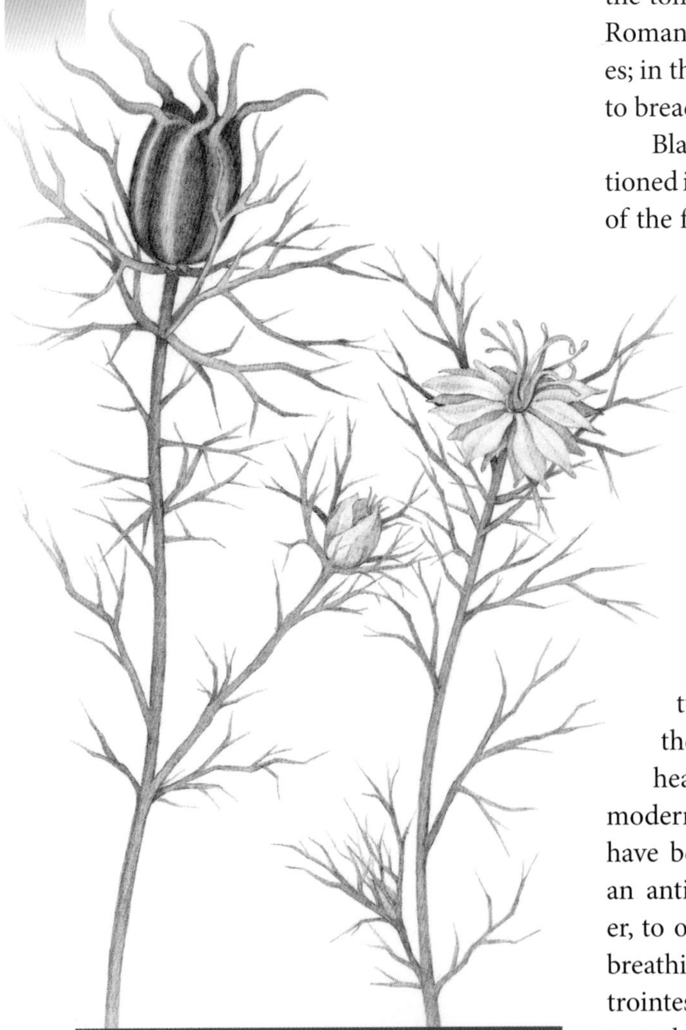

Black cumin is a Bible plant mentioned in Isaiah chapter 28, the parable of the farmer. Here Isaiah gives glory to God for the knowledge he has bestowed on the farmer in knowing when to till, seed, and harvest. In verses 25 and 27, he specifically mentions the seeds of *Nigella sativa*, using the familiar name of cumin.

The seeds of this determinedly prolific annual, also classified as an herb, have been known for centuries in Islamic tradition as the "remedy of the prophet," that heal all things "except death."[36] In modern herbal medicine the seeds have been used as an antimicrobial, an anti-inflammatory, a pain reliever, to open air passages and improve breathing in asthmatics, to heal gastrointestinal issues, and to help protect the kidneys and liver. Quite a claim to fame!

Nigella damascena

The "mist" in its common name,

love-in-a-mist, comes from the thread-like foliage, whose mass forms what appears to be a delicate, fog-like cloud.

Its reference to St. Catherine of Alexandria came from the imagination of the faithful who thought the delicate blue flowers resembled the wheel that broke at her martyrdom. The "mist" of leaves symbolized her deep love of Jesus that she maintained throughout her suffering.

Symbolism:
- healing
- openness to love

Prayer Garden Theme:
- Bible
- saint

CULTURE

An annual that vigorously reseeds, *Nigella damascena* cultivars are hardy in Zones 2–11, requiring full sun and appreciating light afternoon shade in warmer climates.

Its water needs are average, and it is tolerant of most loose soils that are well drained and consistently moist. It is often more floriferous in poor soils, but it is not drought tolerant and will rapidly decline if left too dry.

For the most impressive display, plant this fast grower in drifts; individual plants have a 12–18″ / 30–46 cm spread by 18–24″ / 46–61 cm height. Several gardeners claim that a long border of *Nigella* species is a significant deterrent to deer browsing.

Nigella's flowers are commonly blue, with cultivars that are white, pink, and shades of rose to purple; blooms appear in late spring and continue through summer.

Love-in-a-mist is one of the easiest annuals to grow and ideal for that cottage garden look if you allow it to reseed throughout your flower beds. Collect the pods and, come spring, sow in the garden as soon as the ground is thawed. Continue with additional sowings in cooler regions until midsummer to encourage flowering into autumn.

If you do not want to collect the seed pods for dried arrangements or decorating Christmas greens, deadhead spent flowers to prolong flowering.

These plants do not transplant well, so where they are sown, leave be.

Lungwort, Bethlehem sage

Pulmonaria officinalis, Pulmonaria saccharata 'Mrs. Moon'

CHRISTIAN REFERENCE

Look to the lungwort when seeking flowering plants for the shade — its leaves make an impressive statement too!

For a damp deciduous woodland garden, consider *Pulmonaria saccharata*, which in the spring offers a delightfully soothing display of flowers. Besides its showy leaves, the drooping clusters of bell-shaped blooms begin in a rosy-red and, as they develop, turn to a rich blue. For this reason, one of its English names is Josephs and Maries, derived from the smaller rosy-red blooms for Mary, and the larger matured blues for Joseph.[37]

There are three familiar legends of tears — all seemingly of European origin — associated with the flower's coloring. One tells us that the flower's transition to blue from red was the plant honoring Mary's tears at the suffering to come for her Son. The other is similar: The blue represents the color of Mary's eyes, and the red the effect from her weeping.[38]

The third legend, much like the second, is told from Calvary, where at the foot of the cross the Blessed Mother's eyes were as blue as the matured blossom, and her eyelids were as red as the buds from her crying. The spots on the leaves are said to be the marks from the tears she shed.[39]

As for the spotted leaves, the plant is also known as Our Lady's milk, for it is said when she stopped in the shade to nurse the Holy Infant, some of her milk spilled

Pulmonaria saccharata 'Mrs. Moon'

upon the plant. This plant, as with the herb rosemary, is significant in that it is referenced at both the beginning and the end of Jesus' life.

The symbolism of this flower, with its specific association to Mary as "the new Eve," is seen in fifteenth-century art depicting the Garden of Eden. In modern renderings, artists also include it in paintings of the Annunciation.

For a Stations of the Cross garden, place this low-growing plant at the Fourth Station, Jesus Meets His Mother, or at the Eleventh through Thirteenth Stations of Jesus' crucifixion.

Symbolism:

- devotion
- Mary's tears
- Mary's milk drops

Prayer Garden Theme:

- Stations of the Cross
- Marian
- Rosary

In the Rosary garden, grow lungwort anywhere within the Sorrowful Mysteries. It is also appropriate in the Joyful Mysteries at the Nativity of Our Lord.

CULTURE

There is a wide assortment of *Pulmonaria* species to choose from, with varying leaf color, shape, and mottling, as well as flowers of white, rosy-red, or blue, and (in some) rose and blue at the same time.

Here I offer *Pulmonaria saccharata* 'Mrs. Moon', which is hardy in Zones 3–8, preferring full shade to high dappled shade. It will not tolerate full sun.

Needing average water, it prefers cool soil that is evenly moist, well drained, and organically rich — the conditions of a damp deciduous woodlands. 'Mrs. Moon' grows 18–24″ / 46–61 cm spread by 9–18″ / 23–46 cm height, flowering in late spring with showy blooms that begin as pink and turn to blue. The plant is self-sowing and creates drifts of color among leaf mulch, with persisting finely speckled fuzzy leaves.

If the woodlands run dry, the leaves will curl inward and brown at the edges, as do most *Pulmonaria* spp. Simply cut back hard to rejuvenate the plant.

Marigold

Tagetes spp., *Tagetes patula* 'Red Cherry'

CHRISTIAN REFERENCE

The garden marigold, *Tagetes* species, and the pot (English) marigold, *Calendula officinalis*, presented in Herbs and Edibles, carry the same emblem of grief and death; and, from the Benedictine nun St. Hildegard of Bingen, the same name of Mary's gold.

Before the apparition of Our Lady of Guadalupe that led to the conversion of much of the Americas, the marigold — called *cempaspuchitl*[40] — expressed a love-filled eternity within Aztec mythology.

Like many cultural traditions and legends that were converted to reflect Christian virtues, this myth was brought to coincide with the Church's All Saints Day and All Souls Day, which honor the lives of the saints and intercede for the dead in purgatory.

The Aztec myth tells of a couple who fell in love as children and would go to a mountain together to play and thank the sun god for all things. As years went by, a war broke out and the two adolescents were separated. When word came back to the young woman that her beloved had been killed, in her grief she went to their cherished mountain site one last time to share her sorrow with the sun god, and asked a favor: to be granted one last visit from her beloved.

The sun god was moved by their love, and with a warm ray of light touched the young woman's cheek and turned her into a fragrant golden flower reminiscent of the sun, and

Tagetes patula 'Red Cherry'

made her beloved a hummingbird. For all of eternity, she and he would be united.

The death of these two, and the great love they shared beyond this life, is said to have led to the flower's use in the Day of the Dead celebrations. The flower is said to represent the sun, which guides the spirit into eternity. The strong aroma guides the spirits back to their loved ones, once a year, on *el Día de los Muertos.*

The myth was easily brought into the Catholic tradition of faith in God, the love of God for his children, and the joy of love throughout eternity after death.

Symbolism:

- death
- eternity

Prayer Garden Theme:

- Stations of the Cross
- Marian
- Rosary

In a Rosary garden, use the marigold among the Sorrowful Mysteries. For a Stations of the Cross garden it would be placed at the Fourth Station, Jesus Meets His Mother.

CULTURE

There are hundreds of *Tagetes* species and cultivars available throughout the world. It's a popular and easily grown annual ranging in height from a few inches/centimeters to nearly 2' / 61 cm, and all cultivars have similar culture requirements. Here I offer the French marigold *Tagetes patula*, a dwarf that displays single, semi-double, double, or crested centered flowers in shades of yellow, orange, red, or bicolor.

An annual grown in Zones 2–11, it requires full sun to light afternoon shade. Watering needs are average. It grows best in fertile soil that is well drained, and is one of the garden plants that will tolerate denser clay soils.

The dwarf French marigold grows 6–9″ / 15–23 cm spread by 6–12″ / 15–30 cm height. It is highly recommended to pinch back young plants to promote thicker growth and better flowering display.

The showy and prolific flowers begin in early summer and continue until frost. In extreme heat, blooming will slow until cooler temperatures resume as autumn approaches. Deadhead spent flowers throughout the season. If you choose to collect seeds to store and plant next spring, allow a few flowering heads to remain on the stalk until dried.

Marigolds are an excellent companion plant in the vegetable garden, and elsewhere. *Tagetes* roots kill nematodes in the soil, and the vegetative body deters slugs and repels white fly.

Michaelmas Daisy

Aster amellus, Symphyotrichum novae-angliae 'Andenken an Alma Pötschke'

CHRISTIAN REFERENCE

"The Michaelmas Daisy among dead weeds / Blooms for St. Michael's valourous deeds."[41]

A dizzying number of lilac-colored asters are associated with Michaelmas celebrations. They are common and found throughout the Northern Hemisphere. Narrowing the symbolism to specific genera is nearly impossible; in Europe the *Aster amellus* is claimed.

Symphyotrichum novae-angliae 'Andenken an Alma Pötschke'

In the legend, the focus is on the autumn-blooming, lilac-colored Michaelmas daisy, which is associated with the feast of St. Michael the Archangel on September 29. Saint Michael is celebrated as a protector from evil and darkness — just as the aster fights against the advancing gloom of winter with gay color in our otherwise declining gardens. This species flowers when daylight hours shorten; this light sensitivity is termed *photoperiodicity.*

Traditionally, Michaelmas celebrations were early harvest festivals that included dancing, costumes, games, and of course lots of food prepared from what grew in the fields and gardens. One of those foods prepared in abundance was anything that included blackberries, which were ripe in many parts of Europe by the end of September. And every good Christian in Europe knew the berries had to be harvested by this day, lest the fiery effects of Lucifer destroy the fruits sent by God. The story told is that when Saint Michael cast Lucifer from heaven, and when the devil landed on earth, he fell into a brier of blackberry canes. The devil spat on those canes, cursed the fruit, and scorched them with his fiery breath — all before Saint Michael could finish the job of sending the devil into hell.[42]

Symbolism:
- protection against darkness

Prayer Garden Theme:
- saint
- angel

CULTURE

There are hundreds of asters throughout the world, cultivated and wild. Narrowing the selection for your garden is a matter of preference, culture, and Zone. Symbolically, choose varieties that flower near the end of September.

Presented here is a rose-pink New England aster with a startlingly long name, *Symphyotrichum novae-angliae* 'Andenken an Alma Pötschke'. The culture information is pretty much the same as for most asters.

It is hardy in Zones 4–8, requiring full sun, but will tolerate light afternoon shade in warmer climates.

Asters are typically not drought tolerant and require regular watering. Soil should be organically rich and evenly moist. This cultivar is said to tolerate drought, and will grow in most soil types including clay as long as the ground is well drained. It is also tolerant of salt.

Fast growing and long lived, this aster grows 2–3′ / 61–91 cm spread by 2.5–3′ / 76–91 cm height. Allow for good air circulation to prevent leaf molds from developing, but avoid windy sites because of its height.

The 2″ / 5 cm rose-pink flowers bloom from early autumn to frost, attracting butterflies and bees in search of late-season nectar.

Asters do well if pinched back twice early in the growing season. This will of course shorten the height, but will allow plants to be more floriferous and sturdy. Remove the branched stalks of spent flowers to encourage additional blooms, keep things tidy, and prevent reseeding.

A unique characteristic of this plant's periodicity is that the blooms close up and droop at night or on cloudy, overcast days.

Morning Glory

***Convolvulus* spp., *Ipomoea purpurea* 'Heavenly Blue'**

CHRISTIAN REFERENCE

Life is short — too short when we want to live on — yet too long as we suffer through our death. The common name for the morning glory came about because this plant's flower unfurls to life at dawn and rapidly declines by midday. This frailty led to the morning glory receiving the Christian symbolism of mortality and the brevity of life on earth.

Ipomoea purpurea 'Heavenly Blue'

When considering plant symbolism, keep in mind the era. Different eras ascribed different sentiments.

The earliest symbolism of the morning glory indicated the brevity of life, and was initially applied to the bindweed *Convolvulus arvensis* and related species. In the Victorian era, the symbolism evolved to the brevity or shortness of love. There is also the theme of sadness at being unable to express love — being bound up, unable to be with the one you loved, thwarted either by circumstances or death. And here the symbolism circles back to death, and an eternally binding love.

Red is one of the colors symbolic of love. Use a scarlet morning glory in the garden as a dedication to the Sacred Heart of Jesus or the Immaculate Heart of Mary.

Blue has long been associated with the Blessed Mother's garments and eternity. Appropriately enough, a rather large flowering morning glory in this color is called *Ipomoea purpurea* 'Heavenly Blue'.

White flowers also symbolize eternity, as well as innocence and virginity. Here a choice for the Marian or Rosary garden could be the moonflower, *Ipomoea alba*. This is a nocturnal fragrant bloomer excellent for a night or white garden.

An *Ipomoea* vine of any color is suitable for a Rosary garden within all four sets of mysteries!

The morning glory can be planted anywhere along the Stations of the Cross as well. It is especially appropriate at the First Station, Jesus Is Condemned to Death, to symbolize extinguished hopes and being bound. At the Fourteenth Station, Jesus Is Laid in the Tomb, it can be used to meditate on death and rebirth.

The nature of the morning glory lends itself to several spiritual meditations. The flower may be delicate and speak to the fragility of life, but the vine persists and is surprisingly strong as it clings upon its support — much as we are supported by Christ as we persist in our faith.

Symbolism:

- mortality
- enduring love

Prayer Garden Theme:

- Sacred Heart of Jesus
- Stations of the Cross
- Immaculate Heart of Mary
- Marian
- Rosary

CULTURE

Ipomoea purpurea cultivars are reseeding annual vines growing throughout Zones 2–11. Because of their nature to reseed and twine around anything, they may become weedy or even invasive in warmer climates.

Morning glories require full sun, though they will grow sparsely in light shade — and flower less. Water needs are average, and they are not drought tolerant.

This plant will grow pretty much anywhere: in light sandy soils, average, or clay, as long as the soil is well drained. Overly fertile soils or the use of fertilizer will often cause the vine to be vigorous but without flowers.

A rapid-growing, twining vine, needing a suitable support on which to cling, it grows 2–6′ / 61 cm–1.8 m spread by 6–10′ / 1.8–3 m height in one season! It has large heart-shaped leaves that form a backdrop for the prolific blooms.

The trumpet-shaped flowers, which range from white to pink, red, magenta, purple, and blue, as well as picotee, mottled, or striped, begin to open in late spring and continue until frost. Depending on variety, some are mildly fragrant, but most are not.

Mum

Chrysanthemum spp., *Chrysanthemum* 'Ruby Mound'

CHRISTIAN REFERENCE

The chrysanthemums we know today began from simple yellow daisies that grew wild in northeastern Europe and eastern Asia. Through two thousand years of cultivation by Japanese and Chinese growers, and continued breeding by other nurserymen, the plant has developed into the diversity of flower types and colors we see in modern time.

Chrysanthemum 'Ruby Mound'

There are many culturally based legends going back thousands of years associated with this plant. In the Christian tradition, it is strongly associated with eternal life through Christ; and with eternity comes grieving by those left behind.

The garland mum, *Glebionis* a.k.a. *Leucanthemum coronarium*, is the ephemeral golden daisylike mum common in Israel. It blooms in the springtime around the same time as the Jewish Passover. Legend has it that it was in bloom when Jesus was laid in the tomb. As a result, for centuries the chrysanthemum genus has been a part of funerals and decorations for graves.

There are several legends about the mum, each culturally based and predominantly Eastern. One legend of the white mum comes to us from Germany.

It was a cold and snowy Christmas Eve in the Black Forest, and a blizzard was blowing. As a peasant family was preparing to sit down to a paltry meal, they heard a mournful sound and thought it was the wind.

The wailing sound continued, and the family, uncertain of what was making the noise, reluctantly opened the cottage door. They were startled to find a poor young beggar, nearly blue from the cold! They hurriedly brought him near the fire, wrapped him in blankets, and brought him a bowl filled with their own meager supper.

Upon the offering, the boy stood and, shedding the blankets, revealed himself as the Christ in brilliant white garments with halo about his head. He then vanished from the home. The next morning, outside the door where he had stood, were white chrysanthemums blooming through the snow. To this day many Germans bring white mums into their homes on Christmas Eve as a symbol of sheltering the Christ Child.[43]

Symbolism:

- eternal life
- grieving

Prayer Garden Theme:

- Stations of the Cross
- Marian
- Rosary

CULTURE

With several genera of mums and thousands of varieties, as well as thirteen different bloom shapes, choosing one may prove more difficult than growing them! (Be aware: The genus *Chrysanthemum* was so expansive that in the twentieth century it was divided into several specific genera, of which *Glebionis* and *Leucanthemum* are included, among other confounding name changes.) Culture is much the same, though Zone tolerance differs. Heights range from less than 12″ / 30 cm to more than 3′ / 91 cm.

Here I offer a hardy cushion-style garden mum, *Chrysanthemum* 'Ruby Mound', selected for its compact growth and deep blood-red color.

Hardy in Zones 5–9, this mum requires full sun though it will tolerate dappled afternoon shade in warmer climates. Too much shade and the plant will become thin and leggy with reduced flowering.

Watering needs are average; too much and basal leaves will rot. Grow in average soils that are well drained, especially in winter. These plants do not like wet feet and appreciate good air movement. This variety is said to tolerate clay soils better than most mums.

This plant is typical of cushion mums, being full and round nearly as wide as tall, growing 16–20″ / 41–51 cm spread by 16–24″ / 41–61 cm height.

The mildly fragrant 3″ / 8 cm flowers bloom from early autumn to hard frost on multibranched stems; the leaves are also fragrant.

As for most mums, pinch back young plants twice in the spring, about three to four weeks apart, to encourage branching. Mums are terminal bloomers, so more branching means more flowers and sturdier stems.

Narcissus, Daffodil

***Narcissus poeticus, Narcissus poeticus* 'Actaea'**

CHRISTIAN REFERENCE

The pheasant-eye daffodil or narcissus, a native spring-blooming flower in Europe, carries several symbolisms in Christianity. These pious references point to new life, beginning with the Annunciation and including the Resurrection.

Narcissus poeticus 'Actaea'

The narcissus is included in scenes of the Annunciation, representing the triumph of divine love and eternal life over death.[44] One legend tells of when, at the resurrection of Christ, the daffodils all at once burst into bloom on that glorious morning. This sense of rebirth also alludes to eternal life after death.

Father Gemminger, in his book *Flowers of Mary*, wrote what could be called a litany of symbolisms for this flower: The upright stalks point toward heaven where she is Queen; its calyx turned toward earth reminds us of her gaze to us from heaven and also of her humility; her Immaculate Heart is represented by the pure white petals; the central circle of gold represents her crown of glory; the fragrance of the daffodil is reminiscent of the fragrance of her love, and her role as refuge of sinners; and its abundant spring flowering calls forth her full blooming of virtues.

Narcissus poeticus cultivars are often mentioned as Our Lady's star. When you look directly into the corona, together the stamen form the six points of the Star of David. Another proposed reason for the symbolism may be a reference to her crown of twelve stars mentioned in the Bible; the center corona of the flower is reminiscent of a crown.

Daffydowndilly[45] is the common name for the double-flowering narcissus variety associated with Saint Colette, whose feast day is March 6 — coinciding with the time when this daffodil blooms. The flower is also associated with Saint David for the same reason; his feast day is March 1.

The salvific purpose of the Incarnation was restoration of God in us through the paschal mystery. With all of the narcissus' symbolisms, this flower can be grown in any number of prayer gardens!

Symbolism:

- new life
- divine love especially after death
- forgiveness

Prayer Garden Theme:

- divine mercy
- Stations of the Cross,
- virtues
- Marian
- Rosary
- Bible
- saints

CULTURE

The pheasant-eye narcissus, *Narcissus poeticus* 'Actaea', is hardy in Zones 3–9 and will grow in full sun to light shade. Like most early spring-flowering plants, locating the bulbs in or at the edges of woodlands is fine as long as they receive direct to dappled light before the trees leaf out.

Watering needs are average; narcissus appreciates being moist during the growing season. The plant will tolerate drought after the leaves have died back. Narcissus grows in most soils, preferring organically rich, evenly moist, and well drained. This cultivar is said to perform better than most in damp and poorly drained soils such as clay or near ponds and rivers.

A single plant of 'Actaea' has a 2–3″ / 5–8 cm spread by 12–18″ / 30–46 cm height; daffodils should be planted in groupings of five to seven bulbs and allowed to naturalize, forming drifts.

This cultivar has fragrant blooms up to 3″ / 8 cm wide from mid- to late spring. It is an early source of pollen for bees. Deadheading is encouraged, where practical for small colonies.

Oxeye Daisy, Shasta Daisy

***Leucanthemum vulgare, Leucanthemum × superbum* 'Alaska'**

CHRISTIAN REFERENCE

The oxeye daisy, also known as the shasta daisy, shares many of the same symbolisms in Christian iconography as other plants whose flowers are similarly constructed, such as the English daisy, *Bellis perennis*. *Bellis perennis* (as previously mentioned on page 50) has small, typical disc flowers on spreading stems, and a reputation ranging from attractive low-spreading ornamental flower to annoying common weed. The oxeye daisy is a showier choice for the cultivated garden, with large upright flowers.

Leucanthemum × superbum 'Alaska'

The daisy was prominent in the borders of the beautifully decorated Flemish manuscript, the Hastings *Book of Hours* from the fifteenth century.[46] Elements from nature — plants, bugs, and animals — were used in the manuscript to illustrate the virtues of the Christian life. The daisy was regularly included around images of the Virgin Mary and the Christ Child.

This flower has a long history of being associated with the Blessed Mother, through its symbolisms of humility, purity, chastity, and innocence. These attributes relate to the Christ Child as well, and are often combined with the added symbolism of salvation.

We are all familiar with the Bible story of the Magi journeying to the newborn King of the Jews (see Mt 2:1–12). A sweet legend is told that by night the wise men were guided by the star, but as the sun rose the star's brightness diminished. The Magi found during their morning travels that a small white flower grew along their path, in the direction that the star had indicated during the night. The brilliant white diminutive daisy was the day star guiding them to the baby Jesus.

The daisy was also an emblem of powerful women, and the Virgin Mary as protectress embodied this role.[47] Not only in manuscripts, but also in art, tapestries, and architecture, the open blooms of the flower frequently accompany her image.

Symbolism:

- patience
- innocence
- chastity
- humility
- salvation

Prayer Garden Theme:

- divine mercy
- Holy Spirit
- Marian

CULTURE

There are several cultivars of oxeye daisy available in the market with varying heights, bloom periods, and longevity of floral display, and flowers that are single or doubled and of different sizes. With a little planning, the daisy can grace your gardens for months!

One cultivar is the compact oxeye daisy, *Leucanthemum* × *superbum* 'Alaska'. It is hardy in Zones 3–9 and requires full sun; dappled afternoon shade is tolerated in warmer climates.

The plant needs low to medium watering, but the soil must be well drained — wet roots are fatal to this daisy. It will grow in most any garden soil: normal, sandy, or clay.

Growing 18–24″ / 46–61 cm spread by 20–30″ / 51–76 cm height, with sturdy stems and a dense growth habit, it does not require staking as do many other cultivars. Showy 3″ / 8 cm flowers bloom terminally on the stalks, and pinching the plant back early will set lateral branches for additional blooms. This of course will also shorten the plant height.

To encourage a longer blooming period, deadhead to the third or fourth set of leaves. This plant does well if divided every three years to maintain vigor.

In late autumn shear back the mound by half and allow the stalks to remain. The stalks of the daisy are hollow and offer an overwintering habitat for certain species of bees and other pollinators.

Peony, Pentecost Rose

***Paeonia officinalis, Paeonia lactiflora* 'Bowl of Beauty'**

CHRISTIAN REFERENCE

Imagine standing with anticipation in the nave of the church as the lilting *Veni Sancte Spiritus* sequence reaches its climax — and then they're released! A shower of fragrant peony petals flame the air with the symbolic fire of the Holy Spirit, and you get goose bumps as the Spirit caresses your soul.

This is the peony's — the Pentecost rose's — moment of glory in celebration of the birth of the Church; a ritual that has continued at the Pantheon in Rome since the tenth century. Today, that dramatic moment recreating a sense of the fiery tongues of flame includes most any red petals, often roses, mixed with some white.

The peony is a native plant in Asia and southern Europe, and flowers late spring to early summer. In the northern hemisphere the *Paeonia lactiflora* cultivars are in full bloom for Pentecost Sunday, beginning to flower in May. Since May is also dedicated to the Virgin Mary, here is the origin of another common name, Our Lady's rose.

The peony is a common medicinal plant, centuries old, and still in use today.

With its association both with Mary and with healing, many early Christians held that not only was the peony medicinally beneficial, it also protected from demons.

In the Holy Lands, the *Paeonia mascula* — which now faces extinction — is a native, dark-red, single-petal peony that blooms in early April.

***Paeonia lactiflora* 'Bowl of Beauty'**

Though not mentioned directly in Scripture, the flowers would have been in bloom during Passover. For this reason, any of the deep magenta to dark maroon flowering cultivars are suitable in a Bible garden.

In a Rosary garden, plant a white or red peony at the Third Glorious Mystery, The Descent of the Holy Spirit. With its symbolism of "ardent love of God," this flower in any color can be grown at the first three Joyful Mysteries, or at any of the five Luminous Mysteries.

Symbolism:

- ardent love of God
- healing
- Pentecost rose
- Our Lady's rose

Prayer Garden Theme:

- Holy Spirit
- Marian
- Rosary
- Bible

CULTURE

The peony is a wonderful plant for the beginner gardener. *Paeonia lactiflora* 'Bowl of Beauty', presented here, is grown in my garden.

Hardy in Zones 4–7, it needs full sun and appreciates light afternoon shade. In warmer regions plant on the east side of a garden to protect the blooms from scorching in the afternoon sun. Watering needs are average and best done at the base when the plant is flowering.

Organically rich, well-drained soil is ideal; but peonies will grow most anywhere, even in clay soil, as long as it is well drained.

This cultivar grows 24–36″ / 61–91 cm spread by 24–36″ / 61–91 cm height, and forms a lovely deep green border when not in bloom. The fragrant flowers appear in late spring through early summer and can be up to 8″ / 20 cm wide on mature plants. If purchased as bare root plants, they may take as long as two years to bloom after planting.

Flowers cut in early morning and placed in a vase of cold water will last four to five days; allow cut flowers to sit in the cool shade for an hour to allow ants to vacate. Many experts hold that the darker the flower the lesser the fragrance, with pinks emitting the most intense aroma.

Peonies do best where there is no root competition from trees or shrubs; they prefer a mid-garden location among other herbaceous plants. These sturdy plants are resistant to most diseases.

In Zones 8 and higher, the herbaceous peony may fail to bloom. This perennial plant needs hundreds of hours (about six weeks) with temperatures consistently below 40°F / 4.4°C for bud formation. An alternative — and one that flowers weeks earlier — is the tree peony, *Paeonia × suffruticosa*. A woody shrub preferring high dappled shade, it does not require a freezing period to form buds, but rather needs a period of dormancy.

Persian Buttercup

***Ranunculus, Ranunculus asiaticus* 'Tecolote Gold'**

CHRISTIAN REFERENCE

Do you remember how children would pick dandelions and present the little bouquet to their mothers, or did you do that yourself? Well, an Italian folk legend (the origin of which is elusive) speaks of a similar show of affection, of a son's love for his mother.

The story is told that Jesus — possibly after he had risen on Easter morning, or after his ascension — wanted to give his Holy Mother a gift that would always be a light on earth of his love for her. He gathered up the tiniest of stars and, transforming them into the five-petal buttercup, scattered them about for her to see wherever she roamed. This is one of the reasons why these bright yellow flowers are used to decorate Mediterranean churches during Holy Week.

One of the native species of buttercup that grows wild throughout the eastern Mediterranean is the *Ranunculus millefolius*. Its common Hebrew name means "to give light, to shine." There are other species of creeping buttercups, including some that are native to moist, open areas and flower in late winter to early spring. Ranunculus species are one of the "flowers of the field" mentioned in the Bible.

Another legend about *Ranunculus* relates to the rainbow, God's promise to Noah. The golden flowers of buttercups are said to grow wher-

Ranunculus asiaticus 'Tecolote Gold'

ever the rainbow touches, which may in turn have led to the story of the "pot of gold" at the end of the rainbow.

Symbolism:

- radiance

Prayer Garden Theme:

- Marian
- Bible

CULTURE

Many wild buttercups are weedy and can become invasive.

The *Ranunculus asiaticus* cultivars are popular in the floral industry. This species is also the most commonly sold, being available in a bag of mixed colors at most big-box stores and garden centers. With an abundance of long-lasting, tissue-thin petals, they look like small peony flowers and come in an array of colors from pale pastels, to saturated warm hues, to deep maroon.

You can grow these and other perennial *Ranunculus* species in the home garden, as they are hardy in Zones 8–10. In northern climates, plant corms in spring and grow as an annual.

Persian buttercups require full sun and dislike high temperatures; they are cool-season flowers that grow best in late spring in warmer Zones. In cooler regions they will flower through most of early summer, and are ideal for coastal areas.

Watering needs are medium — it prefers to be evenly moist and well drained; a light sandy loam is best. If the soil stays too wet the corms will rot.

Growing about as wide as tall, *Ranunculus asiaticus* 'Tecolote' varieties grow 14–16″ / 36–41 cm spread by 14–16″ / 36–41 cm height.

Before planting, soak corms in room-temperature water for three to four hours, allowing the water to trickle slightly during the process for better oxygenation to the clustered corms. These root structures will often double in size once soaked. After planting pre-soaked corms, the long-lasting 3–6″ / 8–15 cm flowers will take up to ninety days to bloom. The plants will bloom for five to six weeks in spring to early summer, before going dormant in summer heat. Deadhead to extend the blooming season. In northern climates, start indoors about three weeks prior to the frost/freeze date for your region.

These beautiful flowers stay fresh in a vase for as long as two weeks. As the buds plump and begin to show color, cut flowering stems early in the day and remove any leaves that would be below the water level in the vase.

Petunia

Petunia, Petunia × atkinsiana (Petunia hybrida)

CHRISTIAN REFERENCE

The wildflower *Petunia parviflora* is a plant native to South America that tolerates adverse conditions and produces an abundance of tiny and highly fragrant blooms. Because of its endurance — and welcoming fragrance — it was thought by the indigenous people of that region to ward off evil.

Petunia × atkinsiana

When we look through the lens of Christianity at the symbolism of warding off evil, it is clear why the petunia was given the characteristics of hope, watchfulness, and promise.

The introduction of the petunia into Europe took place during the Renaissance. The artists of that period, the Old Masters, would often include the petunia in still lifes to indicate anticipation; a watchfulness in life looking forward to what waits in eternity.

But conflicting symbolisms are not uncommon in floriography, and in some instances a flower can end up evoking the opposite emotions. During the Victorian era, deciphering a plant's meaning had as much to do with the flower itself as with how it was presented.

This may be the case with the petunia, which had an opposing symbolism of anger or resentment during the Victorian era. When the hope and promise of a future with the beloved recipient is rejected, those intentions can be turned to disappointment, which could account for the negative connotations.

Adding this flower to a Marian garden, or within any of the four sets of mysteries of a Rosary garden, reflects this sense of hope and promise in eager anticipation of God's hand in all things. Use a red or deep purple petunia at the Fourteenth Station, Jesus Is Laid in the Tomb.

With this flower's striking array of colors and patterns — from a delicate blue representing the heavens or the Virgin Mary, red and white striped signifying divine mercy, or a deep velvety purple for preparation and penitence — petunias can be utilized in most any prayer garden.

Symbolism:
- hope
- watchfulness
- promise

Prayer Garden Theme:
- Stations of the Cross
- Marian
- Rosary

CULTURE

There are four main categories of *Petunia* × *atkinsiana* cultivars, all of which have similar culture requirements. Grown as annuals, hardy only in Zones 9–10, they require full sun but will tolerate light afternoon shade as long as they receive five to six hours of direct sunlight. Petunias need average, well-drained, and evenly moist soil; they are not drought tolerant.

All are fragrant, some cultivars more than others. These plants benefit from being pinched back early to encourage branching, as well as in midseason if they become leggy. Hummingbirds and butterflies are attracted to the trumpet-shaped blooms.

Grandiflora have large flowers up to 5″ / 13 cm across and bear fewer blooms. Growing 12–15″ / 30–38 cm tall, this category of petunias needs protection from winds. Watering these plants from the base is encouraged since the large blooms are sensitive to being wet.

Multiflora have numerous smaller 2–2.5″ / 5–6 cm flowers with blooms that hold up better and last longer than grandiflora cultivars, and with stronger stems tolerate windy conditions better. They are an impressive mass of color whether in a garden bed or cascading over walls, and are frequently — and preferentially — used in hanging baskets.

Milliflora, as the name indicates, produce copious amounts of small 1–1.5″ / 2.5–3.8 cm flowers on mounding 7–9″ / 18–23 cm spreading plants. This miniature petunia is the earliest to bloom, and its compact nature makes it excellent for container growing. A similar looking plant is the genus *Calibrachoa*.

Spreading petunias are considered a ground cover, and are sometimes referred to as Hedgiflora. Only about 4–6″ / 10–15 cm tall, they can spread up to 5–6′ / 1.5–1.8 m. They form an impressive display with 2–3″ / 5–8 cm flowers all along the stem and hold up nicely in both heat and humidity.

Poppy

Papaver rhoeas, Papaver orientale

CHRISTIAN REFERENCE

This plant's Christian symbolism begins with Jesus' Jewish heritage. Nisan is the first month of the Jewish religious year and coincides with spring. It is thought that *Nisan* comes from the Hebrew *nitzan*, meaning "bud." In Arabic, *nissan* designates a group of red flowering plants (including *Anemone*, *Tulipa*, *Ranunculus*, *Galcium*, *Papaver*, and *Adonis*) that bloom in the spring in succession, rather than collectively.[48]

Papaver orientale

The month of Nisan is also the time of year when the crucifixion took place. The blood-red flowers of *nissan* include the poppy, and it along with the others has long been associated with the blood of Christ.

A pious legend about the field poppy *Papaver rhoeas*, or corn poppy *Papaver umbonatum*, tells of this flower growing where drops of Jesus' blood fell at the foot of the cross.

Since it often grows among grain fields — this plant reseeds readily in recently disturbed soil — the poppy came to symbolize the Eucharist, both the Body (wheat) and Blood (poppy) of Christ.

The deep red Turkish poppy, also known as the opium poppy, *Papaver somniferum*, grew throughout Asia and has long been known for its ability to induce sleep and dreams — among its other employments. In Christian art this poppy came to represent eternal sleep and death, and was often included in still lifes opposite items representing new life.

The poppy's association with death continued throughout Europe due to the poppy fields that bloomed after battles. Again, it was the disturbed earth of the battlefield that allowed for the seeds of *Papaver rhoeas* to sprout up and appear as if blood covered the land where so many lives were lost. The poppy was soon adopted to represent the blood of fallen soldiers, and paper poppies are worn on Remembrance Day, or Veterans Day.

Symbolism:

- passion of Christ
- eternal sleep/death
- sacrifice

Prayer Garden Theme:

- Stations of the Cross
- Rosary
- Bible

CULTURE

A favorite poppy in the garden is the *Papaver orientale* cultivars.

Hardy in Zones 3–7, it requires a period of dormancy and does not do well in warmer regions. It easily tolerates summer's heat and humidity in the designated Zones.

Grow in full sun. Watering needs are average, preferring to stay evenly moist in fertile, organically rich, well-drained soil. This poppy will adapt to grow in clay soil that does not stay wet. Soils that are poorly drained during the winter can be fatal.

Growing 18–24″ / 46–61 cm spread by 2–3′ / 61–91 cm height, it flowers in midsummer on sturdy pubescent stems. The showy crepe-paper flowers — depending on cultivar — can be up to 6″ / 15 cm across!

This species can reseed, but the following generations of plants often do not grow true to the parent plant. To continue growing the same cultivar, divide mature plants after leaves die back in late summer. Deadheading before seed pods set is encouraged and will also extend the bloom period. Some gardeners allow the end-of-season pods to mature and add them to dried arrangements.

Plan ahead with the Oriental poppy; after flowering, the foliage becomes unsightly and dies back, leaving behind a fairly large visual gap in the garden. Grow any number of late-blooming perennials or annual bedding plants to cover the bare spot left behind.

In late autumn, the poppy will grow a mat of basal leaves that persist through winter. Mulching around this crown of leaves is a good winter practice.

Primrose

Primula vulgaris

CHRISTIAN REFERENCE

The low-growing, pale yellow *Primula vulgaris* grows wild in moist woodlands throughout southern Europe, western Asia, and northern Africa. Its cousin the polyanthus, *Primula veris,* is the primrose that brings the association of keys to this genus, which legends reference.

The polyanthus looks similar to the primrose, except that instead of bearing flowers individually like the primrose, the polyanthus has thicker stems with multiple flowers (an umbel) that eventually droop down and appear like keys on a ring.

"The [polyanthus] … have an interesting history. In the Old Norse times the flowers were dedicated to Freya and symbolized the keys to that goddess's treasure palace. Christianized to 'Our Lady's keys,' they eventually came to be associated with that most famous of key-holders, St. Peter. A north European legend tells that they sprung up where Peter, shocked to find that a duplicate had been made, dropped the key of Heaven to earth!!"[49]

The *Primula veris* flowers hang down to one side of the stem, looking like keys, which — having been discarded by Saint Peter — alludes to the concept of forlorn.

This bowed-down appearance, and that it grows so close to the ground, soon evolved to mean the virtue of humility. A portion of a poem from the 1800s reveals this sentiment:

"Lorn tenant of the peaceful glade, / Emblem of virtue in the shade."[50]

Primula vulgaris

The Latin name *primula* means "little earliest one," or first, referring to the primrose's early spring flowering. Since *Primula* species were one of few flowers in bloom during the Minor Rogation Days, days of prayer and fasting prior to Ascension Thursday, they were and still are considered a necessary flower to decorate the altars throughout much of Europe — like the Easter lily in other regions.

The sturdy upright stems and array of blooms have also been given the moniker of Our Lady's candle. Here the Blessed Mother became the "candle" modeling confidence and trust during the dark days until Easter, and illuminating her Son's earthly visits until his ascension.

Symbolism:

- humility
- trust
- confidence

Prayer Garden Theme:

- Marian
- saints

The primrose, because of its time of flowering, is also associated with several saints: St. Catherine of Siena, Saint Agatha, Saint Alice, and of course Saint Peter.

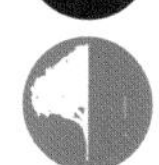

CULTURE

There are a wide range of *Primula vulgaris* cultivars to choose from. They hybridize easily with a startling array of flower colors — solid, bi- or tri-colored, pastels or richly hued. Some cultivars have lost their scent or become short-lived and are treated as annuals. The general consensus is that the yellows to cream-colored blooms are more fragrant. Zone tolerance is cultivar specific, with hardiness ranging through Zones 4–8. Most cultivars grow 3–9″ / 8–23 cm spread to 3–9″ / 8–23 cm height.

In general, primroses need part to full shade in evenly moist, fertile, well-drained soil; they are not drought tolerant and prefer deep woodland mulch. Good air movement is important for many of the modern hybrids.

Flowers are borne singly — though umbels have been developed through hybridizing with polyanthus species — and rise from a rosette mound of leaves in late winter or early spring through midsummer. Bloom period is also cultivar specific. Deadheading is encouraged.

Deer browsing is rare, but does occur regionally.

Resurrection Lily

Lycoris, Lycoris squamigera

CHRISTIAN REFERENCE

I'll begin this entry by clearing up confusion about a few plants that all have the common name of "Resurrection lily" — as well as half dozen other names — and none of them are in the *Liliaceae* family! But any of these plants could be used symbolically for new life through Christ, and the resurrection of Our Lord.

The *Lycoris squamigera*, indicated here, originated from China, and has a broader range of hardiness. The six petals with the larger gap at the bottom indicate the incompleteness of man — whom God created on the sixth day — until he has new life through Jesus. The yellowing of the petal blade that forms the iridescent keel represents the leading light of Christ, and the bluing tips signify the eternity to which we are destined.

Amaryllis belladonna, which is only hardy in warmer climates, comes to us from Africa. (The amaryllis house plant familiar to many of us at Christmas is not a true *Amaryllis* but actually of the genus *Hippeastrum.*) Similar in appearance, *Amaryllis belladonna* has a different flower formation and lacks specific symbolism, though it too represents new life.

A third plant that is sometimes called a Resurrection lily is the *Colchicum autumnale*, a low-growing, autumn-blooming bulb that looks much like an oversized crocus.

All of these plants exhibit the same tendency to emerge, then

Lycoris squamigera

flower devoid of leaves months later, a behavior called *hysteranthous*. When the leaves and flowers appear together, the usual behavior we expect from flowers, it is termed *synanthous*.

The disappearance of the leaves on *Lycoris squamigera* offers an easy reflection of Our Lord's descent into the recesses of darkness at the end of the crucifixion — seemingly dead to the world. At the moment Jesus was placed in the tomb, his followers waited in hope for the Resurrection. And we can meditate on this event with a similar, though lessened anticipation, as we wait for the flowers to come forth.

Symbolism:

- new life
- resurrection

Prayer Garden Theme:

- Sacred Heart
- divine mercy
- Rosary
- Bible

CULTURE

The *Lycoris squamigera* is hardy in Zones 5–9 (in cooler regions of Zone 5, grow near a foundation protected from winter winds, and mulch heavily). It prefers full sun though will tolerate dappled afternoon shade.

The Resurrection lily grows well in drier areas of the garden, where the soil is organically rich and well drained; it tolerates loose clay soils. The plant requires average watering when leaves are present, needs to be dry through the summer, and then requires average watering again in early autumn when the flowers begin to emerge — which they do rapidly!

The foliage grows 18–24″ / 46–61 cm spread by 12–18″ / 30–46 cm height and appears in late spring, dying back by early summer. The flowers rise to 24″ / 61 cm in early autumn.

Each stalk forms an umbel of four to seven fragrant, trumpet-shaped flowers up to 3″ / 8 cm across. The time from when the stalks emerge until they flower is startlingly quick, only four to five days to reach 24″ / 61 cm and fully bloom. The flowering display lasts for two weeks (some gardeners have reported blooms lasting for as long as three weeks).

The Resurrection lily will naturalize, and the colonies do not like to be disturbed. If you are dividing bulbs or setting new ones, the relocated plant may take two to three years to establish before sending up flowers.

The colonies will leave a bare spot in the garden once the leaves have died back. Mark bulb location to prevent disturbing the plant, and overplant with annuals that will not inhibit shoot growth. Wind protection is encouraged.

Rose Campion

Lychnis coronaria (a.k.a. *Silene coronaria*)

CHRISTIAN REFERENCE

The brightest-burning lights before the Light of the World took his place were the lights of the Blessed Mother and St. John the Baptist, the rousing forerunner to Jesus.

Lychnis coronaria

The symbolism of the rose campion derives from its botanical name. The genus name *Lychnis,* meaning lamp, comes from the Greek, and was ascribed by the physician Dioscorides (AD 40–90, in his *De Materia Medica*). The word *lychnis* is used because the dried wooly plant leaves were wound together and used as a wick for oil lamps.[51] The species name *coronaria* refers to a crown.

To be used as a wick in a lamp is to bear light. Here the reference to St. John the Baptist is clear. He was the one sent in advance to light the way for Jesus (see Mt 3:1–6). "The scarlet *Lychnis coronaria* is, in the Catholic Church, dedicated to St. John the Baptist, and the text in which he is described as 'a light to them which sit in darkness,' being taken in a literal sense, the flame-coloured flower was said to be lighted up for his day, and was formerly called *Candelabrum ingens*."[52] A portion of a poem from the 1800s also made that point, "The scarlet Lychnis, the garden's pride, / Flames at S. John the Baptist's tide."[53]

Include the rose campion in the Rosary garden at the First Luminous Mystery, the Baptism in the Jordan. It would also be appropriate planted at the Second Joyful Mystery, the Visitation, or at the Third Joyful Mystery, the Nativity of Our Lord — here honoring the holy family caught up in the light of the Incarnation.

Other associations with the Blessed Virgin Mary come from the silver-blue woolly leaves indicative of the eternity to which she guides us, and the flower representing a crown on or nimbus about Mary's head as the Queen of Heaven.

Saint Joseph is included in these symbolisms as he provided for the Light of the World and was given a saint's crown as Jesus' earthly father.

Symbolism:

- to light up with love
- Mary's rose
- Saint Joseph
- St. John the Baptist

Prayer Garden Theme:

- Marian
- Rosary
- saints

CULTURE

The rose campion is a biennial hardy in Zones 4–8, and readily reseeds. It requires full sun and is nearly intolerant of any light shade; gardeners in warmer climates claim that high or dappled shade in mid-afternoon is fine.

Watering needs are low, and if kept too wet or when rain is excessive the plant will rot. It is an excellent plant for rock gardens and gravelly slopes — drier soils produce a thicker woolly leaf and better silver color. It needs average, well-drained soil especially in winter.

The coarsely branched flowering stems emerge from basal leaf mounds and grow 12–18″ / 30–46 cm spread by 2–3′ / 61–91 cm height. Reseeding is necessary for this biennial; deadheading early on will encourage additional blooming and should be discontinued midseason to allow seeds to ripen.

When buying potted *Lychnis coronaria*, or any biennial plant, do so over two seasons to allow for a cycle of flowering — potted biennials are often sold during the flowering cycle. Follow the same two-season schedule if planting seeds.

The vivid rose-magenta flowers have a long bloom period; they first appear in late spring and continue through midsummer.

This is a plant that you will either love or hate. A small colony in front of dark evergreens is striking, and easier to keep clean as basal leaves die back. A large planting will begin to look messy and eventually decline as reseeding is inhibited by the mat of decaying fuzzy leaves.

Sea Holly

Eryngium* spp., *Eryngium planum

CHRISTIAN REFERENCE

The sea holly is a native plant through central and southeastern Europe and in central Asia. It has a prickly appearance though it lacks barbs, being a more polite plant than a thistle, which carries the same symbolisms. Both are often used in prayer gardens as a way to contemplate the crown of thorns.

The *Eryngium* symbolisms all point to the passion of the Christ. When we consider how Jesus suffered, there is little doubt that his strength and courage to endure through the cross was only maintained through his divine nature — human nature alone was not enough.[54]

We have read in the Bible that the torture endured by Our Lord during his passion began with cruelty at the hands of Pilate's soldiers (see Jn 19:1–2). It was those brutes who gave Our Lord his first crown — that of thorns — which became, along with the cross, a symbol of victory over evil.

The sea holly, and the thistle listed in the Herbs and Edibles chapter, not only signify the crown of thorns; but they also carry the colors of blue for eternity and purple for mourning, preparation, and penitence.

In a Rosary garden, the sea holly is appropriate at any point along the Sorrowful Mysteries. This is also the case for the Stations of the Cross. A large colony at the First Station, Jesus Is Condemned to Death, is a signifi-

Eryngium planum

cant reminder of the passion to come — especially when a companion planting of red flowers is added.

Symbolism:
- moral courage and strength
- endurance
- fortitude
- victory

Prayer Garden Theme:
- Stations of the Cross
- Rosary
- Bible

CULTURE

There are several *Eryngium* species and cultivars to choose from. All have the characteristic coarse appearance, varying in height and hue, and all require the same care.

The *Eryngium planum* presented here is known as the flat sea holly. A perennial hardy in Zones 4–8, it requires full sun and does exceptionally well in any harsh, sun-baked areas of your garden.

Watering needs are low, and if too wet the plant will easily rot. It prefers poor dry soils that are sandy and well drained. It will become leggy and need support if the soil is overly fertile. *Eryngium* species are also salt tolerant.

Forming clumps and looking like an airy shrub, flat sea holly grows in an open branching pattern of 1–2′ / 30–61 cm spread by 1–3′ / 30–91 cm height. Its blue-violet stems and silvery foliage last all summer and are an impressive back-of-the-border addition.

The steel blue flowers, which appear on the tips of widely angled stems, start in early summer and continue throughout the season. Including the colorful bracts — modified leaves — the flowers can measure up to 2″ / 5 cm across. To encourage blooming, deadhead regularly unless planning to use in dried arrangements.

The *Eryngium* species have a long central tap root that allows for them to survive in drought conditions. Because of this the plant does not transplant well.

It will reseed if conditions are right, forming small colonies and, unlike the thistle, is not invasive.

Snowdrops

Galanthus nivalis

CHRISTIAN REFERENCE

In the fifteenth century, Italian monks brought their beloved little alpine snowdrop with them as they set out to establish monasteries in England. They planted the little bulbs in their new monasteries' gardens, and the diminutive snowdrop soon naturalized in the warmer climate of Europe. The love of this harbinger of spring is closely associated with the Catholic Church, and this long-standing affection is seen in its growing around the ruins of churches and monasteries.

The *Galanthus nivalis* begins to bloom in late winter, and its flowering coincides with Candlemas and Imbolc. Imbolc (sometimes spelled Imbolg) is an ancient Celtic festival indicating the beginning of spring, which includes Saint Brigid's Day. Candlemas, celebrated on February 2, is the day set aside to honor both Mary's purification and Jesus' presentation in the temple. It was on that day that Simeon made the first reference to Jesus being the Light of the World (see Lk 2:29–32).

The presence of the small nodding flowers and delicate leaves after a cold, dark winter, often appearing while snow is still present, is seen as a symbol of triumph over adversity and the eternal life to come. In a woodland Stations of the Cross garden — where the snowdrop can be allowed to naturalize — plant this flower near the Fourteenth Station, Jesus Is Laid in the Tomb. *Galanthus* are indicative of hope over death, and resurrection.

Snowdrops are also referred to as Candlemas bells, and are said to have bloomed when Mary and Joseph took Jesus to the temple; you

Galanthus nivalis

can include them in a Rosary garden at the Fourth Joyful Mystery. They can also be planted at the Second Glorious Mystery, The Ascension, to signify the consolation that comes to those who are filled with hope.

Another name for the snowdrop is fair maids of February. This is from a tradition observed in early February, when it was customary for maidens dressed in white to walk in procession at the feast of the Purification (Candlemas).[55] Snowdrop festivals are still wildly popular throughout Europe as the display of white flowers blankets gardens from January through March.

A lovely sonnet written by William Wordsworth in 1819 expresses this delight in the snowdrop's awaited coming. It is, in part:

To a Snowdrop
Lone flower, hemmed in with
snows and white as they
But hardier far, once more I see
thee bend
Thy forehead, as if fearful to
offend,
Like an unbidden guest.
Though day by day,
Storms, sallying from the
mountain-tops, waylay
The rising sun, and on the
plains descend;
Yet art thou welcome, welcome
as a friend.[56]

Symbolism:

- consolation of hope
- watchfulness
- promise

Prayer Garden Theme:

- Stations of the Cross
- Rosary

CULTURE

The genus *Galanthus* is subtle in its diversity of twenty species and seven hundred cultivars.[57] All of them are showiest when massed in sweeping drifts where they have naturalized.

Galanthus nivalis is hardy in Zones 3–7 and will grow in full sun to part shade, which seems irrelevant since it appears in late winter (and dies back in early spring) before trees leaf out.

Water needs are average; snowdrops prefer an evenly moist environment typical of woodlands, offering good leaf mulch from deciduous trees. This environment makes clear the type of soil — organically rich, well-drained, humus-y. (Humus is decomposing organic material within soil; a high humus content usually means the soil is rich with nutrients.)

A small cluster grows 3–6″ / 8–15 cm spread by 6–9″ / 15–23 cm height, and will spread by bulb offsets or seed for as far as a suitable environment allows.

The mildly fragrant white flowers appear in late winter through early spring, and the plant's grass-like leaves will die back before summer arrives.

The bulbs are short-lived in warmer climates, and colonies may decline in unusually hot drought conditions in higher Zones.

Solomon's Seal

Polygonatum spp., *Polygonatum odoratum* var. *pluriflorum* 'Variegatum'

CHRISTIAN REFERENCE

One of the rings of King Solomon is depicted as bearing a hexagram — two equilateral triangles atop one another forming a star. This six-pointed star in Jewish tradition is known as the Star of David and, in the nineteenth century, became a symbol of Jewish identity equal to the menorah.

The appellation of Solomon's seal was given to *Polygonatum* for several reasons, depending on the source. The plant bears flat round marks on the rhizomes (from leaf stalk scars) that resemble the seal from a ring, and on some species resemble a hexagram. It was more recently found that the vascular structure of the arching stem — when cut transversely — appeared to form a six-pointed star as well.

Polygonatum odoratum var. *pluriflorum* 'Variegatum'

The name Solomon means "beloved by Yahweh" or "peaceful." In the Bible when Yahweh spoke to Solomon in a dream (see 1 Kgs 3:5–13), the new king asked only for wisdom enough to rule God's people well. King Solomon listened with his heart, and through his abundant wealth and writings attempted to instill God's peace and prosperity in his subjects.

So here is another reason for the appellation, which refers to this plant's medicinal use for healing wounds — like King Solomon who, by following God's law, helped heal the wounds of Israel.

The Solomon's seal's unique architectural growth habit is reminiscent of cathedral arches and forms a canopy of leaves that protects the flowers and allows for more abundant fruiting — a lovely metaphor for how the Church protects us in a way that allows us to be fruitful.

The characteristic shape of this plant is colloquially known as Our Lady's tresses. If you look underneath the plant when it is in bloom, it looks like a curved comb, similar to one the Blessed Mother may have used. Other folktales tell of the plant looking like waves of her hair.

Symbolism:
- healing
- Our Lady's tresses

Prayer Garden Theme:
- Marian
- Bible

CULTURE

A smaller Solomon's seal — with a very long name! — is the *Polygonatum odoratum* var. *pluriflorum* 'Variegatum', featured here.

This lovely *Polygonatum* has a broad hardiness in Zones 3–8, though some growers claim as warm as Zone 9. Like all in this genus, it requires part to full shade and average watering. This, or any Solomon's seal, would be an excellent addition to a rain garden.

It is a woodland plant, and needs soil that is consistently evenly moist, well drained, and organically rich. It appreciates deep leaf mulch.

A single potted plant has 10–12″ / 25–30 cm spread by 20–24″ / 51–61 cm height. This genus grows by rhizomes forming sizable colonies in optimal growing conditions. It is not a good choice for border beds, needing room to roam … which it will.

'Variegatum' blooms in late spring through early summer, with pairs of creamy-white bell-shaped flowers tipped in pale green arranged neatly beneath arching stems.

With a somewhat unidirectional growth habit, it is an impressive architectural plant in any shade garden. The leaves are dark and light green variegated, streaked with cream predominately on the margins, with leaves wider and more substantial than the common species. Alternately arranged atop curved branchless stems, the leaves turn a soft gold in autumn.

The stems can be cut and used as greenery in floral arrangements. Select branches with tips not yet fully unfurled, and strip lower leaves so none will be underwater. I've enjoyed a vase with a few stems of 'Variegatum' with no need for additional flowers.

Star of Bethlehem

Ornithogalum* spp., *Ornithogalum umbellatum

CHRISTIAN REFERENCE

The Star of Bethlehem is the common name for this white flowering species, and comes from the stellate blooms resembling the star that appeared when Jesus was born. The blooms signify the innocence, purity, and hope so often associated with white flowers.

Ornithogalum umbellatum

In the Holy Land, there are five species of *Ornithogalum.* One of the legends of this flower pertains to *Ornithogalum trichophyllum*, which grows in abundance in Israel and flowers December through February — coinciding with the Latin tradition of forty days of Christmas.

The story is told that at the Nativity, when the child was finally swaddled in the manger, the little plant joyfully burst into blooms throughout the land, some say as an earthly reflection of the natal star — like the oxeye daisy mentioned previously, it guided by day as the star did by night. This little flower continued to bloom until the Holy Family left Bethlehem for the temple, for the Presentation of Jesus and purification of Mary.

The symbolism of Mary's tears has several possibilities involving two species. The *Ornithogalum trichophyllum*, referenced in the story above, has a second legend in that when Mary wept with joy at the side of the manager, the flower sprung up where her tears fell. Another species, *Ornithogalum narbonense*, which blooms in March through April, is connected to the crucifixion:

when Mary's tears fell and landed on the flower along the way to the crucifixion, the blooms closed in solidarity with her sorrow. Following the same vein, where her tears fell the flower took root as a comfort to recall the divine plan in the birth of her Son.

The connection to Saint Joseph has to do with the Star of Bethlehem being in bloom on his feast day, March 19. It resembles a miniature version of the lilies that twice flowered on his staff, confirming he was God's chosen one to marry the Virgin Mary and to be the foster father of Jesus.

Symbolism:
- innocence
- purity
- hope
- Mary's tears
- Saint Joseph

Prayer Garden Theme:
- fruits of the Spirit
- Marian
- Bible
- saints

CULTURE

A caveat about this plant: It is classified as noxious and an invasive exotic plant in several states, and is nearly impossible to eradicate. It is poisonous to livestock, pets, and children. It is presented in this book solely because of its name and the associated legends. Now that you are forewarned, the culture information is hesitantly given below — though I strongly discourage planting until checking with your county extension services.

Ornithogalum umbellatum is hardy in Zones 4–9 and will grow anywhere except deep shade. Watering needs are average. It does not like to be kept wet.

It will grow in any well-drained soil, including clay, preferring organically rich soil.

A single plant has a 2–4″ / 5–10 cm spread by 6–10″ / 15–25 cm height. It will naturalize — exponentially — by bulblets and reseeding, forming expansive colonies. As a ground cover, it creates beautiful white drifts at the edge of woodlands, under shrubbery, and on slopes.

The six-petal white flowers, with a broad green band on the backside, form on 4–6″ / 10–15 cm long stalks bearing three to fifteen buds on a cyme-like raceme resembling an umbrella, hence the species name, *umbellatum*. It blooms in early summer, and the flowers are photonastic during stormy days and at night. Like many bulbous plants, the leaves die back after flowering.

Strawflower, Golden Everlasting

Xerochrysum bracteatum

CHRISTIAN REFERENCE

The strawflower, formerly named *Helichrysum bracteatum*, is an Australian native, with three additional species on the oceanic continent. In the eighteenth century it was brought to Europe and cultivated, where it was loved for its brightly colored, papery, and densely petalled flowers — which are actually bracts — that bloom all summer.

Xerochrysum bracteatum

With the symbolism of unending love, strawflowers are an excellent long-lasting cut flower to be used for the altar. When properly preserved they are used in dried arrangements, with the flower heads lasting for years — hence its second common name of everlasting.

Like many other flowers that maintain a semblance of their former beauty after they have died, it is easy to make the association with eternity. Given the broadness of its symbolism of an eternal embrace, this is a lovely plant for every prayer garden!

Relatively recent in its symbolism, this flower is also associated with the Virgin Mary, as the "flower that never fades." Plant the strawflower within any of the mysteries of the Rosary, though it is particularly fitting with this connotation of endurance to be planted throughout the Sorrowful Mysteries — or for that matter, the Stations of the Cross.

A traditional Ukrainian wreath, woven by young women and worn about the head, would include any of twelve medicinal plants, one of which was the strawflower symbolizing health — both physical and spiritual — and eternity.

CULTURE

Diverse in plant size and flower color, the blooms can have either an open central disc like a daisy or a tightly assembled Fibonacci-like petal formation — all species have the familiar papery bracts. Strawflowers are varied in colors from pastels to deep saturated hues.

Symbolism:
- immortality
- never-ending embrace
- never-ending love

Prayer Garden Theme:
- Sacred Heart
- Stations of the Cross
- Marian
- Rosary

Grown as annuals, some cultivars are hardy in Zones 8–10. Strawflower requires full sun, though it may tolerate light afternoon shade; too much shade will cause loose and floppy growth with reduced flowering, and a susceptibility to mildew.

Strawflower is an excellent plant for a xeriscape or desert garden since it has low to average watering needs. The soil needs to be well drained, slightly acidic, and nutrient rich. Like the sea holly, it's a perfect choice for a garden site that is often too hot for most flowers.

Growth is cultivar specific, averaging 6–18″ / 15–46 cm spread by 2–3′ / 61–91 cm height.

The native species is either white or yellow with a central disc, typical of flowers in the *Asteraceae* family. It can span 1–2.5″ / 2.5–6 cm. The plant will bloom continuously from late spring until frost, and do especially well with deadheading.

To harvest strawflowers for dry arrangement:

1. Select flowers that have not completely opened; they will continue to develop during the drying process.
2. Cut stems about 10″ / 25 cm long and gently remove all leaves
3. Using a rubber band — wrapped hair ties without metal crimps work well too — bind a small cluster of six to eight flowering stems, about 2″ / 5 cm from the end, to a floral stick or pencil to keep stems straight
4. Hang upside down on a line in a dry, cool, and dark location with good air movement. A small clip-on fan will help produce low air movement.
5. In about three weeks, drying should be complete.

A second method uses a 10–12″ / 25–30 cm length of 22 gauge / 0.65 mm floral wire. Cut a partially opened flower from its stem and slide the wire up and back down through the bloom. Stick the wire into a Styrofoam board and follow the basics of drying indicated above.

Sunflower

Helianthus annuus, Helianthus annuus 'Ring of Fire'

CHRISTIAN REFERENCE

Many sunflower species, when the plants are young, are known for the physiological mechanism of moving with the light. In both the plant and animal kingdom, this is called heliotropism, and is often confused with phototropism, which is a directional leaning toward a light source.

In the nineteenth century, the sunflower was called the symbolic flower of faith because of its heliotropism. It was believed then that the flower turns its face unfailingly toward the sun and follows it throughout the day, and when darkness comes, turns expectantly toward where the sun will return. So we too, with faith, turn our gaze toward the light of divine love, and when we face our own dark nights, we return to the source of illumination.

Helianthus annuus 'Ring of Fire'

The moniker of Mary's gold — a colloquial name for many yellow flowering plants — is related to this concept of looking toward the sun. The Blessed Mother (and Saint Joseph, for that matter) always looked to the Light of the World with devotion and faith as she lived and moved through the mystery of God's plan. When the darkness of the cross came, she turned to God and waited with faith for her Son's return.

The sunflower is also known as Saint Bartholomew's star. Saint Bartholomew was one of the Twelve Apostles, identified by scholars as the Canaanite Nathanael, and carried the Gospel through many dangerous territories until he was martyred. His feast day is August 24, and at that time of year the sunflower is in bloom. He too turned toward the Light of the World, and like the stars reflected that light.

Symbolism:

- adoration
- devotion

Prayer Garden Theme:

- virtues
- Marian
- saints

CULTURE

There are several sunflower species and cultivars to choose from that have the familiar yellow petals encircling a dark center of seeds. The cultivar presented here is *Helianthus annuus* 'Ring of Fire'. It is an annual that grows easily in Zones 2–11.

Requiring full sun, its watering needs are average. The soil needs to be organically rich, well drained, and evenly moist. The key for vibrant bicolor petals is the soil; poor soils will show bands of dulled burgundy-brown instead of dark red.

This sunflower is fast-growing to a 2–3′ / 61–91 cm spread by 4–5′ / 1.2–1.5 m height. It is well-branched and produces multiple large flowers. Because of the number and size of the flowers, it is best to locate this plant at the back of a sunny border where it will be protected from winds. Otherwise, consider staking the plants, even though this cultivar has sturdy stems.

'Ring of Fire' blooms later in the summer than most sunflowers, and will often continue to flower until frost. The bicolor flowers begin to open as a rich saturated red and soon develop their signature golden tips on blossoms up to 5″ / 13 cm across.

Many of the larger sunflowers tend to have leaves brown out as the flowers mature, leaving a disheveled mess and gaping hole in the garden. This cultivar's late flowering and multiple branching habit allow it to maintain its leaves longer and prevent that disordered condition.

The seed heads can be left on the stalks through the winter as food for wildlife; or you can remove the heads, dry them, and rub off the seeds for the feeder. For human consumption, choose a cultivar that produces larger seeds intended for harvesting.

Tulip

Tulipa spp., *Tulipa* 'Prinses Irene Parkiet'

CHRISTIAN REFERENCE

The *Tulipa* genus includes more than three thousand cultivars, hybrids, and varieties as of this printing, and fortunately was simplified into fifteen divisions. This genus has a natural range throughout much of Europe, North Africa, and west and central Asia, predominantly in Turkey — the name *Tulipa* is derived from *toliban*, a Persian word for turban.[58] The tulips we are familiar with today were cultivated in the sixteenth century by the Dutch.[59]

Tulipa 'Prinses Irene Parkiet'

In all its diversity, the tulip carries the same symbolisms: divine or perfect love, and the brevity of life.

In Flemish art, the tulip is a predominant symbol of the shortness of earthly life. The book *Nature and Its Symbols*, in reference to the "tulip mania" of the seventeenth century, states "Many still lifes with tulips … are clearly connected to this phenomenon and the financial collapse that ensued. … Its 'costly' beauty, appears in many vanitas paintings … on the theme of the transience of earthy possessions in the face of death."[60]

The tulip is also referred to as Mary's prayer, referencing how the flower petals fold up when darkness comes — a motion called nyctitropism. When we reach out to our Blessed Mother, whether in darkness asking for guidance or with gratitude, we are practicing the virtue of prayer. Mary perfectly expressed this virtue; she was in prayer when Archangel Gabriel came to announce God's plan for her, and we can be assured her hands were often folded in prayer through all her circumstances in life, especially so during the years with Jesus.

The tulip's petals reopen when light comes, which signifies the soul's opening to the light of God.

The blooms of the tulip decline without sunlight — as all flowers will. But because of the rapidity of the tulip's deterioration, it also symbolizes how the soul declines if kept from the divine light.

Symbolism:

- divine or perfect love
- Brevity of life
- Mary's prayer

Prayer Garden Theme:

- Sacred Heart
- virtues
- Marian
- Bible

CULTURE

The genus *Tulipa* comes in a dizzying array of flower types. The blooms can be smooth or fluffy, with broad petals or long and thin, and in nearly every color in the rainbow as solid or multicolored. Usually blooming single-stemmed from the bulb, a few species have a branched flower pattern.

Shown here is a parrot tulip commonly called Princess Irene. As a Division 10 species, it is hardy in Zones 4–6. The plant requires at least five hours of direct sunlight, and so does best with morning sun and light afternoon shade, especially in warmer climates.

It needs average watering, and a cool, moist winter; it requires organically rich and well-drained soil, though it does grow well in soils with nutrient-rich clay.

A single bulb will produce a plant of a 3–6″ / 8–15 cm spread by 12–20″ / 30–51 cm height; it is recommended that all tulips be grown en masse rather than singly or in a line.

As a Division 10 tulip, Princess Irene will bloom late in the season. No two flowers will be exactly the same, but all will have the familiar fluttered petal edge and the same array of colors. Because the parrot tulip has large and heavy blooms it is best to plant it in an area with wind protection. The blooms are mildly fragrant and make excellent cut flowers.

Culture requirements are specific for most non-species tulips, if you want them to rebloom for more than a couple years. For this reason, many gardeners treat the tulip as an annual.

For more reliable perennial tulips, grow Darwin Hybrids (Division 4), *Kaufmanniana* (Division 12), *Fosteriana* (Emperor, Division 13), or *Greigii* (Division 14).

Oh, and tulips are a favorite dessert of deer.

Veronica

Veronica, Veronica spicata 'Blue Charm'

CHRISTIAN REFERENCE

If one pieces together the stories belonging to this multiple-species flower, they point to the fidelity of Saint Veronica. Some scholars associate the plant with the woman Berenike, who touched the hem of Jesus' garment. Upon Berenike's healing, she became a disciple of Christ.

Veronica spicata 'Blue Charm'

The name *Veronica* is said to be a derivation of the Greek name *Berenike*, and to have come from the Latin *vera*, meaning true, and Greek *eikon*, for image.[61] The tradition of our Catholic faith places Saint Veronica as one of the many women present during the passion of Our Lord. She is depicted in the Sixth Station of the Cross, where the face of Christ remained on the cloth she offered.

I've reflected on that station often, and on the courage of Saint Veronica. There she stood, and there Jesus labored to take yet another step; the weight of our grievous sins heavier than the weight of the tree pressing deep into his shoulder. The sense of evil made present by the Roman soldiers reigns dominantly over this scene.

Veronica saw how great an effort it was for Christ to remain upright. The anguish in her heart mirrored that of his bloodied, beaten body. The image of the man before her was tortured; yet she would not look away. She would not falter in the presence of such human destruction. The brutality of what had been done strengthened her to move with compassion. The only action available was kindness, and so she stepped into fear, doing what she could.

Reaching out to the face of God, she wiped away the bloodied grime of an imposed evil. An eternity passed in that moment with God as she steadily met this man's suffering gaze — his eyes a little clearer as recognition validated their courage. The cross revealed the coexisting dichotomy of deep compassion and the presence of unutterable evil.

And here at the death of Christ we see the symbolism for this flower's other common name, speedwell, which means goodbye.

Symbolism:

- fidelity
- goodbye

Prayer Garden Theme:

- Stations of the Cross
- Holy Spirit
- Marian
- Rosary
- Bible
- saints

CULTURE

Of all the plant families, *Veronica* is the largest group, with hundreds of species. Plants vary from annual or perennial, as a 3″ / 8 cm groundcover to 4′ / 1.2 m tall spire, flowering singly or on long spikes, growing in polite clumps to being invasive. *Veronica spicata* 'Blue Charm' is one of the taller cultivars, with gently nodding spires of young flowers.

Hardy in Zones 3–8, it requires full sun — at least six hours directly on its leaves — and will tolerate light afternoon shade. Shallow-rooted, it is not drought tolerant and needs average and consistent moisture. The soil should be organically rich and well drained.

Usually planted in groups at the back of a border garden, this clump-forming plant grows 12–18″ / 30–46 cm spread by 24–36″ / 61–91 cm height. With its continuous blooming, form, and size it is a dramatic landscape planting on its own.

The long terminal racemes of lavender to deep blue flowers begin in early summer and often continue into autumn — especially if regularly deadheaded. The single flowering spike should be removed when about three quarters of it has bloomed and the lower portion is beginning to decline. Deadhead down to the next node where there is a flowering stem or set of leaves.

To encourage branching, and more flowering spikes, pinch back young plants as soon as they begin to sprout in spring. You can pinch back again by about a third after three weeks, if you prefer an even bushier plant. This will reduce the height but, considering the size of 'Blue Charm', this really isn't much of an issue.

Violet

Viola odorata

CHRISTIAN REFERENCE

We have often seen the white lily in art portraying the annunciation, but have you noticed the tiny violet flowers in a few of those paintings?[62] Legend has it that the violet was in bloom outside the Virgin Mary's window when she, with humility and trust, gave the Archangel Gabriel her fiat to God's plan of the Incarnation. As the angel left, he stopped to bless the tiny flowers that Mary so loved, and bestowed on them a delicate sweet fragrance as a reminder of the sweetness of Mary's humility.[63]

Viola odorata

The *Viola odorata* has long been a symbol of humility, because it is a low plant that blooms among more prominent species. Saints and scholars alike have written that the sturdy, diminutive *Viola*, with flowers delicately nestled among its leaves, was a clear example of Mary's unassuming beauty and her humility toward God's plan as she persevered with her Son to his death.

The white violet is also ascribed to Saint Fina (Seraphina) who lived in San Gimignano, Italy. With a humble and pure heart, found so often among the poor, she devoted herself to helping others in greater need than herself until she became gravely ill. Unable to move or leave her bed, she devoted herself to Christ as a supplicant for others. She died on March 12, 1253, at the age of fifteen. It is said that when her body was lifted after the moment of her death, white violets were found under her body growing from the board on which she had lain.

According to another legend, the violet is one of the flowers upon which the shadow of the cross fell; in acknowledgment of the event, the violet dropped its head in sorrow. Its purple bloom is reminiscent of the Church in mourning. Purple is strongly associated with spirituality and the mystical, and is also used to convey authority and purpose. Place this plant at the Twelfth Station, Jesus Dies on the Cross; by its nature the violet will reseed throughout the Stations of the Cross.

Though there is no direct mention of *Viola* spp. in the Bible, it is native to Palestine and, more than likely, a flower of the field — though not as prominent as lilies or grasses — as mentioned in Matthew 6.

Symbolism:
- humility
- perseverance

Prayer Garden Theme:
- Stations of the Cross
- fruits of the Spirit
- Marian
- Rosary
- Bible
- saints

CULTURE

The wildflower *Viola odorata*, known as sweet or wood violet, is hardy in Zones 4–8; it grows in sun to full shade, preferring protection from intense afternoon sun. Its watering need is average, and it will grow in most any well-drained, evenly moist soil, including heavy clay.

It grows 8″ / 20 cm spread by 4″ / 10 cm height, though it reseeds and spreads readily along hedgerows, woodlands, and fields. The fragrant purple flowers (white and pink are not uncommon) appear in spring through summer, and are an early food source for bees.

Herbals indicate that the flowers and young leaves are edible, and the plant has been used medicinally for centuries.

The purple violet is native throughout Asia and Europe, having been introduced to North America and Australia. You can easily allow this wildflower to spread in your gardens, or purchase pansies, *Viola tricolor*, for a more controlled look.

Yarrow

***Achillea millefolium, Achillea millefolium* 'Paprika'**

CHRISTIAN REFERENCE

The yarrow's medicinal properties have been known for centuries, and documented for as long as there have been written texts. In ancient Britain and surrounding areas where yarrow grew, the plant was part of military deployments; it was used to stop bleeding and heal wounds made by metal weapons.[64]

Achillea millefolium 'Paprika'

This military sense of doing battle with an adversary was a main feature in the yarrow's association to Christ, as was its ability to heal wounds — symbolically, the wounds of sin. The red yarrow's colloquial name Our Lord's back is a reminder of the scourging at the pillar, and the continued assault while he carried the cross to Golgotha. Plant the red yarrow anywhere along the path of a Stations of the Cross garden, or among the Sorrowful Mysteries in a rosary garden.

In healing from sin, a mission of evangelization and conversion of hearts takes place — and isn't that the charge for us and all saints? Here are two familiar saints, united together in their association with field plants.

Saint Benignus has several patronages, including that of meadow flowers. We celebrate his feast day on November 9. Benignus was a dedicated disciple of Saint Patrick, eventually following in his footsteps. As a boy he met Saint Patrick, and after being baptized, Benignus watched over the older man while Patrick slept in the shade of the garden. He sang for Saint Patrick and, while traveling with him, sang at all of his Masses. Benignus noticed that insects were being attracted to the dust from the road on Patrick's clothes. To help Patrick rest, the young boy picked strongly scented plants from the garden and field and placed them around the sleeping Patrick to keep the flies and bugs away. One of those plants was the native yarrow.

With that in mind, a garden dedicated to Saint Patrick should include the yarrow in any color — not only for its symbolism of doing battle against the devil, but also because this flower is seen as a tool of evangelizing. Evangelists draw others to the Faith, just like the yarrow is a highly desired food for bees and butterflies.

Symbolism:

- healing
- inspiration
- new beginning or new life
- evangelization

Prayer Garden Theme:

- Stations of the Cross
- Rosary
- saints

CULTURE

Achillea millefolium 'Paprika' is hardy in Zones 3–8 and, like all yarrows, requires full sun all day.

With initial planting it needs average watering; but soon, once established, its watering needs are low. It prefers dry conditions and is drought tolerant. A sandy loam that is well drained is best, but yarrow will grow in most poor soils. In overly moist or fertile ground the stems become floppy; partial shade has the same effect. The leaves are fragrant, though the flowers are not.

It forms clumps and spreads, averaging 20–25″ / 50–64 cm spread by 24–30″ / 61–76 cm height when in bloom. The blooms appear in midsummer and continue into autumn, especially when spent flowers are removed (allow a few to remain as winter food for birds). The corymbs — a group of flowers forming a flat or slightly convex head, each 2–3″ / 5–8 cm wide — open to a saturated red-orange with a distinct yellow eye in each tiny flower, and fade to a dusty pink. Cut back stems in late spring before flowering to reduce overall plant height and encourage more blooms.

The rhizomatous roots of *Achillea* species are deep and wide, forming dense mats. This allows them to be drought tolerant, and they can be used to stabilize hillsides and loose soils, or loosen clay. They are tolerant of salt and grow well in coastal gardens.

Yarrow spreads aggressively by root and seed and in some regions is considered a weed — so keep it in check! In a home landscape, promptly remove stray seedlings. Mature plantings will need to be dug up and divided every three to four years.

Herbs and Edibles

Angelica

Angelica archangelica

CHRISTIAN REFERENCE

The herb that cured the plague? A monk guided by an angel to the plant that saved thousands from the Black Death? It's quite the enduring legend in European history.

Unlike many herbs, *Angelica* has only been recorded with this one name — meaning "from the angel." A legend is told that in 1665 a monk — possibly Benedictine, for they were the epicenter of education about horticulture and herbal medicine — was in great distress that he couldn't find a cure for those dying from the plague. His prayers for insight were answered one night when, either visited by an archangel or in a dream of one, the plant that would be the curative was revealed.

After the encounter with the holy being, it is said that the monk added the name *archangelica* to the plant *Angelica*. Interestingly, during a previous European plague in the fourteenth century, the herb was used in a medicinal drink called "Carmelite Water."

Another theory for angelica's name comes from the date around which it blooms — May 8, formerly the feast of St. Michael the Archangel. For centuries, this plant was a curative for many ailments, and was considered one of the most powerful herbs both medicinally and spiritually. All parts of the herb were used for health, and believed to be a protection against evil because, well, Saint Michael is the Great De-

Angelica archangelica

fender. Before being named by the monk, the herb was known as "root of the Holy Ghost," as it seemed to be a cure-all gift from God.

There are more than fifty species of Angelica. The roots and fruit of the Eurasian species *Angelica archangelica* yield oil used to flavor liqueurs and in perfumery, and the tender shoots are used in making aromatic sweetmeats. Tea made from the roots and leaves is a traditional medicine for respiratory ailments. In Iceland, where the plant grows abundantly and was a lifesaver during times of famine, it is considered a vegetable.[1]

Symbolism:
- root of the Holy Spirit
- defense
- inspiration

Prayer Garden Theme:
- Holy Spirit
- angels

CULTURE

Angelica archangelica is hardy in Zones 3–7, and grows in full sun to light shade in rich loam that is consistently moist. It grows best in wetlands, on river banks, or in rain gardens that do not dry out. A large plant, at 2–4′ / 61 cm–1.2 m spread by 3–6′ / 91 cm–1.8 m height, it is an excellent backdrop with its showy leaves and impressive globe flowers blooming in early summer. It can naturalize by reseeding.

Angelica is a biennial and dies back after producing a crop of seeds — producing leaves in the first year, flowering and producing seeds usually in the second to third years, then dying back. The cycle of dying back is easily disrupted by cutting off the flower stalks every year before the plant sets seed. This way your *Angelica* will continue to grow for many years.[2] All of the plant is aromatic.

Do not gather *Angelica* from the wild. It looks very similar to the poisonous water hemlock, *Cicuta maculata*.

Purple-flowering cultivars with dark leaves are available: *Angelica atropurpurea*, *Angelica sylvestris* 'Ebony', and *Angelica sylvestris* 'Vicar's Mead' are a few.

Apple

Malus pumila, Malus domestica 'Haralson'

CHRISTIAN REFERENCE

In the Bible, there are many conjectures about the nature of the fruit from the tree of the knowledge of good and evil in Eden. Some writers suggest it was a pomegranate, quince, orange, or apricot, based on descriptions in Old Testament verses.[3] Whichever fruit it was, the apple has been its representative in art for centuries.

In the J. Paul Getty Museum book series *A Guide to Imagery*, Mondadori Electa writes: "In some still lifes … one or more apples, sometimes with clear signs of decay, are intended as an allusion to Original Sin. An apple in the hands of Christ child or the Virgin, however, has the opposite meaning, becoming a symbol of salvation and redemption."[4]

There is a wonderful legend about Saint Francis and an apple tree. While Francis was walking down a farm lane one early winter day, he was deeply frustrated about his inability to reach the souls of many townspeople. As he approached a leafless apple tree, he raised his hand, grabbed a barren limb, and shook it in frustration, shouting, "Teach me of God!" As the miracle is recorded, the tree immediately burst into bloom.

A sweet story tells that St. Abundantia of Spoleto, as a child of eight, saw a painting of the Child Jesus holding a golden apple. She — as most children do — really wanted that apple; the Christ Child reached from the painting and gave it to her. Abundantia was so excited that she wanted to give Our Lord flowers in return, and bolted outside into the

Malus domestica 'Haralson'

winter's day. The second miracle was that there *were* flowers, and so she picked a bouquet for the altar.[5]

The apple, when cut in half, is an excellent catechetical tool to teach of the Holy Trinity: skin, flesh, seed as three in one.

Symbolism:

- temptation
- the Fall of Man
- redemption
- eternal love
- immortality

Prayer Garden Theme:

- Bible
- saints

CULTURE

In the genus *Malus* there are about thirty-five species and upwards of 7,500 cultivars — and growing! "The accepted scientific name is *Malus pumila*, but is also referred to as *Malus domestica*, *Malus sylvestris*, *Malus communis*, and *Pyrus malus*. ... Thus, there is much debate in the botanical world over species separation and inclusion."[6]

With this in mind, I've selected three semi-dwarf cultivars suitable to the home garden or small orchard. All require full sun, average watering, and soil that is deep loam, moderately fertile, slightly acidic, and well drained. All require a second tree within 100′ / 30.5 m with the same bloom period for fertilization; the second tree can be a crabapple. All apple trees require annual pruning in late winter.

Malus domestica **'Freedom'**: hardy in Zones 4–8, grows 12–16′ / 3.7–4.9 m spread by 15′ / 4.6 m height. It has large fruit that is crisp and juicy; excellent for table, cooking, or juice/cider. Usually bears fruit in two to five years, late summer harvest, disease resistant.

Malus domestica **'Haralson'**: hardy in Zones 4 (3)–7, grows 12–15′ / 3.7–4.6 m spread by 12–15′ / 3.7–4.6 m height. It is a heavy producer of medium-sized fruit with hard, crisp, white flesh, mildly tart, and juicy; good for table and cooking, though not for saucing. A beautiful tree in the spring landscape, fragrant, and highly disease resistant. Bears fruit biennially starting at about four years old; midseason harvest; the best storing apple, keeping as long as five months.

Malus domestica **'Liberty'**: hardy in Zones 4–7, grows 10–12′ / 3.0–3.7 m spread by 12–15′ / 3.7–4.6 m height. It is a small- to medium-sized fruit with yellowish flesh that is juicy and crisp; excellent for table or baking, the flavor improves with storage. Usually bears fruit in two to five years, late autumn harvest, fully immune to scab and fireblight, and resistant to other disease.

Basil

Ocimum spp., *Ocimum basilicum* var.

CHRISTIAN REFERENCE

Basil, *Ocimum basilicum*, is known as the holy Communion plant. Its name comes from the Greek word for king, *basileios*. It was often strewn at the foot of a cross, as well as strung on Communion rails on holy days — especially in Greece on Saint Basil's feast day. *Basilicum* is also the root word for basilica, which is the heart of Catholic church architecture.

Ocimum basilicum

Basil has been a sign of love for centuries. Not only of the love of the Creator, but also romantic love — in times past in Italy a woman would put a pot of basil on her balcony to indicate her openness to suitors, and a man would present a woman with a sprig of basil to attract her as a spouse.

Basil is said to have grown at the site of Christ's crucifixion. There is a story of Saint Helena's journey to the Holy Lands that may have been the origin of this legend. It is told that Saint Helena had arrived in Jerusalem on her pilgrimage in quest of the true cross. She believed that God had told her she would find the holy relic and restore it as a symbol of Christian worship. Saint Helena had been searching for weeks before she noticed a stand of a sweet-smelling plant — basil — growing on a barren hill outside Jerusalem. She immediately gave instructions to her entourage to dig under the plant, where it is said she discovered the cross on which Jesus had been crucified.

"Orthodox Christians believe the herb sprung up where Jesus' blood fell near his tomb, and ever since basil has been associated with the veneration of the cross, particularly during Great Lent. The priest uses basil to establish and purify the holy water, and a bunch of its leaves to sprinkle the water onto the congregation. The cross, decorated with fragrant bouquets of the herb, is taken in procession around the church and small bunches are handed out. Many people will place their bunch in water until it develops roots, so they can replant the basil as a blessing in their own home."[7]

There is another story that the women who came to Jesus' tomb with their anointing herbs found it empty after the Resurrection. When they entered the tomb, they found basil growing inside when the two angels appeared. This is why basil is the symbol of new life.

In a Rosary garden, you can plant basil at the Fifth Luminous Mystery, The Institution of the Eucharist; at the Fifth Sorrowful Mystery, The Crucifixion; and at the First Glorious Mystery, The Resurrection.

It is appropriate to plant basil at the Twelfth Station of the Cross, Jesus Dies on the Cross, and at the Fourteenth Station, Jesus Is Laid in the Tomb.

Symbolism:

- holy Communion plant
- love
- eternal life
- new life

Prayer Garden Theme:

- divine mercy
- Stations of the Cross
- Rosary
- saints
- angels

CULTURE

The *Ocimum basilicum* cultivars are popular for culinary use, and include 'Genovese', 'Napoletano', 'Italian Large Leaf', and 'Lettuce Leaf'. All have the same culture. There are dozens more!

Grown as an annual usually from seed, basil is hardy only in Zones 11–12. It requires full sun, average watering, fertile, well-drained soil, and good air movement to prevent downy mildew. Depending on cultivar, the plant can be between 10–24″ / 25–61 cm spread to 16–36″ / 41–91 cm height.

To keep your plant productive and the leaves sweeter, frequently pinch off the top four leaves of stems to prevent the plant from setting flowers; lateral flowering buds should also be removed.

Chamomile, German

Matricaria recutita

CHRISTIAN REFERENCE

"God's passionate love for his people is so great that it turns God against himself, his love against his justice."[8] This quote, from Pope Emeritus Benedict XVI in his letter *Deus Caritas Est*, concisely reveals God's mercy and patience, that we are his beloved. The sweet little chamomile is symbolic of being a "loved one." Its botanical name, *Matricaria*, is derived from Latin: *matri-* meaning mother, *cari* meaning "dear" or "my loved one." The sweet chamomile is symbolic of both Saint Anne and her daughter, our Blessed Mother.

Patience is one of the fruits of the Holy Spirit, and fortitude (persistence) is a cardinal virtue. The chamomile was often used to teach of patience, and an English Renaissance poet writes that "The Camomile [sic] shall teach thee patience, / which riseth best when trodden most upon."[9] For those of us so bold as to pray for patience, we know how trials teach this lesson!

In a Rosary garden it can be used at the Fifth Glorious Mystery, The Coronation of Mary as Queen of Heaven and Earth, or at the Second Joyful Mystery, The Visitation, where we read of her cousin Elizabeth's proclamation, "Blessed is the fruit of your womb" (Lk 1:42).

Matricaria recutita

"The popular chamomile, *Matri-*

caria recutita, is an annual herb commonly grown for the harvest of its flowers used to make tea. This herbal tea is a mild sedative used in several ways including calming nerves, relaxing tense muscles, alleviating stress, dispelling insomnia, and treating indigestion."[10]

Another chamomile, *Chamaemelum nobile*, is the Roman chamomile. This smaller perennial chamomile is indicative of persistence in adversity; it can withstand a great deal of foot traffic and often develops more roots where it has been broken. Use this herb at the Seventh Station of the Cross, Jesus Falls a Second Time. It too can be grown in a Rosary garden, at the Third and Fifth Sorrowful Mysteries for courage and patience.

Symbolism:

- beloved mother
- patience
- Saint Anne
- persistence in adversity

Prayer Garden Theme:

- divine mercy
- Stations of the Cross
- fruits of the Holy Spirit
- Marian
- Rosary
- saints

CULTURE

Hardy in Zones 2–8, *Matricaria recutita* is a reseeding annual whose roots will not persist through winters. It requires full sun to light shade, and is tolerant of dryer conditions; but if you are harvesting blooms, regular watering will obtain a higher yield. Well-drained, light, and sandy soil is best. It will grow 1–2′ / 30–61 cm spread by 2–3′ / 61–91 cm height, and blooms early summer to frost. The fragrant white flowers with bright yellow centers attract pollinators. For herbal uses, harvest the flowers when fully opened and petals recurved; they can be used fresh or dried. The leaves and stems are also aromatic.

Chamaemelum nobile is a somewhat evergreen perennial hardy in Zones 4–9, with the same culture requirements as *Matricaria recutita*. *Chamaemelum nobile* forms an aromatic durable mat where each rooting point can grow to 12–16″ / 30–41 cm spread by 3–6″ / 8–15 cm height; it can be weedy. It is excellent to grow between pavers and in optimal environments can be grown as a lawn.

Cucumber

Cucumis sativus, Cucumis sativus 'Straight Eight'

CHRISTIAN REFERENCE

We read in Isaiah 1:8–9: "The daughter of Zion is left / like a shanty in a vineyard, / like a shed in a cucumber field, / like a city besieged. / Had Yahweh Sabaoth not / left us a few survivors, / we should be like Sodom, / we should be the same as Gomorrah" (New Jerusalem Bible). Here Isaiah uses the image of a small shelter in the midst of a cucumber field to paint a charming scene of a small place in a lush garden, even while chaos reigns beyond the edges of the garden. Here cucumbers are a delight, while corruption and destruction are outside of the tended fields.[11]

In this verse, the shelter in the garden is associated with the Virgin Mary to imply that though she was surrounded by sin, she was never touched by it, preserving her purity as the Mother of God.[12] When the cucumber is included in images of the Virgin Mary, it signifies her immunity to sin.

Cucumbers are also mentioned as a longed-for food when the discontented among the Israelites complained about only having manna to eat after their exodus from Egypt (see Nm 11:5–6). It is here that the cucumber acquires its opposite, negative connotation of perdition or sin — it is prolific and spreading.

The cucumber in the era before Christ was not the one we find at the market. The traditional and ancient vegetable *faqqous* (also *faqous*, *faqus*), also known as snake melon (*Cucumis melo* var. *flexuosus*), is a small, sweet

Cucumis sativus 'Straight Eight'

cucumber that thrives in the rich soils of the Mediterranean area.[13] It is still grown there and is eaten raw, pickled, or cooked.

Symbolism:

- redemption
- perdition

Prayer Garden Theme:

- Marian
- Bible

CULTURE

There are numerous species and cultivars in the genus *Cucumis*. Your reason for growing the cucumber — for slicing fresh for the table or pickling — will help narrow your search.

The cucumber is an annual grown from seed each season, requiring full direct sun for at least eight hours a day. It must be planted in fertile, well-drained soil that is consistently and evenly moist; about one inch of water per week minimum, more in arid climates. Good air movement around the plants is essential to prevent powdery mildew and other related diseases.

Its size varies by cultivar, which will be either bush or vining.

Bush varieties usually grow to a 3′ / 91 cm spread by 1′ / 30 cm height, and are good for small spaces, containers, greenhouse growing, or hydroponics.

The typical vining cultivars can take up a lot of space in the garden if grown flat from a mound. From the center of the mound some varieties will grow to a 6′ / 1.8 m spread or more with a 1–2′ / 30–61 cm height. Trellises help in the smaller garden, and when the vines are trained early they easily attach to the frame by curly tendrils.

The best pickling varieties, according to the *Old Farmer's Almanac*, are 'Boston Pickling', a favorite heirloom variety bred especially for pickling; disease resistant 'Sassy' or 'Calypso' for early yields; and long, thin 'Parisian Pickling' for making gherkins (a.k.a. cornichons).[14]

'Straight Eight' is a high-yielding plant for the home garden, and my favorite. The plump 8″ / 20 cm fruit is thin skinned with a fine-grained flesh that is rarely bitter. It matures in sixty to sixty-five days, or less if seeds are started indoors.

'Burpless Bush Hybrid' is a popular cucumber with 8–10″ / 20–25 cm long fruit, and short vines of 24″ / 61 cm long. It matures in fifty to sixty days.

Cucumbers, since they are mostly water, do not store well and should be eaten or processed within a few days of harvesting.

Fig

Ficus carica var., *Ficus carica* 'Chicago Hardy'

CHRISTIAN REFERENCE

In the Bible, the fig tree is the first tree recorded on earth, beginning in Eden (see Gn 3:7), and is the last tree mentioned in Revelations (6:13). It's the most frequently mentioned tree in biblical metaphors and parables because of its familiarity in the Jewish culture; it was and is a common and essential plant. Every household would have at least one fig tree, which could produce fruit up to three times a year.

Ficus carica 'Chicago Hardy'

The symbolism of stability is ascribed to the fig trees for a few reasons. It was a source of domestic security because of its material and medicinal uses, and abundance of highly nutritious fruit that could be eaten fresh, cooked, dried, or sold. The tree's expansive root system and physical strength would secure it in any soil — even when stripped of leaves during powerful storms. The fig tree's resilience is clear in a recent event of rejuvenation that took place in the late nineteenth century:

> When the Indonesian island volcano Krakatoa erupted in 1883, the waves it sent forth crashed into Bantam, some 50 kilometers away in western Java, and flattened forest for a distance of more than 300 meters inland. All that remained standing, said French scientists who visited a year later, were tall fig trees, their bare branches reaching skyward.
>
> Back on Krakatoa there was no trace of life. Much of the island had vaporized, and

what was left was buried under a 60-meter deep blanket of ash. Yet before long, several species of fig trees grew there too. They had arrived as seeds defecated by wandering birds and bats.

The characteristic of endurance — and its frequent biblical use as a metaphor for persisting in faith — makes the fig tree an excellent addition to a Stations of the Cross garden. It also can represent Mary's endurance and faith during the passion. When this tree is painted in nativity art, according to one interpretation it signifies Mary and Joseph as a new Adam and Eve.[15]

Our faith, like the fruitfulness of the fig tree mentioned in Luke 13:6–9, relies on proper cultivation. If left unattended, we fail to bear the fruits of the Holy Spirit.

The final connotation of the fig mentioned here alludes to sin. Medieval legend tells that Judas Iscariot hung himself in a fig tree. When branches of this tree are included in paintings of the passion, it is a sign of the sin that Jesus came to redeem humanity from.

Symbolism:
- stability
- fruitfulness
- sin, to be redeemed

Prayer Garden Theme:
- Stations of the Cross
- virtue
- Marian
- Bible

CULTURE

The common fig, *Ficus carica*, is hardy in Zones 8–10, needs full sun and will tolerate light afternoon shade. Fig trees require average watering, and because of an expansive though shallow root system, are able to grow in a wide range of soils. The fig prefers well-drained, evenly moist, rich and organic soil, and does well with a heavy mulch in winter.

Size is cultivar and Zone specific; trees average 10–18′ / 3–5.5 m spread by 10–20′ / 3–7 m height. Fruiting in summer on new wood, sometimes twice a year, the fruit is ready to eat when there is a slight give when squeezed. A small drop of nectar often appears from the fig's "eye" when mature.

Ficus carica 'Chicago Hardy': Zones 6–10, Zone 5 if situated in a warmer microclimate and given heavy mulch in winter. The stems will die back and in spring send out new shoots, and roots will persist hardy to -20°F / -29°C. The fruit has light brown to deep purple skin, with sweet pink flesh that ripens in late summer. It will only grow 3–4′ / 91 cm–1.2 m tall in cold climates because of die-back; otherwise, 9–12′ / 2.7–3.7 m spread by 10–15′ / 3–4.6 m height. This fig is also known as 'Bensonhurst Purple'. Another cold-hardy cultivar is *Ficus carica* 'Brown Turkey'.

Gourds

Cucurbita spp., *Lagenaria siceraria*

CHRISTIAN REFERENCE

According to DNA studies, the hard-skinned bottle gourd, *Lagenaria siceraria*, originated in Africa, and seeds of this genus are found to have grown on nearly every continent. Among other means of dispersal, many were carried around the globe by humans. It was one of the first cultivated plants, though not for food — it was grown for use as a container.[16] In Greek *lagenos* means flask.

The wayfarer would use a gourd to carry water, and as such, "It is the special attribute of St. James the Great, and of the Archangel Raphael and is sometimes given to Christ, who, dressed as a pilgrim, joined the two Apostles on their way to Emmaus."[17] The gourd also appears in scenes of the flight into Egypt.

The gourd was a sacred symbol in Judaism and as referenced in the Old Testament represents new life and a journey toward God; the plant is fruitful, growing in the most inhospitable of conditions. Twice in 1 Kings we read of its significance in the temple: "The cedar in the interior of the house was carved in the form of gourds and open flowers" (1 Kgs 6:18), and again, "Under the brim, gourds encircled it for ten cubits around the compass of the sea; the gourds were in two rows and were cast in one mold with the sea" (1 Kgs 7:24).

In the story of Jonah, the Lord grew a gourd plant to shelter his servant, "Then the Lord God provided a gourd plant. And when it grew up

Lagenaria siceraria

over Jonah's head, giving shade that relieved him of any discomfort, Jonah was greatly delighted with the plant" (Jon 4:6).

In the medieval garden, as today, roses and vines were used to cover an arbor. The gourd vine has been included here as a possible alternative to cover a garden path, as a symbol of God's attentiveness to comforting his people.

In art, when the gourd vine is painted with an apple it symbolizes salvation; the apple as a symbol of sin and evil, and the gourd a growing toward God.

Symbolism:

- journey
- new life
- fertility
- salvation
- delight

Prayer Garden Theme:

- divine mercy
- Bible
- saints
- angels

CULTURE

The hard-skinned *Lagenaria siceraria*, known as bottle gourd or calabash, has over a dozen cultivars in this species. The fruit size of different varieties can be anywhere from large enough to hold five gallons of water to palm-size, long-necked, or bulbous.

Grown from seed, this annual plant requires full sun, and appreciates light afternoon shade in hotter climates. It prefers light sandy or loamy soils, well-drained though evenly moist, and is tolerant of hot and humid summers. The gourd vine grows 10–16′ / 3.0–4.9 m spread by 12–18′ / 3.7–5.5 m height. It is a night bloomer, so hand-pollinate for better fruit set. The calabash needs a long growing season for mature fruit; starting seeds indoors is advised in cooler Zones. Mature fruit develop best when grown on a trellis or arbor.

Members of the soft-skinned *Cucurbita* species include squash as well as gourds; some are edible and others ornamental. These are easily grown annuals, but be sure to research the cultivars suitable for your purpose and gardening Zone.

Plant by seed in spring when all chance of frost has passed and soil temperature is at least 68°F /20°C. They require full sun, and average to low watering at plant crown; avoid wetting the leaves. They are not drought tolerant. Plant in well-drained, organically rich soil with a generous amount of compost. They are heavy feeders, but go light on the nitrogen content.

For all gourds, trellising is best for forming uniform fruits — and saving garden space! It is recommended to cut back vines once they reach 8–10′ / 2.4–3 m to encourage lateral branching and increase harvest.

Grapes

Vitis spp., *Vitis labrusca* 'Eastern Concord'

CHRISTIAN REFERENCE

Of all plants with Christian symbolism, the grape is the most iconic. We were catechized early on its symbolism: the manner of its growth, its fruit, and that fruit's transubstantiation into the Eucharistic Blood of Christ.

In Christian art the inclusion of the grape in landscapes, portraits, or still lifes conveys various allegories:

Vitis labrusca 'Eastern Concord'

- Laborers in a vineyard — good Christians working for the kingdom
- The leaf and vine in architecture — emblem of Christ, who said, "I am the true vine" (Jn 15:1–5)
- Clusters of grapes hung on a wooden beam — Christ hung from the cross
- Grapes and wine, especially with bread — the Last Supper, the passion, Eucharist
- In images of Madonna and Child, or occasionally of saints — union with God
- Drunkenness of Noah, or inebriated workers in a vineyard — abandoning the call to increase the kingdom

Grapes are especially meaningful for a Rosary or Stations of the Cross garden. For the Rosary garden, it is significant in the Second and Fifth Luminous Mysteries, The Wedding Feast at Cana and The Institution of the Eucharist, and for the Sorrowful Mysteries in general. For Stations of the Cross, place the grapevine at the Twelfth Station,

Jesus Dies on the Cross, or on a structure at the end of the Way.

A patron of vintners, St. Vincent of Saragossa (c. 304) was a Spanish martyr. There are several allusions to why Saint Vincent is the patron of vine growers, the first being because his name in French, *vin sang*, could be interpreted as "the blood of the wine." Another is that his feast day, January 22, falls between the vine's dormant state and appearance of new growth, when pruning is to begin.

There is also a legend that tells about his donkey. During his travels throughout Spain, Vincent stopped by the edge of a vineyard to talk with the men working there. While he chatted, his donkey nibbled at the young vine shoots. Come the next harvest, it was discovered that the vine stock that had been browsed had produced more fruit than all the others. Saint Vincent's donkey had invented the art of vine pruning.[18]

Symbolism:

- Blood of Christ
- union
- fruitfulness
- sacrifice
- faith

Prayer Garden Theme:

- Jesus
- Sacred Heart
- Stations of the Cross
- Rosary
- Bible
- saints

CULTURE

Cultivar selection is determined not only by Zone, but also by the purpose of the grape: table or wine.

All *Vitis* species require full sun, good air circulation, and well-drained and deep, organically rich soil; planting on a slope is best. Grapevines do not tolerate wet roots, needing about 1″ / 2.5 cm of water weekly, enough to soak soil 6–8″ / 15–20 cm deep. All require pruning in late winter of up to 90 percent of previous growth; fruiting occurs on new growth. A mature table grape vine can produce 15–25 lbs / 6.8–11.3 kg of fruit.

Vitis labrusca are table or juice grapes, though not very good for wine. The three common cultivars in the States are red 'Catawba', white 'Niagara', and purple 'Eastern Concord'. These are hardy in Zones 5–7 and adapted to the shorter growing season, with 'Eastern Concord' having good pest resistance.

Vitis vinifera are European cultivars good for wines, but compared with grapes native in the United States, are less cold hardy and more susceptible to diseases.[19] These need a warm, dry climate with extended growing season in Zones 7–10.

Vitis rotundifolia is a Muscadine grapevine well suited to the warm, humid southern states, with its long growing season in Zones 7–9; depending on cultivar it is good for either table or wine.

Lavender

Lavandula spp., *Lavandula angustifolia* 'Hidcote'

CHRISTIAN REFERENCE

Lavender is one of only a handful of plants with ancient documentation. It is included, along with papyrus, lilies, and grapes, in hieroglyphic texts from ancient Egypt. Its grammatical pictorial sign detailed its uses for cosmetics and embalming. Lavender was a common additive to Greek and Roman bath waters and scented soaps — much the same as it is used today. The lavender plant is also included in manuscripts from the fifteenth century.

The genus name, *Lavandula*, comes from the Latin root *lavare* for "laundry" and "to wash," because it was used to scent washed fabrics as well as baths. In Medieval Latin it is thought that the common name "lavender" may have come from Latin *lividus* — "bluish, livid" — indicating the color.[20]

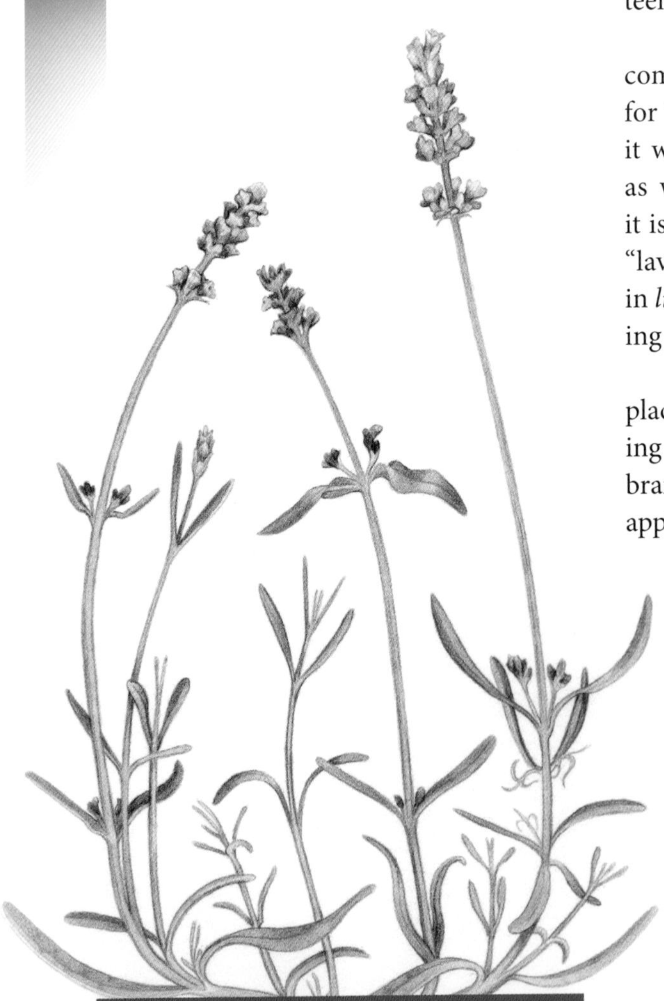

Legend has it that Mary would place the freshly laundered clothing of the baby Jesus upon lavender branches to dry (the same legend is applied to the rosemary bush). The species *Lavandula spika* (*Lavandula latifolia*) is a sturdy perennial shrub of the Mediterranean Basin that grows 3–4' / 91 cm–1.2 m tall and nearly as wide.

Saint Gabriel, Messenger of God, is depicted with lilies or a scroll, and his colors are silver or blue. The lavender plant with its symbolism of protection, silver leaves, and bluish flowers, works well in a garden dedicated to this archangel.

Lavandula angustifolia 'Hidcote'

There has been misinformation

over the centuries by Bible plant writers between spike lavender, a common native plant in the Middle East, and spikenard, the highly priced oil mentioned in the Bible. Spike lavender, *Lavandula latifolia*, is a small, aromatic shrub that belongs to the *Lamiaceae* plant family. Spikenard, *Nardostachys jatamansi*, belongs to the *Valerianaceae* plant family. "The Greeks referred to spike lavender by the name *Nardus*, after the city of Naarda, whereas the Romans referred to spike lavender as *Asurum*."[21] It seems the common names — nard (spikenard) and nardus (spike lavender) — contributed to the confusion.

Symbolism:

- protection
- devotion

Prayer Garden Theme:

- Marian
- St. Gabriel the Archangel

CULTURE

Lavandula angustifolia 'Hidcote' is an excellent garden variety lavender for small spaces. Hardy in Zones 5–8, it requires full sun all day. Watering needs are low, and once established, the plant is drought tolerant. Loose, well-drained soil is essential; it will not tolerate wet feet. In areas with poor drainage, create a raised mound or row for the plant.

'Hidcote' will grow to a 30″ / 76 cm spread by 24″ / 61 cm height. It is considered the most fragrant of the lavenders, and has a long blooming period from late spring to midsummer.

This cultivar needs good air circulation, with which it will be more tolerant of humidity, wet winters, and coastal environments of salt and wind.

In late winter to early spring, prune back to about 8" / 20 cm, allowing branches to remain through winters with heavy snow to protect the crown. Flowering occurs on new growth.

Lemon Tree

Citrus medica, Citrus limon 'Eureka'

CHRISTIAN REFERENCE

The citron fruit *Citrus medica* is a primary species that led to the cultivation of lemons, and citron is desired for its peel, which is 70 percent of the fruit.[22] Also known as *etrog* (or *ethrog*), it is widely grown in Israel because of its importance in the Jewish religious ceremony Sukkot. This plant has a long history in Greek, Roman, Persian, and Jewish culture.

In Jewish culture:

> The etrog is said to represent the heart (because of its shape), and also said to represent the ideal kind of Jews, who have both knowledge of Torah and good deeds (because it has both a pleasant scent and a pleasant taste). One midrash [biblical exegesis by ancient Judaic authorities] suggests that the etrog, not the apple, was the forbidden fruit in the Garden of Eden. ... [The misnomer in Western culture was] because the ancient Greeks called this fruit the Persian apple, Median apple or golden apple.[23]

Citrus limon 'Eureka'

The main products currently obtained from citron are candy, liqueurs, and oil — a minor product used as a flavoring in sweets and beverages.

The lemon tree was considered a powerful antidote to illnesses and poisons, and for this reason in Christian art is symbolic of salvation, recalling Christ as the curative for sin.

A similar association is attributed to the Virgin Mary, referring to the lemon's "sweet-smelling fruits of pleasant appearance and also rich in curative properties, acting, according to some, as a potent antidote."[24]

In both of the above references, the lemon tree depicted growing in the sun represented salvation, in that both Jesus and Mary grew in the light of God.

The flowers of the lemon tree, and possibly the fruit, which can remain attached for more than a year, are representative of Mary and her fidelity in love. She bore all sufferings for the love of God.

Symbolism:
- salvation,
- fidelity in love

Prayer Garden Theme:
- Jesus
- Stations of the Cross
- Mary
- Rosary
- Bible

The lemon tree, *Citrus limon* 'Eureka', like all *Citrus* species, is cold-sensitive and has a limited hardiness in only Zones 9–10. It requires full sun and wind protection and average watering once established, and is not drought tolerant. Deep-rooted, it is adaptable to most any evenly moist soil that is well drained — *Citrus* species will not tolerate wet roots. It requires acidic fertilization twice a year.

CULTURE

Size varies, especially in the landscape, 15–20′ / 4.6–6.1 m spread by 18–20′ / 5.5–6.1 m height, and considerably smaller in containers with 4–5′ / 1.2–1.5 m spread by 10–12′ / 3–3.7 m height. Considered an evergreen, its fragrant white flowers appear all year, and so will bear fruit all year with main production in spring and summer.

In Zones 4–8, grow lemon trees using containers in greenhouse or home environments. Purchase dwarf cultivars like 'Meyer' for container growing. In general, container-grown plants require full sun, and should be planted in exceptionally well-drained soil. Allow soil to dry between watering, and then thoroughly drench soil. Fertilize every three months. Grows up to 3–4′ / 91cm–1.2 m spread by 8–10′ / 2.4–3 m height (rarely this big in home environments). Keep plants out of drafts and away from heat sources; they prefer high humidity, so mist the leaves often. The flowers are self-fertile; help pollinate by gently shaking the branches, or you can use a cotton swab or small soft paintbrush and pretend to be a bee. Repot when necessary, about every two to three years, and trim back by about 25 percent.

Parsley

Petroselinum spp., *Petroselinum crispum* var. *neapolitanum*

CHRISTIAN REFERENCE

Parsley grows wild in rocky areas and is native to southern Europe and the Mediterranean regions; it is thought to have originated on the island of Sardinia, Italy. Its genus name *Petroselinum* means "rock celery"; from Greek *petro,* "stone" or "rock"; and *selinon,* "celery."

This herb is a little powerhouse of nutrients. It has been cultivated for centuries — medicinally and culinarily — for its leaves and root as a flavoring, in salads, for teas, as a breath freshener by the Romans, and to promote appetite by the Greeks, which is why we often see it served with our meals.

The symbolism of death is attributed to the Greeks, and related to mythology; it was used as a funerary wreath and tossed into the graves of the deceased. Christianity carried on this association with death by ascribing parsley to the apostle Peter — he has the designation as warder of the gates of heaven.[25] The expression "to be in need of parsley" was an indication that a person was actively dying,[26] possibly coming from the herb's known health value.

As a Bible plant it is one of several bitter herbs mentioned in Exodus 12:8 and Numbers 9:11; the Israelites were commanded to eat the paschal lamb with unleavened bread and bitter herbs. "Originally in the primitive Passover … these were probably merely salads; the simplest

Petroselinum crispum var. *neapolitanum*

and quickest prepared form of vegetable accompaniment to the roasted lamb. … Cucumbers, lettuce, water-cress, parsley and endive are some of those commonly used. Later on the Passover ritual (as it does today) laid emphasis on the idea of "bitterness" as symbolical of Israel's lot in Egypt."[27]

Parsley's symbolism of victory goes beyond simply a festive celebration. When planted along the Stations of the Cross, it draws our attention to Jesus' victory over sin and death.

In the Marian garden a similar connotation, attributed to parsley's health benefits, is that of overcoming sin and death — Our Lady's motherly care for the health of our soul. This herb also carries the moniker Our Lady's lace and signifies Mary's purity, as is common of many delicate white flowered plants; herbal parsley (*Petroselinum* spp.) evolved from "fool's parsley" (*Aethusa cynapium*) in this symbolism.

Symbolism:

- victory
- death
- Our Lady's lace or little vine
- bitter herb for Passover

Prayer Garden Theme:

- Stations of the Cross
- Marian
- Bible

CULTURE

Flat-leaf parsley, *Petroselinum crispum* var. *neapolitanum*, is a biennial grown as an annual, hardy only in the temperate climates of Zones 9–10, though it will languish in hot, humid summers. It requires full sun though it will tolerate light afternoon shade. Parsley needs average watering in rich, evenly moist and well-drained soil. It will grow 12–15″ / 30–38 cm width by 18–24″ / 46–61 cm height.

This herb is grown from seeds, which take four to six weeks to germinate. It has a deep tap root (central root stem) that makes it nearly impossible to transplant.

Generally, flat-leaf parsley has a more robust flavor for cooking, whereas curly leaf — minus the stems — is used fresh in salads.

Parsley is a larval food for the black swallowtail butterfly. From experience, I can assure you if you live in a region where this butterfly lives, you will need to plant a second crop once the butterfly has passed that life stage. Deer also love this herb.

Peach

Prunus persica, Prunus persica 'Reliance'

CHRISTIAN REFERENCE

The peach was the first of the fruits associated with and symbolic of the Holy Trinity — the fleshy fruit, the pit, and the seed inside the pit representing the Three Persons. This three-in-one aspect comes from Pliny the Elder's *Natural History*, written in the first century.[28] Since that time other fruits have been associated with the Trinity for the same reason, especially the apple.

Prunus persica 'Reliance'

There is a sweet legend that during their flight into Egypt, the holy family stopped to rest under the shade of a peach tree. The Blessed Mother saw the ripened fruit, but it was too high to be reached, even by Joseph. The baby Jesus, knowing his mother's desire, spoke to the tree, which then bent low its branches for Joseph to pick the fruit and give it to Mary. In some retellings of the story, angels appeared and plucked the fruit closest to heaven for the holy family. In art, this legend has been portrayed with a fig tree and more commonly the date palm.

In paintings where the Madonna and Child are depicted, the peach in the hands of Jesus carries significance as the fruit of salvation.[29] There are also paintings that include the image of a rotting, half-eaten peach, here symbolizing an immoral woman who has tarnished her reputation.

In a haunting image by El Greco, *The Holy Family with Mary Magdalen*, the Virgin Mary feeds Jesus from a bowl held by Saint Joseph fruit that is full of symbolic meaning: The apple represents the fall of man; cherries, the blood of Christ; peaches, salvation;

and pears, the sweetness of Christ's virtue.[30]

The virtues of constancy and good works are virtues particularly associated with Saint Joseph, a righteous man. In art a righteous man is often depicted with the image of a peach and its attached leaf. St. Francis de Sales shares,

> As with God doing and saying are the same, so our saying must be doing, and our words must be immediately followed by works. For this reason, when the ancients wished to represent a virtuous man, they made use of the comparison of a peach, upon which they laid a peach-leaf, because the peach is the shape of a heart, and its leaf that of the tongue, and thus they wished to show us that the wise and virtuous man has not only a tongue with which to speak well, but that he should never speak except as his heart wishes him to do.[31]

Symbolism:

- Holy Trinity
- fruit of salvation
- silent virtue
- truth

Prayer Garden Theme:

- Jesus
- Stations of the Cross
- fruits of the Spirit
- virtues
- Saint Joseph

CULTURE

The cultivar *Prunus persica* 'Reliance' is hardy in Zones 5–8, requires full sun and appreciates regular watering. Fertile, evenly moist and well-drained soil is best. Its size depends on whether it was grafted onto a dwarf root stock or standard. If dwarf it will be 8–10′ / 2.4–3 m spread by 8–10′ / 2.4–3 m height; a standard tree will grow 10–15′ / 3–4.6 m spread by 12–15′ / 3.7–4.6 m height.

The self-pollinating, showy pink blooms open in late spring, and like most peach trees, its flower buds are sensitive to harsh winters and late-spring frosts. A freestone cultivar, its fruits are harvested in late summer.

Peach trees are high maintenance, and if you're up to it, worth the effort. They are prone to a number of diseases and pests; pesticides are needed — organic or otherwise. It is essential to keep up a regular schedule of spraying, watering, and fertilization, and the trees must be pruned yearly.

A strong caveat: All but the fruit is poisonous — leaves, stems, bark, and pit. Plant where livestock (and children!) are unable to browse on its limbs.

Plum

Prunus subgenus Prunus, Prunus salicina 'Santa Rosa'

CHRISTIAN REFERENCE

History records the plum as one of the earliest domesticated trees along with olives, figs, and the grapevine. In some cultures it is considered the tree of life and conveys virtues similar to Christian values: The plum blossom has been an important symbol in Chinese culture. As a "friend of winter," the plum blossom most vividly represents the value of endurance, as life ultimately overcomes through the vicissitude of time. The fragrance of plum blossoms "comes from the bitterness and coldness," as the Chinese saying goes. Souls are tempered in the depth of experience, growing in inner strength and unyielding courage.[32]

When the plum is depicted in Christian art, it is usually included in images of the Madonna and Child Jesus. Often the Madonna is reaching for or handing a dark purple plum to the child, indicating her awareness of his purpose, with a watchfulness and fidelity to God's plan for her Son.

With the symbolism of hope, watchfulness, and promise, the plum tree can be planted in a divine mercy garden. The dark purple plum also indicates the passion of the Christ and his death, and so it is appropriate planted anywhere within a Stations of the Cross garden.

The fruits of the Spirit are associated with the various colors of plums:

Prunus salicina 'Santa Rosa'

Jesus' chastity is represented by a yellow-orange plum, his charity a red plum, and his humility by a white (a pale yellow pulp) plum. These fruits of the Spirit are made all the sweeter with, as St. Francis de Sales wrote, "heavenly love raises [spiritual fruits] to higher and higher perfection; as the sugar in preserves seasons all fruits with its sweetness."[33]

Symbolism:

- charity
- fidelity
- hope
- watchfulness and promise
- independence

Prayer Garden Theme:

- divine mercy
- Holy Spirit
- Marian

CULTURE

Plum trees are easy to grow, but before you choose a tree be aware that for most plum trees it is necessary to have a specifically matched pollinator tree. Pairing them appropriately is essential, or you will have a sterile, nearly fruitless tree.

The red plum *Prunus salicina* 'Santa Rosa' comes from Santa Rosa, California, named after St. Rose of Lima. This plum tree is a Japanese species hardy in Zones 5–9, needs full sun and average watering, and will adapt to most any well-drained, evenly moist soil. Average size is 15–20′ / 4.6–6.1 m spread by 15–20′ / 4.6–6.1 m height.

It requires minimal yearly pruning, which should be done after flowering and before the tree leafs out. Prune out central limbs to allow sun to reach the interior. This will encourage new growth for the next seasons' fruit. The standard is to remove about 20 percent of the growth each year to rejuvenate the tree and manage its spread. Never prune in winter! A good book on pruning will be helpful.

The 'Santa Rosa' plum is self-fertile, though will bear more fruit if a second plum tree is nearby. Fragrant white flowers appear in spring, with fruit harvest in late summer. It requires three hundred to four hundred chill hours[34] to set flowers and will bear fruit in about three to five years.

According to the Arbor Day Foundation, you should plant plum trees at the highest point of your garden to discourage frost from settling around the base, as it can damage the tree. Plum trees do well in areas that are a bit sheltered from wind exposure. Water newly planted trees weekly and continue to water well into late autumn to encourage stability during the winter.[35]

Pomegranate

***Punica granatum, Punica granatum* 'Granada'**

CHRISTIAN REFERENCE

The pomegranate grows prolifically throughout the Holy Lands. Its Hebrew name is *rimonim*, and it is mentioned throughout the Bible, and as one of the seven most bountiful agriculture products of ancient Israel. In Judaism it serves as a symbol of righteousness and fruitfulness, as declared in the Rosh Hashanah expression, "May we be full of merits like the pomegranate." It is also associated with fertility and sensuality, and is mentioned six times in the Song of Songs.[36]

Punica granatum 'Granada'

The abundance of seeds, which root quickly, was easily interpreted as being prosperous and fertile, which is strongly associated with a right marriage of love. Shakespeare's placement of a pomegranate tree beneath Juliet's window clearly indicated the love and hope for marriage of the young lovers.

During the Middle Ages, the pomegranate became the symbol of the Resurrection and the hope for eternity when it was depicted being held in the hands of the baby Jesus. This association comes from the Jewish roots, to be filled with virtues as the fruit is filled with seeds.

The fruit alludes to chastity when depicted in the hands of the Virgin Mary. This symbolism comes from Songs of Songs 4:13, "Your branches are a grove of pomegranates, / with fruits of choicest yield."

For Christians, the fruit as a whole signified the Church uniting many people in one Faith across cultures.[37] St. Francis de Sales speaks to this unity and God's love when he writes:

> The pomegranate, by its bright, red colour, by the number of its closely serried grains, and by its beautiful corolla, aptly symbolises, says St. Gregory, holy charity, which is all crimson in the ardour of its love for God, adorned with a variety of virtues, and bearing the crown of the everlasting recompense. But the juice of the pomegranate, which is, we all know, very agreeable to both the sick and the healthy, is so mixed up with bitterness and sweetness, that it is hard to tell whether it pleases the palate by its sweetish bitterness or by its bitter sweetness. Just so, Theotime, love is bitter-sweet, and as long as we are in this world its sweetness is never perfectly sweet, because love itself is never perfect, and never purely and perfectly sated and satisfied. Nonetheless, love is even here exceedingly pleasing, its bitterness rendering more delicate the suavity of its sweetness, while its sweetness makes more keen the charm of its bitterness.[38]

Symbolism:
- love/marriage
- fertility/fruitfulness
- hope
- immortality
- resurrection
- virtues

Prayer Garden Theme:
- Stations of the Cross
- Holy Spirit
- Marian
- Bible

CULTURE

The *Punica granatum* 'Granada' is the new favorite because it fruits one month earlier than 'Wonderful'; otherwise they are much the same. Hardy in Zones 8–11, requiring full sun, it does well in locations where other plants would scorch. The tree is drought tolerant, but if grown for fruit requires average watering. It will adapt to most soils, but prefers fertile, organically rich loam that's well drained.

Mature size is 6–8′ / 1.8–2.4 m spread by 8–15′ / 2.4–4.6 m height. The flowers are a vibrant red-orange, with fruit ready for harvest in six to seven months. The tree will bear fruit in two to three years. Fruit does not ripen off the tree, and must be cut — not pulled — from the branch.

This shrub is a lovely addition to the landscape with its amazing flowers, which attract hummingbirds, and bright yellow fall color. It needs minimal care; prune in late winter if needed, and two to three times a year to remove root suckers.

Pot (English) Marigold

Calendula officinalis, Calendula officinalis 'Geisha Girl'

CHRISTIAN REFERENCE

St. Hildegard of Bingen dubbed the *Calendula* "Mary's gold" in the twelfth century. The pot marigold is not the same as, though often confused with, the modern marigolds from the *Tangetes* family. *Calendula* was a common utilitarian herb for centuries and a desired herb in the medieval and monastic pottage.

Traditionally the flower had a monetary value based on its use in medicine and food. In many cultures, it was "more precious than gold" because of its curative properties. It makes sense then that these "flower coins" were said to have been carried by Mary during the flight into Egypt.[39]

Early Christians placed these valued blossoms as a prayer offering to our Holy Mother. After the sixth century, the gold blossoms represented the nimbus about her head. Because this flower is photonastic — opening with sunlight — it was easily associated with following Holy Light.

The pot marigold reseeds readily on loosened soil and was frequently found nearly carpeting fresh graves; here is its association with grief. In some cultures the flowers were placed on the eyes of the deceased, and on the Day of the Dead (October 31–November 2), the scattering of the petals on the walkway and stairs leading to an altar or to the family house was thought to lead family spirits home.

From the 1858 book *Flowers of Mary*, a poem by Rev. Louis Gem-

Calendula officinalis 'Geisha Girl'

minger connects the sentiments of the *Calendula*:

Wither not, O Marigold,
But thy petals e'er unfold;
Thou that symbolizeth death,
Increase our faith with every breath.
Warn us of that dreadful day
When from earth we'll pass away;
That each day we may prepare,
And of cursed sin beware.[40]

The expanded symbolism of "a mother's grief" — for what mother doesn't grieve for the loss of a child — makes this herb appropriate for growing at the Fourth Station of the Cross, Jesus Meets His Mother. You can add this herb anywhere in a Rosary garden; it is especially significant among the Sorrowful Mysteries.

Symbolism:
- grief

Prayer Garden Theme:
- Stations of the Cross
- Marian
- Rosary

CULTURE

There are multiple varieties of *Calendula* all having the same basic culture, though size and appearance differ. *Calendula officinalis* 'Geisha Girl' is a semi-double flower, dark yellow to rich orange with a darker eye appearing light brown to nearly black.

'Geisha Girl' is an annual grown from seed, and like most pot marigolds reseeds readily in warmer climates. Hardy in Zones 10–11, it requires full sun and appreciates light afternoon shade in warmer climates. It needs average watering and will grow in most soils that are well drained. It has a spreading habit, growing to 12–20″ / 30–51 cm in width and height.

The genus name is indicative of its blooming habit; in Middle English, from Latin, *kalendae* is the "first day of the month." The pot marigold blooms almost continuously from late spring to hard frost. To encourage blooming, deadhead regularly. The flower is not fragrant, though the leaves are.

The more branches the plant has, the more flowers will be produced; in spring, pinch back early growth. At times the plant will languish during the growing season if too hot and dry, or if it is in too much shade. Simply trim back to about 1″ / 2.5 cm from the ground for new growth and late-season color.

Rosemary

Rosmarinus officinalis, Rosmarinus officinalis **'Tuscan Blue'**

CHRISTIAN REFERENCE

This herb was present at the beginning and the end of Jesus' life. During the time of Mary and Joseph, the rosemary was a common and relatively large shrubby herb found throughout the Middle East. It's not mentioned in the Bible because it was a utilitarian herb used for maintaining a household and would be like writing about dish soap — something functional, necessary, and completely irrelevant to the story.

One of rosemary's many uses was to repel insects. It would be strewn on interior floors, and incorporated into straw mattresses. Joseph, having been a bachelor for most of his life, would have known well about adding this herb in his own bedding.

When it came time for Mary to give birth, Joseph was the one preparing a bed in the manger for the newborn. More than likely he only had to step a few feet outside the stable to find this bush. Snapping off a few tender, oily sprigs, he would have added them to the stable's straw in the manger to protect the baby from bugs.

The rosemary bush was commonly used when drying clothing. Mary would have laid their laundry upon its branches to dry. The heat of the sun against the clothing drew the oils into the cloth to freshen and, again, protect. Throughout Jesus' life, from childhood and into his min-

Rosmarinus officinalis **'Tuscan Blue'**

istry, his clean clothes carried this fragrance.

For centuries brides wore wreaths of woven rosemary sprigs in their hair or carried them in their bouquets as symbols of domestic love.

In the religious practices of Jews at that time, copious amounts of rosemary were strewn in the tombs of the departed, possibly helping to mask the odor. The holy women coming after the Sabbath to anoint Jesus' body would have carried armloads of this herb, and in all likelihood thrown it aside when they discovered the Risen Christ.

What a beautiful plant to have present in our homes during Christmas, recalling the Nativity. It will help us call to mind the life of Jesus, and his Holy Mother Mary, from the time he was born until the empty tomb.

Symbolism:

- remembrance
- friendship
- love

Prayer Garden Theme:

- Stations of the Cross
- Marian
- Rosary

This herb is appropriate for any Rosary garden, especially so at the Third Joyful Mystery, The Nativity of Our Lord; the Fifth Sorrowful Mystery, The Crucifixion; and at the First Glorious Mystery, The Resurrection.

For the Stations of the Cross garden, plant at the Fourth Station, Jesus Meets His Mother, or at the end of the garden where we leave his passion, looking forward to the Resurrection.

CULTURE

Most cultivars of rosemary can be used in cooking; those with broader leaves have more of the oils that provide the distinctive taste. Cultivars that smell of pine or turpentine are best avoided for cooking purposes. A few favorite cultivars for the kitchen are 'Blue Spires,' 'Tuscan Blue,' and 'Spice Island.'

Presented here is the culture for *Rosmarinus officinalis* 'Tuscan Blue', which is excellent for cooking and lovely in the landscape.

Hardy in Zones 8–11, it requires full sun, average to low watering once established but needs a bit more in extreme heat; this herb is not drought tolerant. Organically rich soil must be well drained, as rosemary is prone to root-rot.

'Tuscan Blue' grows 2–4′ / 61 cm–1.2 m spread by 5–6′ / 1.5–1.8 m height. Site it well since, like all rosemary, it does not like being transplanted. In cooler Zones, site where it is also protected from cold winds.

A good foundation plant that is not bothered by reflective light from buildings, it blooms rich periwinkle blue flowers spring through summer.

Saint John's Wort

Hypericum calycinum cvs.

CHRISTIAN REFERENCE

The June celebration of the pagan fires of Midsummer — an offering of light to strengthen the declining sun — were beliefs deeply ingrained in the customs of early societies. The Church in its wisdom "baptized" this practice and turned it in a different direction. During the fourth century the Church began the transition from Midsummer to the feast day of St. John the Baptist.

Hypericum calycinum

Saint John was not the Light but was sent to bear witness to that Light (see Lk 1:14–17, 76–79) and so the celebrations of Midsummer were transformed and became the light of goodwill among communities. "Bonfires were lit in the streets … and the richest folk set out tables of food and drink before their doors and invited neighbors to partake. Quarrels were made up … feuds forgotten."[41]

As a result, yellow flowers symbolic of sunlight were used in dedication to the Forerunner of the Light. The one flower that stood above all others was the *Hypericum calycinum*, Saint John's Wort (the word *wort* means plant in Old English). The plant's already established medicinal uses — it was known as "heal all" — was easily transferred to the Baptist's cry that Jesus would heal all spiritual wounds.

It is easy to see how this flower can be added to a Rosary garden; the First Luminous Mystery is the Baptism in the Jordan. Here Saint John takes part in the revelation of Jesus as the Light of the World. There are traditional and modern colors associated with each mystery (see Supplemental Catholicism, p. 259), and the modern color for the Luminous Mysteries is yellow.

If you are creating a Bible garden, not only can the *Hypericum* be used for the Baptism of the Lord; its red fruit is also symbolic of Christ's sweat in the Garden of Gethsemane.

The genus name comes from the Greek *hyper* meaning above, and *eikon* (icon) for picture. A common practice was to hang these flowers above images or windows.

Symbolism:

- Devil's flight
- grace of God
- heal-all

Prayer Garden Theme:

- Rosary
- Bible
- saints

CULTURE

In general, *Hypericum calycinum* is hardy in Zones 5–9, and requires full sun but will tolerate afternoon shade. It needs average watering in well-drained areas, and is tolerant of most any soils. It grows 18–24″ / 46–61 cm spread by 12–18″ / 30–46 cm height.

Its bright yellow flowers bloom mid- to late summer, depending on cultivar. It is sensitive to rot in hot and humid climates, and will benefit from good air movement.

To rejuvenate plants, mow them down every two to three years in late winter to early spring, to about 2″ / 5 cm above ground.

A ground covering herb classified as deciduous shrub, it is truly beautiful in mass plantings. Many landscape designers consider it to be one of the best groundcovers available. Because of its spreading root system, it is used in naturalized plantings, and is effective on slopes and embankments to stabilize soil, and at edges of woodlands where it competes well with the shallow roots of trees. Depending on the cultivar, in some areas it can be invasive — so be sure to read plant labels carefully or check with your county cooperative extension service.

Spikenard

Nardostachys jatamansi, Aralia racemosa

CHRISTIAN REFERENCE

The spikenard mentioned in the Bible, *Nardostachys jatamansi*, grows in the Himalayas and surrounding regions, and has a specific soil requirement to survive; it is a small herb that belongs to the *Valerianaceae* plant family, and today is considered an endangered species.

The essential oil derived from its woody rhizomes has been used since ancient times in religious ceremonies and in traditional medicines by the Egyptians, and Romans reportedly used it in perfumed oil called *nardinum*. This expensive oil is mentioned in all four Gospels[42] of the Bible, as the oil that Mary extravagantly anointed Jesus with before the Last Supper.

In Songs of Songs where referencing "a garden enclosed," symbolic of the Virgin Mary, the spikenard is placed among other "finest" plants. "Your branches are a grove of pomegranates, / with fruits of choicest yield: / Henna with spikenard, / spikenard and saffron, / Sweet cane and cinnamon, / with all kinds of frankincense; / Myrrh and aloes, / with all the finest spices" (Sg 4:13–14).

It is from this biblical description of an enclosed garden that a small fence or enclosure is commonly placed around Marian gardens. Saint Fiacre, who created the first Marian garden, is believed to have placed a low wattle fence around that garden, which began the tradition.

Aralia racemosa

A legend from ancient Jewish teachings tells of the spikenard as the only plant permitted to be taken by Adam and Eve when expelled from the Garden of Eden. "Its possession was to be for them a reminder of the joys that had been theirs in their original created state and, hence, also a reminder of the goodness and beauty of God and of his readiness to be reconciled to them and to reestablish them in a condition of undiluted bliss."[43]

This herb carries the symbolism for spiritual certainty, which was a virtue of Saint Joseph, who listened carefully to the messages sent by God. The Blessed Mother also displayed this certainty throughout her life, and especially so during the passion.

Symbolism:

- spiritual certainty

Prayer Garden Theme:

- Marian
- Bible
- Saint Joseph

CULTURE

Nardostachys jatamansi is an endangered species, and difficult to grow, so the American spikenard, *Aralia racemosa*, will be offered as a substitute.

American spikenard is a medium-sized, low-maintenance, shrubby herb hardy in Zones 3–8, which prefers light shade but will tolerate full shade. Watering needs are average, but it can withstand occasional drought when mature. It grows in a wide range of evenly moist soils, including clay and rocky; fertile humus-y loam is best.

Mature size is 3–5′ / 91 cm–1.5 m spread by 3–5′ / 91 cm–1.5 m height. White umbel-shaped blooms appear in three to five years in midsummer, and produce dark blue-black berries desired by birds.

The large, dramatic compound leaves, rising from dark maroon stems, do best in sheltered areas protected from winds. This shrub can naturalize and in some regions is considered weedy, forming thickets by way of seed and rhizomatous roots. It makes an excellent stand-alone specimen plant or in woodland garden with dappled shade.

The roots of the American spikenard are used much like sassafras to flavor root beer or in teas. It was formerly used medicinally as a poultice for skin ailments.

Strawberry

***Fragaria × ananassa* var.**

CHRISTIAN REFERENCE

The strawberry is cultivated on nearly every continent for its fragrant and sweet juicy fruit. Though it's not directly mentioned in the Bible, some hold that the plant was one of the fruits of the Garden of Eden that God allowed to continue to grow beyond its gates to nourish man — an "earthly delight" as a continual reminder of paradise.

The allusions to strawberries in Christian art are numerous, and begin in the spring of Christianity with the Annunciation. Mary's conception of the Incarnation was established near the end of March, by counting back from Christmas — a date chosen by Pope Julius I in the mid-fourth century with the additional effect of incorporating the traditions of pagan celebrations. In many regions, the strawberry begins flowering by late March, near the date of the Annunciation.

The plant and its fruit are also seen in images of the Nativity, where the Magi and shepherds are portrayed adoring the Child. The symbolisms here are to Jesus' Incarnation, and his death as the Christ; the red color of the paradisiacal fruit alludes to the passion and blood shed for our salvation.

The strawberry's white flower signifies the humility and innocence of both Mary and Jesus. The three-branched leaf, like many other trilobed plants, alludes to the Holy Trinity.

Fragaria × ananassa

From these symbolisms, the strawberry, in all its botanical forms in art, was also included in the margins of manuscripts as well as sculpted designs on altars and pillars in cathedrals and churches.

Symbolism:

- incarnation
- passion
- Trinity
- innocence
- humility

Prayer Garden Theme:

- Stations of the Cross
- Holy Spirit
- fruits of the Spirit
- Marian

CULTURE

As of the writing of this book, there are some 250 cultivars that grow within Zones 3–10. Choosing the right variety begins with where you live and the properties of your climate.

Common cultural needs of strawberry plants are:

- full sun to light afternoon shade (strawberries may go dormant in the heat of summer)
- average water for plumper fruit
- organically rich, fertile soil that is well drained (a sandy loam)
- a strong dislike of humidity, which makes them prone to diseases and pests

Strawberries spread with great abandon by runners that root and send out more runners. You will need to diligently maintain a bed suitable for harvesting.

These are a cool season perennial that grows best in spring and autumn. White flowers appear in mid-spring, and depending on cultivar may have a second flush in late summer.

Listed below are considerations for selecting cultivars, in addition to climate and Zone:[44]

June-bearing (Early Summer): typically produce the largest strawberries in their second year, and do so over a period of two to three weeks.

Short-day: a subset of June-bearing/early summer that will set bud in cooler temperatures when daylight is shortened mostly used by commercial growers.

Everbearing: generally produce two harvests per year: one in the spring and another in the late summer or fall on year-old plants.

Day-neutral: often planted on a hill system, will produce a good yield of smaller fruit in the first year they are planted.

Tansy

Tanacetum athanasia (a.k.a. *Tanacetum vulgare*), *Tanacetum balsamita*

CHRISTIAN REFERENCE

The fern leaf tansy, *Tanacetum athanasia*, with its little yellow flowers, is dedicated to Saint Athanasius; this saint proved the falseness of the Arian heresy at the Council of Nicaea in 325, which led to the formulation of the Nicene Creed.

In Greek *athanasia* means immortality. The tansy was bestowed on Saint Athanasius either because its flowers — which seem to not wilt — continue to bloom for what seemed like "an eternity" (all summer to frost); or because of its aromatic properties, used by the ancients to disguise the smell or possibly preserve dead bodies from corruption by pests.

Another yellow-button flowering tansy, *Tanacetum balsamita*, is also known as Bible-leaf, costmarie, and maudlin (from Magdalene).

The fragrant oblong leaves of *Tanacetum balsamita* are large and relatively durable, and once pressed and dried, were used as bookmarks for Bibles. Their odor helped repel the book lice, silverfish, and beetles that would eat away the pages — a serious issue when considering the cost of books in earlier centuries.

In the fourteenth century the common name of costmarie signified the Virgin Mary. From Latin, *costum* was an aromatic plant; and of course *marie* was our Holy Mother Mary. The "fragrance of Mary" in our world is that of compassion and unwavering, ardent love of God.

St. Mary Magdalene also had an

Tanacetum balsamita

ardent love for the Christ. For this reason, during the Middle Ages the tansy also carried the common name of maudlin-wort. Wort, as previously mentioned, simply means an herbaceous plant, and "maudlin" was for Magdalene, who was thought to be the repentant woman who wept at Jesus' feet, and anointed him with expensive oil (see Spikenard). Today's definition of "maudlin" continues to carry the connotation of sad and sentimental crying.

For a Stations of the Cross garden, place the tansy at the Fourth Station, Jesus Meets His Mother, or at the Eleventh Station, Jesus Is Nailed to the Cross.

Symbolism:
- immortality
- compassion
- ardent love

Prayer Garden Theme:
- Jesus
- Stations of the Cross
- fruits of the Holy Spirit
- Marian
- saints

CULTURE

There is a great deal of confusion with the *Tanacetum* genus, as many species are weedy and invasive. The tansy described here is *Tanacetum balsamita*, which has a leaf shape that is a solid, elongated oval, and is commonly called costmarie or Bible-leaf. It is a bit more polite in its growing habit.

This perennial herb is hardy in Zones 5–9, requiring full sun to light afternoon shade in hotter environments. Watering is average to light in organically rich, well-drained soil, though it is adaptable to most any soils that are dry. It is somewhat drought tolerant, preferring warm, sunny locations.

Tansy spreads by rhizomes, though a single cluster is generally 2–3′ / 61–91 cm spread by 2–3′ / 61–91 cm height. The leaves carry a distinct fragrance similar to a combined eucalyptus and mint aroma.

The flowers are small, bright yellow buttons that grow in branched umbel clusters. The plant is highly attractive to pollinators.

Though tansy is classified as an edible herb, and historically was used in medicine, brews, and salads, approach it with caution. Its oil is potent and can be toxic.

Thistle

Asteraceae family, Echinops ritro

CHRISTIAN REFERENCE

The use of thistle in art and legend has more to do with epithet than botanical name. Several genera, mostly from the *Asteraceae* family, are included in the symbolism of thistle in art — here are just a few:

Echinops ritro

Carduus and the ***Gundelia tournefortii*** are the thistles found on the Shroud of Turin (see Supplemental Catholicism, p. 259).[45]

Cnicus benedictus **(blessed thistle)**: Benedictine monks grew the blessed thistle as a cure-all; it was believed to be especially effective in curing smallpox. It is a yellow-flowered thistle that has been used medicinally for more than two thousand years.

Cynara cardunculus **(cardoon or artichoke thistle)**: The stems of this plant are recorded in Greek and Roman cuisine; it remained a popular food throughout the region until the nineteenth century. In art, it is an allusion to man's need to labor for his food after the expulsion from Eden, when God said to Adam "In toil you shall eat [the earth's] yield all the days of your life. Thorns and thistles it shall bear for you, and you shall eat the grass of the field" (Gn 3:17–18). To avoid confusion, the globe artichoke whose petals we eat is *Cynara scolymus*.

Onopordum acanthium **(Scottish thistle)**: This easily recognized thistle carries the symbolism of protection. It is said that invading armies to Scotland were thwarted by this plant's defensive nature. The Order of the

Thistle was founded in 1540 by King James V, who created the royal title for himself and twelve of his knights, "in allusion to the Blessed Savior and his Twelve Apostles."[46]

***Silybum marianum* (milk or holy thistle)**: It is said in a legend of King Charlemagne that his army was dying of the plague. An angel appeared to him in a dream and told him to shoot an arrow into the air; whatever plant the arrow landed upon, he was to feed his soldiers with. Charlemagne did as the angel instructed; his arrow landed in a patch of thistle. He had all his men eat the plant, and all were saved and continued the holy fight for Christianity.

In a Rosary garden, the thistle is appropriate for spiritual courage at the Transfiguration in the Luminous Mysteries, and at any point along the Sorrowful Mysteries. For the Stations of the Cross, the thistle is planted at the beginning of Our Lord's passion, when Jesus is condemned to die. When we think of the cardinal virtue of fortitude, which enables one to conquer fear, the ultimate gift of love is one's life.

The reference to salvation comes by way of the goldfinch, *Carduelis* spp., whose name comes from Latin *carduus* meaning thistle, since this is one of their favorite foods. In art, "the goldfinch, usually a symbol of the soul, is nourished by the thistle, which stands for the Passion of Christ."[47]

Symbolism:
- endurance
- suffering
- passion
- crown of thorns
- salvation

Prayer Garden Theme:
- Stations of the Cross
- virtues
- Marian
- Rosary
- Bible

CULTURE

Thistles are listed as invasive weeds. An ornamental genus, less prone to become a nuisance, is the globe thistle, *Echinops ritro.* It is hardy in Zones 3–8, and requires full sun, low to average watering, and well-drained soil.

Growing 2–3′ / 61–91 cm spread by 3–4′ / 91 cm–1.2 m height, it may need support in fertile soils. This thistle is excellent for the back of the bed, with smaller plants in front to hide its ratty lower leaves.

Globe thistle flowers are a steely blue in midsummer; deadhead spent flowers to reduce spreading. Cut plants back to basal foliage after flowering, to encourage a repeat bloom.

Thyme

Thymus praecox, Thymus vulgaris

CHRISTIAN REFERENCE

Thyme is one of the fragrant herbs we most appreciate when it is trodden upon along a garden path; it releases its scented oil when crushed or burned. The name *thyme* goes back to Greek *thymon*, usually referencing smoke, and as a verb *thyein* as a smoke cure, or incense sacrifices.[48]

Thymus vulgaris

Often the smoke sacrifice of thyme was offered prior to battle by warriors for courage, and if a warrior was wounded, the herb was thought to be a powerful aid in the passage through death. Thyme was used for centuries as a funerary herb to help the soul transition, and possibly, like other fumigatory herbs, used to preserve bodies by repelling pests. The symbolism of safe passage into eternity was, like many pagan customs, adopted into Christianity.

Monasteries served as the keepers of medicinal knowledge, and made frequent use of thyme in their breads, soups, and roasts. In the days before refrigeration, adding thyme to recipes gave some protection against spoiled meat and food-borne disease.[49] Because of its antimicrobial properties it was also used as an antiseptic on bandages.

Thyme, like other herbs, was used to repel insects, either by burning or combining tender branches with bedstraw. It was also eaten by livestock, so in all probability it was present at the Nativity and may have also been in the manger with rosemary branches. Here is the reason for thyme also being called Mary's bedstraw. A pious legend also claims that thyme burst into gold blooms when it came into contact with Jesus' head — the first revealing of his nimbus.

In a Rosary garden, plant this herb near the Third Joyful Mystery, the Nativity of Our Lord; the Fourth Luminous Mystery, the Transfiguration, where we meditate on spiritual courage; or the First and Fifth Sorrowful Mysteries, the Agony in the Garden and the Crucifixion, respectively.

St. Francis de Sales wrote in *Love of God* how bees gathering pollen from not only large blooms, but more frequently by also visiting the smallest of flowers like the thyme, making better honey. "It is quite certain that if we practice many small acts of devotion, we will also practice charity, not only much more frequently, but also more humbly, and, therefore, in a useful and holy manner."[50]

Symbolism:

- courage
- strength
- nativity

Prayer Garden Theme:

- Holy Spirit
- Marian
- Rosary

CULTURE

Thymus vulgaris is the species most frequently used for cooking. Hardy in Zones 5–9, it requires full sun, minimal watering, and grows best in light, shallow, and rocky well-drained soil. It will not tolerate wet feet, and will promptly rot.

A shrubby herb, it grows 6–12″ / 15–30 cm spread by 6–15″ / 15–38 cm height. Its leaves are most fragrant prior to blooming, which takes place from late spring to midsummer.

Thyme does best with frequent trimming; cutting back stimulates new growth and, when done each spring, helps reduce woody stems. This herb becomes woody as it ages, and after a few years will need replacing.

It is an excellent potted windowsill herb, and, considering its broad use in the kitchen, a good one to keep on hand!

Grasses and More

Clematis, Virgin's bower

Clematis flammula, Clematis terniflora

CHRISTIAN REFERENCE

"The clematis, the favour'd flower
Which boasts the name
of virgin-bower."

Sir Walter Scott

Clematis flammula is native in southern Europe, northern Africa, and the Middle East. A common and rapidly growing vine, often seen as a massive ground cover or liana, it has a delightful story associated with the Virgin Mary.

To understand the story, an explanation of the other part of the common name for this clematis may help. The word "bower" as a noun means a pleasant, shady place under trees or climbing plants in a garden or wood; and as a verb it means to shade or enclose a place or person.

The pious legend is told that during the holy family's flight into Egypt, they were pursued by soldiers who were ordered by King Herod to kill all male children aged two and under (see Mt 2:13–16). As the family journeyed, the Virgin Mary needed to rest and attend to the baby Jesus. Wherever she dismounted the burro and sat upon the ground, a clematis bower sprung up and sheltered her from sight of the soldiers. The soldiers were looking for a family and

Clematis terniflora

were not interested in Saint Joseph, traveling alone with a pack animal, and so continued on their hunt.

From this story comes the symbolism of "traveler's joy," for the bower — now called the Virgin's bower — was a joy to the holy family in their journey.

Another possible reason for the clematis being named after the Virgin Mary is that the wild species, *Clematis vitalba*, found throughout Europe, the Mediterranean, and Middle East, comes into flower around midsummer near the feast of the Assumption on August 15.

In a Rosary garden, plant *Clematis terniflora* at the Fourth Glorious Mystery, the Assumption of Mary into Heaven. To use this vine as part of an enclosure for a Marian garden, let it trail across an open rail fence, one that will be easy to remove old vines from when pruning.

Symbolism:

- journey
- traveler's joy

Prayer Garden Theme:

- fruits of the Spirit
- Marian
- Rosary
- Saint Joseph

CULTURE

Clematis terniflora is a large vine hardy in Zones 5–9, needing full sun to half shade. It requires average watering and is somewhat drought tolerant when matured and sited in afternoon shade. It tolerates loamy soils but prefers average soils that are well drained, and needs additional fertilizing early in the growing season. This is a rapidly growing vine and in one season can reach 15–30′ / 4.6–9.1 m spread by 15–30′ / 4.6–9.1 m height.

Blooming late summer through late autumn, it is highly fragrant and a source of late-season food for bees. It can be grown on an open trellis, along a rail fence, or cascading over a rock wall. It attaches by way of leaf tendrils for support. The flowers produce long, silvery, plume-like seed heads.

Clematis terniflora is in Group 3 for pruning (see page 257 on clematis pruning in Gardening Basics) and, like all clematis in this group, flowers on the current year's growth. In late winter or early spring cut back all of the old stems to the first (lowest) pair of live buds — measuring from ground level, this is usually about 8–10″ / 20–25 cm up the stem.

Because of its pruning needs and rapid growth rate, keep this clematis away from ornamental trees and shrubs. If it's being grown as a liana in large mature trees, make sure you will be able to remove old vines each year.

Grasses, Ornamental

***Calamagrostis* spp., *Chasmanthium* spp., *Miscanthus* spp., *Pennisetum* spp., *and others. Pennisetum setaceum* 'Rubrum'**

CHRISTIAN REFERENCE

The lowly grass is spoken of frequently in the Old Testament, second only to trees, but lags in our memories when we think of flowers. Though often taken lightly, the grass family, *Poacea*, is the fifth largest plant family and provides crops, forage, building material, and fuel today as it did in ancient times.

The Hebrew words for grasses more often indicate their function rather than a species. *Eastons Illustrated Bible Dictionary* offers four basic categories in the Old Testament, [1] and their lessons for relationship of us to God are worth contemplation.

From a root word meaning "greenness," the verses in 1 Kings 18:6, Job 40:15, and Psalms 104:14 convey the meaning of bringing forth food, to be ripe and fit for use. We see the symbolism of green grass and flourishing from good rains, as when we take in the word of God, in Genesis 1:11–12, Isaiah 66:14, and Deuteronomy 32:2. Grasses are also a reminder of the brevity of life (see Is 40:6–7; Ps 90:5–6). And, last, grasses remind us of how those who do not heed what the Word brings forth prove themselves weak and easily destroyed (2 Kgs 10:26; Ps 129:6; Is 37:27).

Their diversity both in culture and Christian reference makes ornamental grasses an easy fit into any prayer garden. They represent a fruit of the Spirit, gentleness; he would not bruise a reed of grass (see Mt 12:20).

Often, I think of the breath of God and its gentle movement in my life when watching the motion of ornamental grasses; like the breeze we

Pennisetum setaceum 'Rubrum'

cannot see, though we can see its effects.

When using grasses in a Stations of the Cross garden, place them around the Tenth Station, Jesus Is Stripped of His Garments. Here the grasses signify submission, because they offer very little resistance as they move and bend in the wind.

Use tall ornamental grasses to surround a Marian garden to create a "garden enclosed."

Symbolism:

- breath of God
- gentleness
- brevity
- submission

Prayer Garden Theme:

- Stations of the Cross
- fruits of the Spirit
- Marian
- Bible

CULTURE

A favorite grass for prayer gardens is the *Pennisetum setaceum* 'Rubrum'.

Grown as an annual, it is only hardy in Zones 9–10. The shiny burgundy waterfall-like leaves are showiest in full sun but will tolerate light shade. It requires evenly moist, well-drained soil and average watering, being more sensitive to drought than most in the species.

'Rubrum' grows 2–4′ / 61 cm–1.2 m spread by 3–4′ / 91 cm–1.2 m height. Its flowers (fronds) are a beautiful arching bottle-brush in pink-burgundy that can exceed 12″ / 30 cm long; it blooms midsummer to late autumn with scape rising an additional 4–6″ / 10–15 cm.

This is a seedless, clumping *Pennisetum* species that is non-invasive, tolerant of juglone toxicity from black walnut trees, and pollution.

Here is a very limited selection of other popular grasses:

***Calamagrostis* × *acutiflora* 'Karl Foerster'.** Zones 5–9, full sun to light afternoon shade, average water and does not like drying out. Rich, evenly moist to wet soil, clay and black walnut tolerant, 2′ / 61 cm spread by 3–4′ / 91 cm–1.2 m height of vertical fronds appearing in early summer, leaves on lower two-thirds of plant.

***Chasmanthium latifolium*.** Zones 3–8, full sun to half shade, average watering to wet, well-drained soil, 1.5–3′ / 46–91 cm spread by 2–4′ / 61 cm–1.2 m height. Blooms late summer through early autumn with drooping flat seed heads on delicate arching stems, which flutter in the slightest breeze. Will spread by seed and naturalize, and can become invasive.

***Miscanthus* spp.** There are several beautiful species within this genus to choose from. Hardiness varies, as does form, size, and appropriateness in a home garden.

***Pennisetum* spp.** Here too are several amazing species to choose among, hardy in Zones 6–9 specific to cultivar. This genus has the familiar bottle-brush fronds.

Ivy, English Ivy

Hedera* spp., *Hedera helix

CHRISTIAN REFERENCE

The ivy is a plant that secures itself upon most any structure. Because of this tendency to cling to its support, it is symbolic of hope and the fidelity of love; the ivy always seeks to be held up.

Hedera helix

In the 1858 edition of *Flowers of Mary*, Rev. Louis Gemminger likens this trait of the ivy to the Virgin Mary. "In like manner, we never see Mary alone. She is always near her God. … Jesus is her stay, her help, her counsel and her consolation. In every situation … she hoped in him. … Let us raise ourselves aloft to the Divine heart of Jesus, clinging to it firmly with the arms of holy hope."[2]

We read about clinging as the ivy in the Book of Sirach, "I bud forth delights like a vine" (24:17). Here the clinging action is related to seeking wisdom, offering foundation in the Holy Spirit. In ancient texts, according to the USCCB,[3] Sirach continues, "Do not grow weary of striving with the Lord's help, but cling to him that he may reinforce you" (v. 23).

Add the ivy to any Rosary garden where you are planning to meditate on the Joyful Mysteries. The ivy is symbolic at all the stages of Mary's (and Saint Joseph's) clinging to God with fidelity, hope, joy, and triumph, from rearing Jesus through his adulthood and ministry.

Author Julia Cameron writes, "As we extend the tendrils of our faith above and through the walls of our resistance, our lives become green, verdant, affirming. … As we cling to our conscious optimism, finding footholds of faith despite opposition, our lives become rooted in the soil of grace. We are nurtured, prospered, and blessed."[4]

Symbolism:

- clinging to God
- triumph
- fidelity of love (spiritual and marital)
- joy
- hope

Prayer Garden Theme:

- fruits of the Holy Spirit
- virtues
- Marian
- Rosary

CULTURE

There are a dozen or more species and numerous cultivars in the genus *Hedera*. They are grown for their climbing or trailing habit and predominantly evergreen foliage. The shape of the leaves vary by species and maturity: lobed, heart-shaped, curly, fans, or bird-foot.

Hedera helix, or English ivy, is hardy in Zones 4–9, requires full to part shade and will not tolerate full afternoon sun. Preferring moist, well-drained, humus-rich, fertile soil, it can tolerate some drought once established.

Depending on species, *Hedera* grows 3–50′ / 91 cm–15 m spread by 20–80′ / 6.1–24 m height trailing or climbing, and 6–9″ / 15–23 cm height as a ground cover.

Hedera species will root at the nodes where they touch the soil. In some regions this plant can be aggressive and invasive.

Climbing English ivy supports itself by aerial roots. Where these penetrate brickwork that is not sound, such as joints or cracks, they may cause structural damage; the main problem with climbing ivy is keeping growth away from gutters and painted trim work.

Hedera helix is an excellent houseplant to filter impurities from the air. Research has shown it is effective at cleansing formaldehyde, benzene, toluene, and xylene from the air, and helps reduce mold.

Jasmine

Jasminum spp., *Jasminum sambac*

CHRISTIAN REFERENCE

The *Jasminum officinale*, being the most common in Europe during the Renaissance, is the variety most portrayed by artists in depictions of the Virgin Mary. Jasmine flowers in May, the month devoted to our Blessed Mother, and its whiteness suggests her innocence and purity.[5] The *Jasminum* has long been regarded as a "flower of heaven," carrying the connotations of grace, divine love, and promise. Not only is it seen in Marian paintings, but it also circles the head of saints, and appears in vases and in the hands of young girls and virgins.

In a garden dedicated to the Resurrection, the jasmine would signify hope, watchfulness, and promise. If you live in a region where this vine is hardy, place an arbor at the end of the Stations of the Cross and plant jasmines to signify "he is not here, for he has been raised just as he said" (Mt 28:6).

The versatility of this plant's Christian symbolisms allows this vine to be a part of many of the mysteries of the Rosary, especially the Joyful and Glorious. For the symbolism of purity, use leafy sprigs in arrangements for weddings and religious ceremonies, especially during solemn or final religious vows. The nature of jasmine flowers would make it difficult to include a flowering stem.

If you are planting a white garden dedicated to the Holy Spirit, consider adding this vine. The flowers open in the evening and the perfume scent adds another dimension to the visual meditation of a

Jasminum sambac

white garden, which at night reminds us of light in darkness.

Jasmine originated in China, then reaching Persia was referred to by the Arabic name *sambac*; its perfumed oils were traded along the silk routes and into Europe.[6] And did you know that the name for girls that originated in Persia, Jasmin or Yasmin, connotes "gift from God"?

Symbolism:

- hope
- watchfulness
- promise
- Mary's purity
- divine love
- grace

Prayer Garden Theme:

- Holy Spirit
- Marian
- Rosary

CULTURE

Jasminum sambac, also known as Arabian Jasmine, is a lush, evergreen, shrubby vine hardy in Zones 9–11. In colder climates it is grown in containers. Requiring full sun, it will tolerate light shade. Watering is average, preferring evenly moist, humus-rich soil that is well drained. This vine does not attach to surfaces or have tendrils for support; it twines around a structure and usually needs ties to secure it to a frame.

It will grow to a 3–5′ / 91 cm–1.5 m spread by 6–10′ / 1.8–3 m height, though in its humid native region — predominantly South Asia — it will grow much larger.

The highly fragrant flowers will bloom throughout the year, with a greater flush in midsummer. Flowers are produced in clusters of two or more at the ends of vining branches; they open at night, then fade to a pale pink as they close in the morning. There are several cultivars available, distinguished by the flower form, with the most fragrant being *Jasminum sambac* 'Mysore Mulli'.

Maidenhair Fern

Adiantum* spp., *Adiantum capillus-veneris

CHRISTIAN REFERENCE

In the Church's evangelization efforts, especially in early centuries, she would identify the natural realities embedded in local customs and myths, and "baptize" them to turn the practices toward the truth of Christ. The maidenhair fern was converted in this way, becoming Our Lady's tresses and the Virgin's hair.

The genus *Adiantum* derived its name from the Greek *adiantos*, which means "unmoistened" — the leaves have the ability to repel water. This property of remaining un-wetted was attributed to the hair of Venus when she rose from the sea. With that association and from Latin we have *capillus*, which means hair — referring to the thin, black stems and emergent fiddleheads — and *veneris*, meaning Venus.

Adiantum capillus-veneris

In the symbolism of plants, maidenhair represents grace, purity, and innocence — to be unaffected by sin. This too comes from its ability to be unaffected by water. When rain or mist comes in contact with the plant, its stems gracefully droop. The layering of leaves allows the water to rapidly run off, preserving its original state, untouched and unaffected.

If you have a Stations of the Cross constructed through a shaded area, consider using maidenhair fern at the Eighth Station, Jesus Meets the Women of Jerusalem. With the fern's nature to remain unwetted, reflect upon Jesus' words: "Daughters of Jerusalem, do not weep for me; weep instead for yourselves and for your children" (Lk 23:28). This fern (or in a sunny location, plant *Asparagus setaceus*, asparagus fern) also recalls the woman who washed Jesus' feet with her tears and dried them with her hair.

Ferns are an ancient group of plants, revealed through fossils. These plants were a fascination of botanical and scientific art illustrators, especially during the Renaissance. This was a study brought about by the confounding nature of ferns; like algae, lichens, and mosses, ferns do not bear flowers or fruit and are classified as cryptogams.

In an article by Dr. Joachim Scheven, the evidence of fossils confirms the catastrophic event of burial — and eventual fossilization — caused by the great flood in Genesis 6. Dr. Scheven states, as any backyard gardener who composts can confirm, that the slow decay of plant materials does not leave behind a "shadow" of its previous form but breaks down to a cellular state. "Fossil ferns … have therefore somehow bypassed the normal processes of decomposition. Instead, they have retained their shape and turned into mineral … that is, 'fossilized.'"[7]

Symbolism:
- grace
- purity
- innocence
- Virgin Mary

Prayer Garden Theme:
- Stations of the Cross
- Marian
- Bible

CULTURE

Adiantum capillus-veneris is commonly called Southern maidenhair, and has a lovely layering of delicate fronds with distinct fan-shaped pinnae (small leaflets of the frond). The Northern maidenhair has the same fan-shaped pinnae, but its stems are forked, appearing as a fan or palm, and are more erect.

Southern maidenhair is hardy in Zones 5–8 and needs half- to full shade that is consistently moist. It prefers neutral to alkaline soils, and can be found growing across boulders on the edges of streams and rivers, and cascading from moist ledges.

This maidenhair grows 12–18″ / 30–46 cm spread by 12–18″ / 30–46 cm height on wiry black stems, with a distinct pendant-like arching habit. It spreads slowly by short clinging rhizomes, and its fine texture adds interest in moist woodland areas.

The Missouri Botanical Garden writes that this fern is native throughout the world in tropical to temperate regions including South America, Europe, Asia, and Africa. In the United States, it is commonly found throughout the southern states, north to California, South Dakota, and Ohio.[8]

Moss

Dicranum spp., *Leucobryum* spp., *Polytrichum* spp., *Hypnum* spp., *Hypnum imponens*

CHRISTIAN REFERENCE

Moss is considered symbolic of the love and charity we should have for our neighbor. The word *moss* is thought to have derived from Egyptian for the male child Moses, named so because he was "drawn out of water."[9] Pharaoh's daughter experienced the innate sense of nurturing toward the baby. Children have this influence over us — to draw out love from us for them.

Hypnum imponens

The Blessed Mother's concern for others was shown perfectly: her haste to see Elizabeth, her seeking help at the marriage feast, and her encouragement of the apostles and Mary Magdalene as the Church began.[10]

We learn this devout sense of charity not only through our Blessed Mother but also through the lives of many saints. One example is Saint Tranquillus, who was abbot at the monastery Saint-Benigne in Dijon, France. There is a wonderful story about Saint Tranquillus and a carpeting of moss over his grave, recounted in *Magnificat*:

"Following his death numerous miracles of physical healing occurred at his tomb. … St. Gregory of Tours (d. 594) relates that the moss growing over Tranquillus' tomb was a particular instrument of such healings, which he was able to verify from his own experience. While suffering from a very painful outbreak of blisters all over his hands, Gregory touched the moss, and was swiftly cured."[11]

There is a legend that moss was originally gray. The story is told that when Jesus was taken down from the cross and laid in his mother's lap, the last of his blood dripped on the moss on which the sorrowful Virgin sat. The moss immediately turned green as a symbol of eternity and the power of the Precious Blood of Jesus. Consider growing moss at the Thirteenth Station of the Cross, or as part of a Rosary garden at the Sorrowful Mysteries.

Symbolism:
- love of neighbor
- love
- charity

Prayer Garden Theme:
- Stations of the Cross
- Holy Spirit
- virtues
- Rosary
- Saints

CULTURE

There are more than twelve thousand species in the *Bryophyta* family, which includes moss. Here I've presented four genera: one for dense shade, another that tolerates light foot traffic, one for heavier traffic, one easily grown and good for terrariums; and a mosslike plant suitable for sunny areas.

Most mosses do not tolerate being covered in leaf litter.

Windswept or rock cap, *Dicranum scoparium*: Hardy in Zones 6–10, requires deep shade and will burn in minutes from direct sun. Will not tolerate being wet; prefers moist, well-drained soil. It spreads and grows to 1–4″ / 2.5–10 cm height, and forms distinctive rounded mounds.

Sheet moss, *Hypnum imponens*: easily transplanted, hardy in Zones 4–9, needs full shade and is intolerant of artificial light. It requires acidic soil, which must be consistently moist, not soggy, and well drained. Spreads 1–4″ / 2.5–10 cm height. More tolerant of air pollution, making it suitable for urban and suburban gardens; will tolerate light to moderate foot traffic when grown between pavers.

Cushion moss, *Leucobryum glaucum*: Hardy in Zones 4–11, grown in part shade. Prefers loose, sandy, well-drained, evenly moist, acidic soil that is and will remain undisturbed. Grows 6″–3′ / 15–91 cm spread by 1–5″ / 2.5–13 cm high in clumps. Good for indoor terrariums.

Hair cap, *Polytrichum commune*: Hardy in Zones 3–11 and will tolerate part sun to full shade. Well-drained, evenly moist, sandy, acidic soil is necessary; it will not tolerate leaf debris or being wet on top. It will grow up to 1′ / 30 cm per year, 6–24″ / 15–61 cm spread by 2–6″ / 5–15 cm height. Will tolerate only slight foot traffic.

Irish or Scottish "moss": Irish moss *Arenaria verna* and Scottish moss *Sagina subulata* 'Aurea' are not true moss, but look-alikes. Grow in Zones 4–8, full sun to light shade (especially in hotter climates), average watering — it will be short-lived with too much or too little water. Needs average, well-drained soil. Blooms tiny white flowers in late spring and does not tolerate foot traffic.

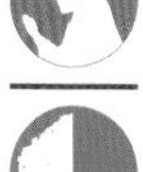

Passion Flower

***Passiflora incarnata, Passiflora incarnata* 'Damsel's Delight'**

CHRISTIAN REFERENCE

The flowering vine *Passiflora incarnata* is one of the few plants that can be traced back to preliterary times as a teaching tool for religious practices. It is an amazing plant rich in symbolism. When we feel ourselves faltering in our faith, we can reflect on this flower and find confidence in the greatest love story ever lived.

The passion flower catechetically has the following meanings:

1. Ten petals represent the ten of the twelve apostles that did not betray Jesus (Judas) or deny him (Peter).
2. The three topmost stigmas as attached to their styles (tiny little stems) recall the three nails that impaled Our Lord to the cross.
3. The five stamens that hold the anthers together signify the five wounds of Our Lord.
4. The anthers alone represent the sponge used to moisten Jesus' lips.
5. The central column of the three stigmas and five anthers signifies both the post to which Jesus was scourged and also the cross on which he was hung.
6. The seventy-two radial filaments are for the number of lashes Jesus received throughout his passion. They are also said to represent the crown of thorns.
7. The leaves of most

Passiflora incarnata
'Damsel's Delight'

species are shaped like a lance and represent the spear thrust into Jesus' side.

8. The red stain on the corona at the base of the central column and the red speckling on the style holding the stigma are a reminder of the blood Jesus shed.
9. The fruit of most passion flowers is round and signifies the world that Jesus came to save.
10. The tendrils symbolize Jesus holding firmly to his purpose and being supported by God's love.
11. The wonderful fragrance is said to represent the spices that the holy women brought with them on the day of the Resurrection.
12. The duration of the flower's life is three days, recalling the time that elapsed before the Resurrection of Our Lord.

Symbolism:

- catechetical
- passion of the Christ

Prayer Garden Theme:

- Stations of the Cross
- Marian
- Rosary

CULTURE

The *Passiflora incarnata* species is generally hardy in Zones 6–9; if planted in an area protected from northwest winds it may survive in Zone 5. Shown here is the cultivar 'Damsel's Delight', which is hardy in Zones 7–11. All cultivars prefer full sun but will tolerate light shade, especially from afternoon sun in warmer climates. 'Damsel's Delight' needs average watering; the soil should be well drained and loose or sandy. Use mulch to keep the soil cool. The passion flower will suffer from root rot in damp soils.

This is a fast-growing vine, 3–6′ / 91 cm–1.8 m spread by 6–8′ / 1.8–2.4 m height that spreads by root suckers. It attaches by tendrils as it climbs trellises or other plants. Train to a framework early. Prune yearly in late winter, and if needed throughout growing season to keep it in check — it is an aggressive vine.

Its intricate, large, fragrant blooms flower all summer, and come in an astonishing array of colors.

The resulting fruit, called maypops, are edible; they are said to taste like a cross between apricots and guava, and are high in antioxidants. The soft pulp separates easily from the skin — which is not very tasty — to eat fresh, and pulp and seeds are cooked down for jellies. The fruit is ripe when it falls to the ground. The fruit is also desired by wildlife.

Periwinkle

***Vinca minor* var.**

CHRISTIAN REFERENCE

This evergreen groundcover has a long association with the holy, and most strongly in *memento mori*, the remembrance of death. In many cultures the *Vinca* species represented a binding love, especially an existence of such love throughout eternity. This association comes from the vine being long-lived and able to secure the earth beneath it, as love secures us while in this realm.

Vinca minor

This symbolism of eternal love, and the assurance of God's mercy and love, made it a popular plant for cemeteries during the nineteenth century. It was a rapidly growing, dense groundcover planted over fresh graves, and at Catholic cemeteries the flowers also represented Mary's mantle.

Like the lilac, when found growing in abandoned areas the periwinkle indicates a place that was once a homestead. It is symbolic of the same type of love as the lilac: enduring, from young love fresh with hope to eternal reunion after death.

In art, the Blessed Virgin Mary is usually depicted wearing a blue veil that resembles the color of the *Vinca* flower — hence the name "Virgin flower." The five petals also represent a star; combined with the color it is reminiscent of the Marian moniker "Star of the Sea."

With such strong religious symbolism, the periwinkle is often seen in stained-glass windows, especially those that include a Marian image.

We know that a circle represents eternity, and evergreen wreaths are particularly significant at Christmas. The *Vinca* was also used to create wreaths and, interestingly enough, baskets — a source of income for many a hermit or religious order.

Symbolism:

- virginity
- binding love
- existence through eternity
- purity and strength of the Blessed Virgin Mary

Prayer Garden Theme:

- Sacred Heart
- divine mercy
- virtues
- Marian

CULTURE

Vinca minor is an evergreen vine hardy in Zones 3–8, and Zone 9 if sited in an evenly moist and shaded environment. It will tolerate part sun in the morning, but prefers full shade. Once established, watering is low, but it grows best in evenly moist, organically rich to average, well-drained soil. It is tolerant of dry, shallow, and rocky soils, where its size will be diminished.

As a groundcover it spreads, dominantly and at times invasively, having only a 3–6″ / 8–15 cm height. Because of its ability to root at every node, forming a dense, nearly weed-free mat, it is used for erosion control. To keep it contained, prune the edges of expansion in early summer. Lawn mowers are not effective in controlling the vine, since the rooting stems grow below the height of mower blades.

There are several *Vinca minor* cultivars to choose from, which include various flower and leaf colors and sizes. Here are a very limited few.[12]

- 'Atropurpurea' — large burgundy flowers with a long blooming period
- 'Blue and Gold' — a clumping variety with blue flowers and variegated gold leaves
- 'Bowles Variety' — a larger *Vinca minor* with blue-lavender flowers, also clump forming
- 'Emily Joy' — tallest of the species at 8–10″ / 20–25 cm with cream-colored flowers
- 'Flore Plena' — double light wine to pale purple flowers
- 'Illumination' — green-edged gold leaves and blue flowers
- 'Miss Jekyll' — petite in many ways, spreading to only 6–8′ / 1.8–2.4 m; smaller leaves and delicate abundant white flowers
- 'Ralph Shugert' — dark green oval leaves with wide, cream-colored margins, sky blue flowers

Rosary Plant

Crassula rupestris, Crassula rupestris* var. *monticola

CHRISTIAN REFERENCE

This little succulent is called the rosary plant because of its string of plump, bead-like leaves, which are particularly tight and round when it is young. It also has the moniker Mary's gold from the eternal rewards gained through praying the Rosary with Mary. Its clustered pink-flowering head of five petals symbolizes the five wounds of Christ, and its darker center the crown of thorns, as well as the crown of final glory upon entering heaven.

The Rosary is a familiar devotion that evokes a sense of peace as we meditate through the pater and mater beads. In the Catholic tradition, October is devoted to the Holy Rosary, and when I pray the Rosary with our Blessed Mother, problems seem to fall like leaves along the path of the mysteries.

The word *rosary* comes from the Latin word *rosarium*, meaning "rose garden." In the mid-1500s, *rosaire* came to mean "a garden of prayers," from the medieval concept of compiling a collection of items, which could include flowers, into bouquets. This apparently originated in the late 1400s with the printing of a prayer book, *Hortulus Animæ*, that literally meant "little garden of the soul." Creating a "bouquet" of prayers eventually led to a string of knots or beads to track one's praying. It was during the fifteenth century that the Rosary evolved into its present form.

Crassula rupestris var. *monticola*

Here is a familiar children's poem (author unknown) to share with the little lovelies that visit and ask about you Crassula:

My Rosary
My Rosary is a silver chain
that binds my soul to God.
My Rosary is a mystic vine
that grows in Heaven's sod.
The Aves from a rose bouquet
of white and red and gold
that stew along Our Lady's way
as each blest bead is told.

The mysteries are
lessons learned
of life's true gain and loss,
and always at the Chaplet's end,
I find and kiss the Cross.

Symbolism:

- eternal reward

Prayer Garden Theme:

- Stations of the Cross
- Marian
- Rosary

CULTURE

In the *Crassula rupestris* species are several cultivars suitable for symbolism as a rosary plant. *Crassula rupestris* var. *monticola*, a native plant on the continent of Africa, is frequently used.

This plant has limited hardiness in Zones 9–11; in colder climates it is grown as a houseplant or in containers and wintered over inside where there is adequate light — it does not go dormant. Like all *Crassula* species, it requires full direct sun for a minimum of six hours to prevent it from becoming leggy and weak-stemmed. In hot, dry, sunny climates, provide afternoon shade.

Watering is low, as it is drought tolerant, but remember that it is not a cactus and will need regular watering. The soil needs to be porous, loose, and well drained. It is excellent in a xeriscape, adding unusual texture and color.

Crassula rupestris var. *monticola* will be larger grown out-of-doors, at 12–15″ / 30–38 cm spread by 8–12″ / 20–30 cm height, about a third less as a houseplant or in containers. The red coloring that edges the plump leaves will also be more intense outside. It creates multiple branches and drapes well over walls and pots. At times the succulent branches become so heavy that they will break off or uproot — a natural means of propagation. They are easily trimmed back as desired.

This succulent has well-formed pink umbel blooms at the ends of branches (a terminal bloom) on plants usually three or more years old.

Royal Fern

Osmunda regalis, Osmunda regalis var. *spectabilis*

CHRISTIAN REFERENCE

The origin of the family name *Osmundacea* goes back centuries and is difficult to trace with accuracy, though there is significant information associating the name with Christianity.

Osmunda regalis var. *spectabilis*

The fern *Osmunda regalis* is large and prominent throughout the European continent and much of the Asian continent. Its stately nature and grand colonies are thought to have been behind naming the species *regalis*. Some sources indicate that this "regal" reference refers to a bishop of nobility who reigned in southern Great Britain,[13] possibly Saint Osmund (Osmer).[14]

The genus name for this fern, *Osmunda*, is also said to honor Åsmund Kåresson, early eleventh century, a Scandinavian and professional writer of runestones who helped prepare the way for the Swedish acceptance of Christianity.[15] This stone master created as many as fifty runestones, still viewed today — many bearing the Latin cross.

There is also the Germanic possibility of its name, as *os* means God and *mund* means protection. These ferns grew so large throughout Europe that they indeed could have protectively hidden a person beneath their fronds.

The root of this fern is said to have been used to clean the mouth of ailments, and from Latin comes *os* meaning mouth, and *mundus* meaning clean. There are other herbal uses for *Osmunda regalis*, including as an astringent, a diuretic, and in the healing of lacerations — the fronds were used to make compresses for external application to wounds and rheumatic joints.[16]

Symbolism:
- protection

Prayer Garden Theme:
- saints

CULTURE

Osmunda regalis var. *spectabilis* is native to the United States and hardy in Zones 3–9, requiring part to full shade in consistently wet environments such as bogs or rain gardens, or along stream beds where the moist soil is rich, humusy, and acidic. It will tolerate some clay soils.

Each mound of this fern will grow 2–3′ / 61–91 cm wide by 3–5′ / 91 cm–1.5 m height, with the scape of seed-fronds — termed sporangia — rising an additional 4–6″ / 10–15 cm above the leaves in late summer. Its leathery leaves and broad architecture make it appear more like a shrub than a fern, especially when "flowering." It is one of the slower-spreading ferns, expanding primarily by rhizomes, though not exclusively.

Royal Fern fiddleheads — the emerging young leaves — like those of several other ferns, are edible, and cooked young fronds are used in Korean cuisine.

Other suitable *Osmunda* species for the symbolism include:

Cinnamon fern, *Osmunda cinnamomea*: Zones 3–9, light to full shade, evenly moist soil that is organically rich and acidic, but will adapt to most soils as long as wet. Grows in clumps of 2–3′ / 61–91 cm spread by 2–5′ / 61 cm–1.5 m height with dramatic, long, upright fronds with impressive sporangia display. Tolerates black walnut trees.

Interrupted fern, *Osmunda claytoniana*: Zones 3–8; part to full shade; moist, acidic, humus-y soil on wet wooded slopes and ledges. 3′ / 91 cm spread by 3–5′ / 91–1.5 m height of open, arching fronds.

Shamrock

Trifolium repens, Oxalis regnellii var. *triangularis*

CHRISTIAN REFERENCE

The most famous of symbolic plants, attributed to Saint Patrick, is the white clover or wood sorrel, *Trifolium repens.* A native plant throughout the British Isles, it is a common perennial ground cover and an important part of forage for grazing animals. During Saint Patrick's time — the late fourth century — cattle were the prominent livestock, and so highly prized that they were guarded by herdsmen, with the largest herds being held by monasteries.

Oxalis regnellii var. *triangularis*

The shamrock, with its three-lobed leaf, was used catechetically by Saint Patrick to teach the Celts about the Holy Trinity:

> There is no evidence that the clover or wood sorrel …were sacred to the Celts in any way. However, the Celts had a philosophical and cosmological vision of triplicity. … Thus when St. Patrick, attempting to convert the Druids on Beltane, held up a shamrock and discoursed on the Christian Trinity, the three-in-one god, he was doing more than finding a homely symbol for a complex religious concept. He was indicating knowledge of the significance of three in the Celtic realm.[17]

The shamrock was initially used to explain the theological concept of the Holy Trinity, rather than as a religious symbol of the three in one Godhead. But this beloved and enduring symbol that indicated unity and, when enclosed by a circle, infinity, soon took its place among other architectural and emblematic forms of the trefoil.

The shamrock is the national emblem of Ireland, and its etymology comes from the Irish word *seamróg* "trefoil," diminutive of *seamar* "clover."[18]

Symbolism:

- joy
- Holy Trinity
- Saint Patrick

Prayer Garden Theme:

- Holy Spirit
- fruits of the Spirit
- saints

CULTURE

The common clover (shamrock) *Trifolium repens* is rarely used in a garden setting, because it is invasive and weedy. Consider other shamrocks, such as *Oxalis regnellii* var. *triangularis*, which is noninvasive and has several cultivars to choose from. Here is one, a purple leaf variety.

Oxalis regnellii var. *triangularis* is hardy in Zones 7–10, and in colder climates may be grown in containers. It requires sun to part shade, especially from afternoon sun. It needs average watering in sandy, humus-rich soil that is well drained — wet feet, especially in winter, is certain death. It is intolerant of salts.

It grows 4–10″ / 10–25 cm spread by 6–12″ / 15–30 cm height, in the smaller range when grown in containers. Depending on the cultivar, the plant will bloom early to late summer, with the fullest flush in early summer.

Often treated as an annual in northern climates, the bulbous roots are planted outdoors in spring. *Oxalis regnellii* var. *triangularis* will go dormant in prolonged periods of excessive heat — simply cut back the leaves, and when the soil is cooler it will regrow.

The leaves are affected by light intensity and will fold up at night, a trait called *photonasty* — and a wonderful Franciscan-style way to endear children to evening prayer.

Trees and Shrubs

Almond

Prunus spp., *Prunus amygdalus* 'Hall's Hardy'

CHRISTIAN REFERENCE

The almond tree is a well-known symbol for resurrection. In Israel, it is the first tree to bloom in spring. "The almond tree has a special significance for the beginning of the 'New Year for Trees' (called Tu B'Shevat) that is traditionally regarded as the time when spring begins in Israel. ... Some scholars have said that originally Tu B'Shevat was a "folk festival" to celebrate the re-emergence [resurrection] of spring."[1]

The Jewish word for almond is *shakeid*, coming from a root word meaning "to watch" or "to wake." There is a play on this word in the Old Testament, in one of the earliest prophecies of a young Jeremiah: "The word of the LORD came to me: What do you see, Jeremiah? 'I see a branch of the almond tree,' I replied. Then the LORD said to me: You have seen well, for I am watching over my word to carry it out" (Jer 1:11–12).

This sense of watching for the Lord is as much a truth for us today as it was for Israel then. Let us, too, awaken from dormancy to the virtue of hope, and the promise of our own springtime of faith.

The nut of the almond is concealed beneath an outer skin. This presents the concept of a divine essence concealed within a thing thought to be of little importance: a woman — the Virgin Mary — carrying the Incarnation, Christ hidden in human form.

The almond tree would

Prunus amygdalus 'Hall's Hardy'

work well as part of a Rosary garden where the tree's symbolisms are indicated in the First and Second Glorious Mysteries, the Resurrection and the Ascension (hope, watchfulness, promise); and the First Joyful Mystery, the Annunciation, the moment of the Incarnation (purity, and again watchfulness and promise).

The tree would also be an excellent metaphor at the end of the Stations of the Cross. St. Francis de Sales explains: "Now, in order to draw the almond and the shell from this outer bark, we crush and break it; and this represents very well our Lord's sacred humanity, which was so broken, crushed, and bruised during his holy Passion. … The almond which is within the nut … represents the Divinity; and the shell … represents the cross upon which our Lord was fastened."[2]

Symbolism:

- resurrection
- watchfulness
- hope
- promise

Prayer Garden Theme:

- Stations of the Cross
- virtues
- Rosary
- Bible

CULTURE

Before you purchase almond trees, be aware if potato, tomato, eggplant, or tobacco (*Solanaceae* family) or cotton (*Gossypium* genus) have been growing where you intend to plant your almond tree. The area must be left clean of those plants for four to five years to minimize the risk of Verticillium fungal infection of young trees.

There are several cultivars available; search for the ones that will thrive in your Zone. If you live in a cooler area at the low end of the almond tree's Hardiness Zone, select varieties that bloom later to prevent loss of flowers to late frost. Speaking of blooms, you will (usually) need two trees for pollination.

The culture information given here is for the cultivar 'Hall's Hardy'.

Hardy in Zones 6–8. Plant in full sun. It requires 2–3″ / 5–8 cm of water per week, less once established, and must be regularly fertilized with nitrogen and phosphorus. The soil should be a sandy loam, allowing for good drainage while retaining some moisture. A relatively fast grower with a mature size of 10–15′ / 3–4.6 m spread by 15–18′ / 4.6–5.5 m height. Plant two trees at least 20′ / 6 m apart, though this cultivar is advertised as self-pollinating.

'Hall's Hardy' requires mild, wet winters and dry, warm summers to fruit properly, and will bear fruit in three to five years. The shell is woody and particularly hard to crack.

It is a lovely, fragrant tree, with its light pink petals and dark pink eye, if being grown singly as an ornamental.

Cedar

Cedrus spp., *Cedrus atlantica*

CHRISTIAN REFERENCE

The impressive and long-lived cedar of Lebanon (*Cedrus libani*), native to Lebanon, Syria, and southern Turkey, is the most noteworthy of trees in the Bible — it is mentioned nearly fifty times throughout Scripture! The cedar had a significant role in ancient culture and was prized above all other trees. Its finely grained wood, though soft and comparatively lightweight, was strong, straight, long, and wonderfully scented. As such it was the first choice for building temples or palaces — it was used to build King David's palace (see 2 Sm 5:11; 7:2) and in the construction of King Solomon's temple (1 Kgs 6).

Cedarwood oil was one of the first ingredients in perfumery. The ancient Sumerians used the oil as a base for paints, and ancient Egyptians used it in embalming practices. Because of the oil's curative properties for skin ailments and as an anti-inflammatory, it was used for both humans and animals. It is still used in homeopathy because of its bactericidal and fungicidal attributes.

The wood was thought incorruptible, an image of eternal life, because insects dislike its oil's distinctive scent and taste. This property also provided for the cedar's resistance to blight diseases.

Because it could withstand the ravages of nature, cedar was also used for the construction of ships, and by the Egyptians for mummy cases. Its wood was so highly prized that the grand forests of the "tree of God" were nearly lost to deforestation.

Cedrus atlantica

CULTURE

The mighty and slow-growing Lebanon cedar is too large for the average garden. If you do choose to grow it, it is hardy in Zones 5–7 and has very specific culture requirements.[3]

There are other species of *Cedrus* to choose from. The two most often used in the garden are *Cedrus atlantica* (Atlas cedar, pictured here) and *Cedrus deodara* (Himalayan cedar).

Symbolism:

- eternal life
- incorruptibility
- healing
- power and strength

Prayer Garden Theme:

- Bible

Adaptable to a wide range of soils, the genus is limited by its cold hardiness. Most *Cedra* species are better transplanted when purchased as container plants.

The landscape value of *Cedrus atlantica* is described as, "A handsome specimen tree, particularly striking when fully matured … surrounded by ample turf and allowed to develop naturally they have no garden rivals; not used enough in the south where *Cedrus deodara* dominates because of its fuller, denser habit and faster growth in youth; unfortunately *Cedrus deodara* will often die back starting at the top of the plant."[4]

Give this evergreen a lot of room and do not prune away the lower branches, allowing them to curve gracefully toward the ground. The tree grows to 30–40′ / 9.1–12.2 m spread by 50–60′ / 15.2–18.3 m height. Its cones ripen in autumn to form "roses" that are used for decorations.

Cedrus atlantica 'Argentea' is pyramidal in shape and has needles that are a silver-blue, almost appearing white. Hardy in Zones 6–8, it requires full sun for better color but will tolerate light shade, and needs average watering. It prefers acid soil, which needs to be loamy, evenly moist but not continually wet; being well drained is important. The tree also needs to be sheltered from strong winds.

Other listed cultivars of *Cedrus atlantica* from the 2015 University of Connecticut database[5] are:

'Glauca': Known as the blue atlas cedar. Most commonly used cultivar and more available than the species. Has blue-green needle color. Seedlings grown from blue-needled plants will exhibit a range of needle colors, from blue to green.

'Glauca Pendula': A weeping form with bluish needles. Must be pruned and staked when young to develop a good form and habit. Typically to 15′ / 4.6 m tall, but individual specimens are unique with cascading branches. Very popular and used frequently in modern landscapes, but can appear awkward if employed improperly.

'Fastigiata': An upright form with blue-green needles.

'Glauca Fastigiata': A narrow, columnar selection with gray-blue needles and a mature of spread of only 10′ / 3 m.

Dogwood

Cornus spp., *Cornus kousa* var. *chinensis*

CHRISTIAN REFERENCE

There is a familiar children's story of the dogwood that is used as a metaphorical teaching tool.[6] It is told that at the time of the crucifixion, the dogwood was comparable in size to the oak tree. Because its wood was firm and strong, it was selected as the timber for the cross, but to be put to such a cruel purpose greatly distressed the tree. The crucified Jesus, sensing the beautiful tree's sorrow at his suffering, said to it,

"Because of your sorrow and pity for my sufferings, never again will the dogwood tree grow large enough to be used as a gibbet. Henceforth it will be slender, bent and twisted, and its blossoms will be in the form of a cross — two long and two short petals. In the center of the outer edge of each petal there will be nail prints stained with red and in the center of the flower will be a crown of thorns, and all who see this will remember."[7]

Dogwoods do not grow naturally in Israel and were not part of the passion; yet the tree is rich in symbolism because of this story, and makes a strong element in any spiritually themed garden.

Dogwood flowers are sturdy and can tolerate adverse weather well, hence the symbolism of endurance. Its wood is remarkably strong and durable, and represents reliability. Both of these appellations reflect fortitude, a gift of the Holy Spirit and a cardinal virtue. Add the dogwood to a Stations of the

Cornus kousa var. *chinensis*

Cross garden because of its associated symbolism, "love in adversity."

The etymology of "dogwood" has little to do with dogs, and more to do with its wood and the making of sharp tools. In its Latin name *cornus* is "tusk" or "horn," which makes clear the hardness of the wood; it was used to make daggers, skewers, and arrows. The Middle English verb *dag* meaning "to pierce or stab" may have led to the common name.[8]

Symbolism:

- love in adversity
- endurance
- reliability
- fortitude

Prayer Garden Theme:

- Stations of the Cross
- Holy Spirit
- virtues

CULTURE

The *Cornus kousa* var. *chinensis* is representative of the old legend of the dogwood. It is hardy in Zones 5–8, will tolerate full sun but prefers part shade, and needs average watering (increase during hot, dry summers). Grows best in organically rich, slightly acidic to neutral soils that are well drained. It will grow 15–30′ / 4.6–9.1 m spread by 20–30′ / 6.1–9.1 m height.

According to the Missouri Botanical Garden, *Cornus kousa* has no serious insect or disease problems and has better disease resistance and better cold hardiness than the more popular *Cornus florida*, and is an excellent alternative to flowering dogwood in areas where dogwood anthracnose is a problem.[9]

Besides its spring tufts of bright green leaves and showy summer flowers — which are actually bracts — it is a fall beauty with purplish-red to scarlet leaves. Its raspberry-like fruit is a food source for birds. The dogwood's patterned bark and nearly horizontal branching pattern in the winter landscape make it a four-season tree.

Bunchberry, *Cornus canadensis*, is a perennial ground cover with the familiar white cruciform flower. It is perfect if your prayer garden does not have room for a tree, but you want the same symbolism. Hardy in Zones 2–6, it requires part shade, and evenly moist, well-drained soils; grows to 12–15″ / 30–38 cm spread by 6″ / 15 cm height.

A fun fact: In the southeastern United States, a late spring cold spell is referred to as a "dogwood winter." Farmers avoided planting their crops until dogwood flowers appeared — the signal that winter was over.

Fir

Abies* spp., *Abies concolor

CHRISTIAN REFERENCE

Because of Saint Boniface, the fir tree has had a long association with Christianity. The story is told that he came across a group of pagans worshipping an oak tree in the druidic tradition. In anger, he swung an ax, eventually cutting down the oak tree, to prove that the false god had no power over him.

To the amazement of the onlookers, a young fir tree[10] immediately sprang up from the roots of the fallen oak. Saint Boniface took this as a sign from God and began to teach the Christian faith saying: "This humble tree's wood is used to build your homes: Let Christ be the center of your households. Its leaves remain evergreen in the darkest days. Let Christ be your constant light. Its boughs reach out to embrace and its top points towards heaven. Let Christ be your comfort and your guide."[11]

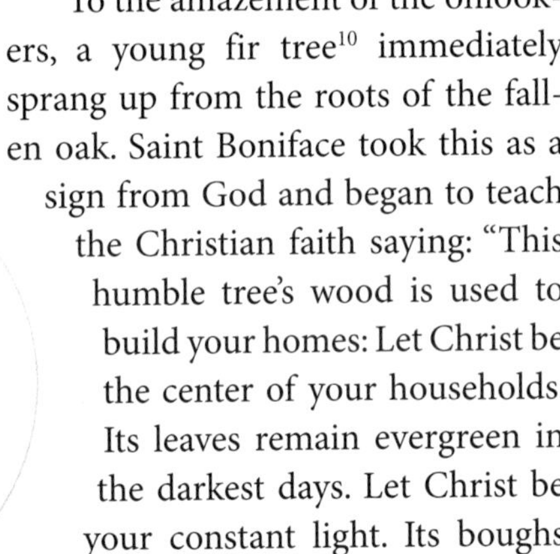

The fir tree mentioned in the Bible is another tree confused by malapropism, and believed to be cypress or, more likely, pine. What can be said about the fir tree, as is true for most evergreens, is that it represents immortality because its needles remain green throughout winter — and green is the color signifying life.

In the Christian tradition, immortality leads us to contemplate the beatific vision. On earth, we can embrace a "lifting up" to God in faith, hope, and fortitude, and in heaven we exist beyond

Abies concolor

our sins and ignorance in an eternity of fidelity with the Holy. Our Lord is patient with us as we weave a life back to eternity with him, and for this reason, the fir tree would fit well into the theme of a divine mercy garden.

Symbolism:
- eternity
- patience
- fidelity
- a lifting up

Prayer Garden Theme:
- divine mercy
- virtue
- Saint Boniface

CULTURE

There are more than fifty species in the genus *Abies*, most bearing the distinct silver bands on the underside of the needles. Found throughout most of the northern hemisphere, this evergreen — which can be anything from towering to shrub-like — requires full sun; evenly moist, well-drained, slightly acidic soil; cool temperatures and high humidity; and most need protection from desiccating winds. They are not recommended for city plantings, as they are intolerant of pollution. When properly placed, fir trees are generally easy to grow, though slow, and make a striking addition to the landscape.

Listed here are some of the more popular species; some have cultivars with distinct attributes such as dwarf, branching pattern, or coloring. Take time to read through resources describing the characteristics of *Abies* spp. to find the one that suits your fancy.

White Fir, *Abies concolor*, pictured here. Hardy in Zones 3–7, 15–20′ / 4.6–6.1 m spread by 40–70′ / 12.2–21.3 m height, most adaptable of the firs, being tolerant of drier soils. Needles are blue-silver with underside greener. Cultivar 'Violacea' is bluest of the larger firs and stunning when new growth appears. 'Cadicans' is also blue-silver, slender, and appears fluffy, with its 2.5″ / 6.4 cm long needles.

Nordmann Fir, *Abies nordmanniana*. Hardy in Zones 4–6, 20–30′ / 6.1–9.1 m spread by 35–50′ / 10.7–15.2 m height, branches are horizontally arranged in tiers, with glossy black-green needles marked beneath by silver bands.

Nikko Fir, *Abies homolepis*. Hardy in Zones 5–6 — a very limited range of temperature tolerance — and grows 20–30′ / 6.1–9.1 m spread by 30–60′ / 9.1–18.3 m height. It is native to the mountainous region of Japan. In early summer, mature trees have narrow purple-blue upright cones that look like candles. It is reported to have a better tolerance of air pollution that other *Abies* species.

Gardenia

Gardenia jasminoides, Gardenia jasminoides 'Crown Jewel'

CHRISTIAN REFERENCE

For centuries the gardenia has held the rank of the most perfect of flowers in beauty and fragrance — a scent that is distinct and alluring. It's primarily native to China, and evidence of cultivation of both wild and double-petal forms of the gardenia has been depicted in historical Chinese painting. This flower is still a popular theme in Chinese landscape art.

Gardenia jasminoides 'Crown Jewel'

The flower has an enduring symbolism of pure love, of someone who is strongly attracted to another in the most honorable of ways, even transcending earthly happiness. In a garden created to reflect the virtues, the gardenia represents several: love, joy, patience, faithfulness, and chastity.

The gardenia's white color contributes to its representation of purity, gentleness, and grace — a perfect description of our Blessed Mother.

Gardenia leaves are shiny and waxy. This is symbolic of clarity and self-reflection, a movement of understanding in that, "what faith alone cannot do, [the Holy Spirit] is able to do with the help of the gift of understanding. This gift surpasses our human way of comprehension and enlightens us in a divine way; it makes us *intus legere*, that is, 'read within' the divine mysteries, with the light, with the understanding of the Holy Spirit himself."[12]

In myths and legends the gardenia is known as moon pearl, moon tears, or moon fruit because its flowers open at night, and the petals seem to glow in the dark even on nights of new moons. Its fragrance is most intense in the evening, not only because that is when the oils are freshest, but also because the cool moist air holds the fragrance closer to earth.

With the symbolism of "transport of joy" and the fact that many of the blooms come forth from darkness, the gardenia would be a lovely addition to a Resurrection or Easter garden. It also works well in a Marian or Rosary garden when meditating on the Joyful Mysteries, especially planted near the Annunciation or the Nativity of Our Lord.

Symbolism:
- purity
- gentleness
- grace
- transport of joy
- attraction

Prayer Garden Theme:
- Holy Spirit
- virtues
- Marian

CULTURE

Gardenias are heat-loving evergreen shrubs hardy in Zones 8–11, needing full sun to dappled or shifting partial shade. They require average watering, and need well-drained, evenly moist, humus-rich, acidic soil. Depending on cultivar, they average 3–5′ / 91 cm–1.5 m spread by 4–6′ / 1.2–1.8 m height.

This shrub's intoxicatingly fragrant flowers bloom throughout the year. The white flowers have a matte texture, in contrast to the glossy leaves.

Gardenias are slow growers and can be fussy, but if properly placed in a landscape — sheltered from winds — are impressive evergreen shrubs. They are heavy feeders and do not tolerate salts in coastal conditions, or treated and softened water. They do not transplant well, disliking disturbance or competition at their roots, so choose a site without tree roots and mulch widely to reduce weeds.

Gardenia jasminoides 'Crown Jewel' is a compact gardenia, 3–4′ / 91 cm–1.2 m spread by 4–5′ / 1.2–1.5 m height. 'Crown Jewel' is claimed to be hardy in Zones 6–11, so is able to withstand temperatures below 32°F / 0°C, and adapts to varying soil types. It has a double white flower 3″ / 8 cm across appearing on both old and new wood.

Hawthorn

Crataegus spp., *Crataegus laevigata* 'Superba'

CHRISTIAN REFERENCE

According to tradition, following the crucifixion of Jesus, St. Joseph of Arimathea was driven from his home and began a journey of evangelizing.

He traveled first to Marseilles and then to Glastonbury, in an attempt to bring Christianity to the Britons. When he and his companions arrived at Wirrial Hill, tired from the journey, he thrust his staff into the hillside as the group lay down to rest. When he awoke, a miracle had taken place: The staff had taken root and begun to grow and flower.

This became the site of the Glastonbury Abbey, where the hawthorn bloomed every Christmas, and in spring, almost always near Easter time.

Legend has it that the original hawthorn was cut down by a Puritan soldier in 1653; numerous other versions of the attempted eradication exist. However, many cuttings were taken from the tree before its destruction. The last hawthorn on the grounds of Glastonbury Abbey was said to be a cutting from the original tree. It was planted in secret after the original was destroyed.[13] Unfortunately the Holy Hawthorn of Glastonbury, *Crataegus monogyna* 'Biflora', has been subjected to repeated vandalism since 2010, until its final loss in May 2019.

This shrub-like tree was a classic selection used in the monastic and medieval garden to form an impenetrable barrier, called a "laid hedge." A ditch was dug along the desired

Crataegus laevigata 'Superba'

border, and on the crest, saplings were planted between stakes that held eddered rails to train growth. Pleaching (braiding) the branches as they grew created a formidable dense wall of thorns against marauders, human or animal.[14]

The hawthorn's flowers were often used by brides because of its symbolism of the "union of love" within which love was protected — as the hawthorn flowers are protected by thorn — and because of its prolific fruiting, symbolic of a hope for a union that would bring forth children.

Adding to these the meanings of promise and watchful hope, the hawthorn is appropriate in gardens dedicated to the Sacred Heart of Jesus, the Blessed Mother, Stations of the Cross, and saints.

Symbolism:

- hope
- watchfulness
- promise
- union of love

Prayer Garden Theme:

- Sacred Heart
- Stations of the Cross
- Marian
- saints

CULTURE

Crataegus flowers come in an assortment of colors: white to reds, solid or with two-tone petals, single or doubled blooms. It can be dangerously thorned or nearly thornless, as is the case with cockspur hawthorn (*Crataegus crus-galli* var. *inermis*) described below.

The cultivar shown is *Crataegus laevigata* 'Superba,' also known as 'Crimson Cloud.' It is hardy in Zones 4–8 and, like all hawthorns, requires full sun. Once established, it is fairly drought tolerant. It will grow in most any soil to a size of 15–25′ / 4.6–7.6 m width by 20–25′ / 6.1–7.6 m height. 'Superba' is intolerant of salt, whether airborne or in soil — in colder climates it should not be planted near driveways or sidewalks. Its drooping branches also make it unsuitable for such locations.

Hawthorns are long-lived, with three seasons of interest: spring flowers, autumn color in certain varieties, and depending on cultivar, a lovely silhouette in winter. It is a food source for pollinators in spring, and its berries feed birds and other animals in winter. Deer love all parts of this tree; they will eat spring buds, summer leaves and twigs, and winter berries.

Crataegus crus-galli var. *inermis* is a thornless tree with single white flowers, abundant red fruit, and silver-gray bark. The foliage is dark glossy green and turns a bronze to purple-red in the autumn. It is more disease resistant than most hawthorns. The bark exfoliates in thin gray strips, and provides winter interest.

Holly (evergreen), Winterberry (deciduous)

Ilex* spp., *Ilex × meserveae

CHRISTIAN REFERENCE

The American holly, *Ilex opaca*, similar in appearance to the English holly, *Ilex aquifolium*, is the species most closely associated with Christmas. Its shiny, deep green leaves and bright red berries are a regular feature in holiday decorations.

Holly carries interrelated symbolisms. In the language of flowers, it means "to foresee," as in "to understand in such a way as to predict, to prophesy." It is also used as a reminder of where Jesus' birth and life will lead; its prickly leaves are reminiscent of the crown of thorns, and the red berries of the blood he shed upon the cross. It is easy to see how branches of this shrub displayed during Advent symbolize the fulfillment of Jesus' human life.

The evergreen species of *Ilex*, like all evergreens, is symbolic of eternal life because the leaves "never die," whereas deciduous trees shed their leaves annually.

In the Stations of the Cross, also called the Way of Suffering from the Latin *Via Dolorosa*, there is a story that the holly berries were at one time white and were stained red by drops of blood as Our Lord walked by, and where he fell. Use holly in a Stations of the Cross garden; it is particularly appropriate when placed at any of the three Stations representing when Jesus fell.

Hollies are an excellent choice for dividing a prayer garden space. The range of cultivars allows personal preference as to their function: Use

Ilex × meserveae

a tall variety to create a sense of enclosure and shade, a smaller one for a hedge, or dwarf cultivars for designating a particular area.

Symbolism:

- eternal life
- to foresee or prophesy

Prayer Garden Theme:

- Stations of the Cross

CULTURE

There are nearly five hundred *Ilex* species, hybrids, and cultivars with an extraordinary array of habit and size: from evergreen to deciduous trees, shrubs, and lianas; varying leaf form, shape, texture, and color; different fruit shape and color. Most are tolerant of air pollution and heavier (clay) soil. The American holly, *Ilex opaca*, includes more than one thousand cultivars! Its Hardiness Zone is broad, from Zones 5–9. Check with local nurseries or university extension services to choose the variety best suited to your region.

Here I offer culture information for the familiar blue holly, *Ilex × meserveae* — referred to as blue because of its deep-colored leaves. Considered the hardiest for northern gardens, Zones 4b–7, this hybrid needs full sun to light shade; it will grow more densely in full sun. It requires evenly moist, well-drained soils that are slightly acidic and organically rich.

The most popular varieties are 'Blue Princess'/'Blue Prince,' with 8–10′ / 2.4–3 m spread by 10–12′ / 3–3.7 m height; and 'China Girl'/'China Boy,' which is smaller at 6–8′ / 1.8–2.4 m spread by 6–8′ / 1.8–2.4 m height and rounded, with a wider tolerance of temperatures.

Like most hollies, these grow best in locations protected from cold winter winds and prefer afternoon shade in hot summer climates.

If you want the shrub to have showy red berries — which are food for birds — you will need to grow both male and female plants of the same cultivar. For *Ilex × meserveae*, plant one male for every five female shrubs placed fairly close, no more than 100′ / 30.4 m apart. Distance and male/female ratio is specific to species, hybrid, and cultivar.

Most hollies are toxic to equines, though, like deer, they tend not to like its taste — but there is always that one horse.

Juniper

Juniperus spp., *Juniperus communis*

CHRISTIAN REFERENCE

The juniper is mentioned by name in the Bible (see Ez 27:5; 31:8; Ps 104:17; Is 60:13) and has a strong identity in art history and legend. In Isaiah 60:13, it is included with fir and cypress as one of the three trees for the Lord's sanctuary.

Juniperus communis

The juniper, like other plants in the Bible, was confused with a similar-sounding word — a malapropism — in this case, with the genus *Genista. Genista* comes from Latin for "broom," and is called *rothem* in Hebrew. It is also known as brushwood and cedarwood, which circles back to the juniper, whose wood is called cedar.

Similar in sentiment to the Lebanon cedar, the juniper was a tree considered to be a symbol of God's strength and glory. This led to it being grown in monastery gardens, not only for its symbolism but also for its beauty.

A cloister garth — a central open area especially found in monasteries — rarely had any other significant vegetation besides a juniper. This tree signified the tree of life, because of its decay-resistant wood and evergreen leaves.

Juniper branches were historically used as an aspergillum to sprinkle holy water in blessings. Considering the amount of water the branch could hold, there was no sprinkling to it! Some parishes still follow the tradition of using the juniper branch during Easter. At one such celebration that I attended, the gasps — and eventual squeals of anticipation — of the congregation were heard as the abundant holy water moved like a mini wave over their heads until it made contact, and drenched hair and faces. The priest was well pleased with the congregants' physical awareness of being awash with the Holy Trinity.

The juniper is associated with the virtue of chastity. Its fruit, a berry, is protected by the plant's sharp, needle-like leaves; for this reason the juniper is often depicted in art in association with virginity of both men and women, and our Blessed Mother.

The thorny branches are also depicted in nativity scenes and in art of the Madonna with child, alluding to the crown of thorns. When using the juniper in a Stations of the Cross garden, place it near the Sixth Station.

The legend of the juniper tree speaks of the time when the holy family fled from Herod and was pursued by his soldiers. The giant juniper tree, *Juniperus thurifera*, miraculously opened up its branches like arms and enfolded Joseph, Mary, the Baby, and the burro so they were safely hidden. In gratitude, Mary gave the tree her blessing, and to this day, juniper boughs are hung in stables and barns on Christmas Day.

Symbolism:
- tree of life/eternity
- chastity
- Christ's passion

Prayer Garden Theme:
- Stations of the Cross
- virtues
- Marian
- Bible

CULTURE

Hardy in Zones 3–9 (cultivar specific), junipers require full sun to light shade; watering is average to light. Average, well-drained soil is best, though they are tolerant of most soil conditions except excessively dry or wet.

Junipers are a striking evergreen in winter, with some cultivars turning purple-red, deep blue, or pink-tipped in cold climates.

To maintain shape, use hand nippers to prune in winter; do not shear with hedge clippers.

The juniper is a diverse evergreen tree or shrub with hundreds of cultivars to choose from, ranging in height from 6″–130′ / 15 cm–40 m tall. It is able to withstand bitter cold or hot and dry environments and is salt tolerant, making it an excellent plant for seashores and alongside walks and drives. It is prone to twig fungal diseases in areas that have a lot of rain and high humidity, and if exposed to excessive overhead irrigation.

For those who suffer from pollen allergies, most *Juniperus* species bloom in late winter. This is good to know for the amateur beekeeper as well; junipers are a source of pollen for bees when few other plants are available for food.

Lilac

Syringa spp., *Syringa vulgaris*

CHRISTIAN REFERENCE

The lilac has a wonderful relationship with Christianity. In many parts of the world it is called the ascension flower because of its bloom period.

Syringa vulgaris

The feast of the Ascension of Our Lord is set forty days after Easter. Nine days later, the sharing of a new form of love from God comes to earth as the Holy Spirit. This day is Pentecost — which means "fiftieth" — and concludes the fifty-day season of Easter. During this time, late spring to early summer, the lilac blooms in its native lands, Asia and Europe.

The etymology of the common lilac, *Syringa vulagis*, has its origin in that region. The word *lilac* comes from the Persian *nilak* and Turkish word *leylak*, meaning bluish, and was incorporated into Spanish, then French, as the name we use today. Lilac was designated as a color in the late 1700s.

The first part of its botanical name, *Syringa*, is associated with shepherds. *Syringa* is derived from the Greek word *syrinx* meaning "pipe" or "tube." Shepherds would hollow out the pith in the center of the stems to make pipes, or flutes. When you look at a nativity scene, there is often a shepherd playing a flute; now you know its origin! We still see this type of flute today, called a pan flute.

The lilac has always had a strong association with love, though different colors of lilacs carry various meanings. The symbolism of love, both new and old, seems to have originated in the Victorian era. Giving the blue lilac indicates a young love and the hopes of courtship developing into more, through the summer weeks ahead. A widow would wear the blue lilac during its blooming season as a symbol of her love enduring beyond the grave.

I like the way the lilac connects the virtue of *caritas*, charity, to marriage. The flowers' beauty and fragrance — like love — draw us in, and the strong roots and eternally flowering branches are enduring. I live in the Midwest, where numerous family farms existed. Often when driving I'll pass abandoned fields, and not far from the road stands a well-established lilac. I can imagine a clapboard house, a young and hopeful couple planting a slip of a lilac next to the porch, and the yearly bouquet set on the family table.

Symbolism:

- ascension
- first emotion of love (enduring to an old love)

Prayer Garden Theme:

- Holy Spirit
- virtues
- Rosary

CULTURE

Syringa vulgaris is hardy in Zones 3–7, requires full sun, and will often develop mildew on the leaves in humid environments, especially with the slightest amount of shade. Watering is average, with mature shrubs being fairly drought tolerant. It is able to withstand a wide range of soil conditions except consistently wet or boggy. This species — as is true for most *Syringa* — spreads by rhizomes and will become sizable: 10–15′ / 3–4.6 spread by 18–20′ / 5.5–6.1 m height.

The fragrant panicle blooms are 5–8″ / 13–20 cm long, and grow in pairs at the terminus of second-year stems (old wood), with a short blooming period of only two weeks — three if the temperatures are cool. It attracts pollinators. Lilacs must have a cold period of dormancy in order to set bud.

There are around twenty-five species of *Syringa*, with thousands of hybrids and cultivars. With so many to choose from, you may be challenged to select just one — I've had five. Though not the most impressive of the species, *Syringa vulgaris* has run the length of my drive for more than thirty years as a screen; I appreciate that it is leggy at the base and denser up top.

Myrtle

Myrtus communis

CHRISTIAN REFERENCE

Myrtus communis was used by prophets to indicate a change on earth, when the knowledge of the Lord shall cover the earth as the waters cover the sea.[15] In Isaiah 41:19–20 we read, "In the wilderness I will plant the cedar, / acacia, myrtle, and olive; / In the wasteland I will set the cypress, / together with the plane tree and the pine, / That all may see and know, / observe and understand, / That the hand of the LORD has done this." Also, in Isaiah 55:13: "In place of the thornbush, the cypress shall grow, / instead of nettles, the myrtle. / This shall be to the LORD's renown, / as an everlasting sign that shall not fail."

From the Old Testament verses, we Christians can understand why myrtle holds a significant and enduring place in Jewish religious traditions and prayers. The myrtle is considered in Judaism to be the symbol and scent of Eden, and is one of the four sacred plants of the weeklong autumn festival of Tabernacles, Sukkot, also known as the Festival of Ingathering.

In Christianity, myrtle is an emblem of the bridal-tie[16] — the vows of love, chastity, and fidelity. This connection to secular marriage translates easily to the bridal-tie of women religious consecrated to Our Lord, and priestly love and fidelity to the Church. It was common to weave crowns of myrtle for brides and grooms,

Myrtus communis

and for branches to be carried or placed in the sanctuary during religious vows.

The divinely espoused heart of the Blessed Virgin Mary is said to be like the myrtle, for she is the "vessel of election of the love of the Holy Spirit"[17] and glorified all his fruits with her life. Legend has it that when Mary and Joseph were married, she wore a wreath of the sacred myrtle braided with roses on her head.

Myrtus communis is native to the Mediterranean region and grown for medicinal and culinary use. Its berries are also used to make mirto, a traditional Italian liqueur from the berries of myrtle. This liqueur originated on the islands of Sardinia, Corsica, and Capraia in the Tyrrhenian Sea.

Symbolism:

- love
- chastity
- purity
- fidelity (marital bliss, a good and prosperous marriage)

Prayer Garden Theme:

- fruits of the Spirit
- Marian
- Rosary
- Bible

CULTURE

Myrtus communis is classified as a broadleaved evergreen shrub. Hardy in Zones 8–11, it requires full sun but will tolerate light shade, though it will have fewer blooms. The bush will need average water when young, but once established it is fairly drought tolerant. It prefers fertile, evenly moist, well-drained soil and will not tolerate having wet feet.

It grows 3–5′ / 91 cm–1.5 m spread by 6′ / 1.8 m height, with some native plants reaching up to 15′ / 4.6 m in height.

The myrtle flowers from late spring to early summer, with an abundance of highly fragrant blooms that have a mass of long, fluffy stamen that nearly cover the small white petals. It requires a long, hot summer to flower properly the next season.

Many cultures consider myrtle an herb. The leaves are used in much the same way as bay leaves; flowers can be added to salads; and its berries are used as a seasoning like peppercorns.

Oak

Quercus spp., *Quercus alba*

CHRISTIAN REFERENCE

The oak has a significant presence in the Old Testament — it is mentioned from Genesis to Zechariah in more than twenty-five verses. In *Eastons Bible Dictionary* there are six Hebrew words rendered in English as "oak," which is often applied to a species of terebinth tree said to be extinct by AD 330.[18] I enter the biblical fray of "oak tree" hesitantly; the identity of trees in the Bible has been a point of controversy for centuries. In Hebrew texts, trees are identified by adjectives, and oak was indicated as strong tree or mighty tree.

Quercus alba

Promises were made under the oak's boughs; royalty buried within its shade; and its longevity — some trees were said to be nearly one thousand years old — was proof of the everlasting goodness of God. Through these concepts the symbolisms of triumph, patience, stability, and strength were assigned to the oak.

Oak wood is often used for constructing church crosses, not only for its durability but also for its symbolism of triumph. Place this tree as a central feature in a Stations of the Cross garden.

The story of oak trees, and the association with the tale of Saint Brigid's cloak, is one that conveys trust in God. One of Saint Brigid's tactics for the conversion of her countrymen was Christianizing their customs. Oak trees held specific ritualized meanings in the druid culture. To debunk those magical associations, Brigid built her monastery from this tree; the site was called the church of the oaks, Cill Dara, or more commonly, Kildare.

There is a folktale about how Saint Brigid acquired the land upon which her abbey was built. The saint had such a reputation for good works that the local chieftain was obligated to fulfill her request for land. Mockingly, he told her she could have as much land as her cloak could cover. With a look heavenward, Saint Brigid confidently swirled her cloak to the ground where it began to miraculously increase and did not stop spreading until it covered the hillside she had prayed to obtain for her abbey.

The oak is a slow-growing tree that develops steadily and will bear fruit, but not until its roots are well established. We, like the oak, grow slowly in our faith, at our own pace, and with well-set roots the fruits of the Holy Spirit grow in our souls.

Symbolism:
- triumph
- patience
- stability
- strength

Prayer Garden Theme:
- Stations of the Cross
- fruits of the Spirit
- Bible
- saints

CULTURE

Quercus alba, according to Dirr, is the standard;[19] a majestic tree by which all other oaks are measured.

Hardy in Zones 3–8, it requires full sun; average watering, though it is drought tolerant once established; and deep, moist, well-drained, acidic soil. This is a massive, long-lived tree, in maturity reaching at least 50–80′ / 15.2–24.3 m spread by 60–90′ / 18.2–27.4 m height. It has an impressively deep tap root that stabilizes the tree, and makes it a poor candidate for transplanting. Choose the site with care, and once placed, leave it set.

The oak provides for wildlife: deer and rabbits will browse tips and branches as well as the acorns, which also feed squirrels, turkeys, pheasants, ducks, and other birds. The acorn starts forming in midsummer, ripening in late autumn, and will not develop in trees less than about fifty years old.

The leaves often turn deep wine-red in autumn.

Oleander

Nerium oleander, Nerium oleander 'Hardy Pink'

CHRISTIAN REFERENCE

A prominent shrub in the Holy Lands, the *Nerium oleander* species name comes from the genus name for the olive tree, *Olea*; their leaves look similar, but that is their only resemblance. All parts of the oleander are highly toxic, whereas the olive is not.

Nerium oleander 'Hardy Pink'

This toxicity is the foundation for its symbolism of sin and caution. We are often deceived into thinking there is something good and inviting about sin: a false good of some personal benefit. Carelessly accepting what we think is good — rather than what is best for us, as God always wants — we find soon after how toxic the act was to our soul. Sin is like the oleander, deceiving in its fragrance and beauty; and if we act without knowledge of the danger it poses, it is deadly.

Oleander also represents the heart, both in love and death. The reason for the symbolism of death is that the toxicity will "stop the heart from beating," but in a symbolic way, the same applies to love. There is a boundary to love; when true love of another is held in high esteem, the trust between lovers is not broken. But woe to the lover who falls to infidelity. The toxicity of that act kills love and breaks the heart.

The oleander also appears in one of the two stories of Saint Joseph's staff bursting into bloom. The one we are most familiar with — and mentioned earlier in this book — is when Joseph stood before the elders of the temple as they were choosing a chaste husband for the Virgin Mary.

Lilies bloomed on his staff as an indication from God that he was the chosen spouse. The other legend is that the Archangel Gabriel brought a message to Joseph that he would marry the Virgin Mary, and confirmed the promise with white oleander flowering on his walking stick.

A miracle of healing from Saint Joseph involves a young girl and oleander. It was written that a Spanish girl lay ill of a fever. Her mother tried everything to cure her daughter, but to no avail. Exhausted by her desperate efforts, the mother fell to her knees to pray to Saint Joseph to spare her child. When she stood, the room was filled with a rosy glow from a male figure bent over the girl. He placed on the child's breast a flowering branch of pink oleander. Then the light faded, and the chamber was empty, except for the child and the mother. But she saw that the girl was in a calm sleep, the first since her illness. The child's recovery was quick, and from that day the oleander became the flower of Saint Joseph.[20]

Symbolism:

- heart (love or death)
- sin
- caution

Prayer Garden Theme:

- Saint Joseph
- Bible
- saints

CULTURE

Nerium oleander 'Hardy Pink' is hardy in Zones 7–11, requiring full sun, and average watering (less once established). It tolerates most any soil if evenly moist and well drained — oleanders will not tolerate wet feet. Rounded in shape and fast-growing, the shrub grows to a 6–10′ / 1.8–3 m spread by 8–15′ / 2.4–4.6 m height.

Its fragrant flowers bloom from summer to autumn. A showy evergreen resistant to salt, wind, and pollution, it is an excellent shrub for coastal or street plantings.

It needs to be pruned annually. The debris must not be burned or go into compost piles, but instead be bagged for disposal. Even a few leaves in a pool of water can kill a dog, and a stick used for roasting a marshmallow will seriously affect a child.

Poplar

Populus alba, *Populus* × *canadensis* 'Robusta'

CHRISTIAN REFERENCE

Poplars are mentioned in the Old Testament and, depending on which version of the Bible you use, are named up to six times. The species mentioned in the Bible are the white poplar, *Populus alba*, and the shrub-like Euphrates poplar, *Populus euphratica*. The white poplar, often called silver poplar, has young stems that are white as they begin growth, a cream to light gray bark, and the undersides of its dark green leaves are silvery from a covering of tomentum — a matted woolly down.

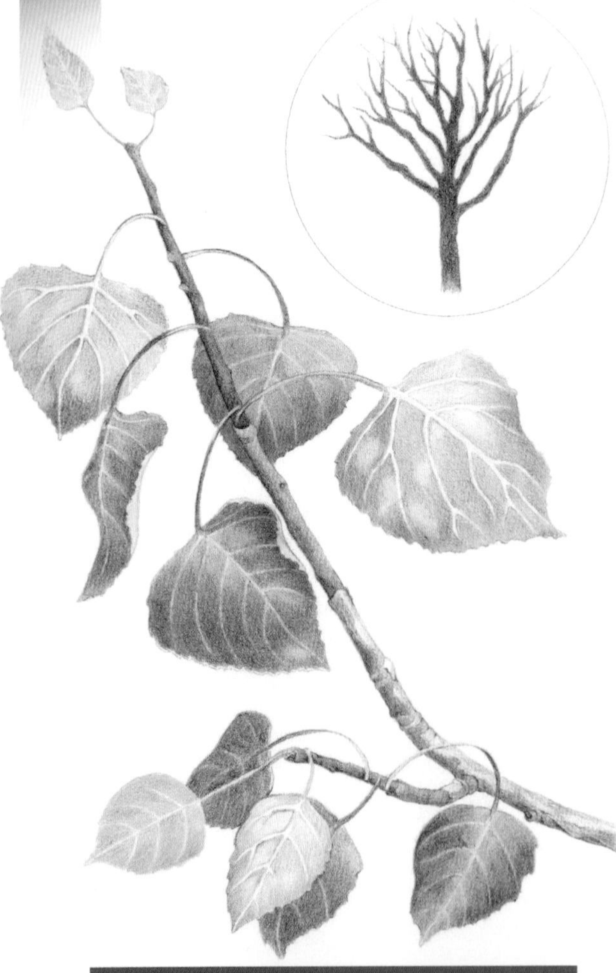

Populus × *canadensis* 'Robusta'

In the Holy Land the poplar, growing near streams, was often a tree of gathering and relief. I have a childhood memory of a beloved silver poplar that grew in my grandfather's front lawn. It was an immense and beautiful tree that provided me with endless play in its branches and under deep shade on summer days — not so unlike the children of the Middle East.

In Israel, the white poplar is found growing in Mediterranean woodlands and shrublands, and along stream beds, but rarely in mountainous areas since the tree requires even moisture. The tree's prolific nature is spoken of in Isaiah 44:3–4 when the Lord speaks to him of descendants: "I will pour out my spirit upon your offspring, / my blessing upon your descendants. / They shall spring forth amid grass, / like poplars beside flowing waters."

The white poplar is also the tree referred to in the genetics experiment of Jacob, "Jacob, however, got some fresh shoots of poplar, almond and plane trees, and he peeled white stripes in them by laying bare the white core of the shoots. The shoots that he had peeled he then set upright in the watering troughs where the animals came to drink" (Gn 30:37–38).

This tree was called the tree of life, referencing eternity. Its prolific, regenerative nature established the poplar as a symbol of victory, strength, and transformation as it repeatedly — and rapidly — reached heavenward.

The poplar has not been designated as a tree representative of martyrs, but its symbolism of deep courage and strength is easily translated to a person of great faith, like so many saints. It would also make a powerful statement in a memorial garden dedicated to those who gave their life in service.

Symbolism:
- deep courage and strength
- victory
- transformation
- reaching heavenward

Prayer Garden Theme:
- Bible
- saints

CULTURE

From the smaller and beloved quaking aspen (*Populus tremuloides*) popular in poetry and essays, to the towering eastern cottonwood (*Populus deltoides*), there is a wide range of poplars to choose among, depending on your Hardiness Zone and preference. I suggest these trees with hesitancy. Depending on the species and cultivars, the *Populus* is typically short-lived and soft-wooded, prone to storm damage, messy, suckering, and potentially invasive.

A sturdier and often-used poplar is *Populus* × *canadensis* 'Robusta.' Hardy in Zones 5–9, it requires full sun, and average moisture — it is drought tolerant when mature, and will take hold in most any soil. It grows fast, making it somewhat weak-wooded, maturing to 40–50′ / 12.2–15.2 m spread by 90–100′ / 27.4–30.4 m height with an invasive root system — so give it ample room to develop away from buildings. If pruning is needed, do so in late summer to autumn. The longevity of this cultivar is fifty to one hundred years. It does not produce "cotton," and is salt, pollution, and wind tolerant.

A smaller poplar is a fairly recent introduction: the seedless (cottonless) male, *Populus deltoides* 'Siouxland.' Hardy in Zones 3–10, 25–40′ / 7.6–12.2 m spread by 60–80′ / 18.2–24.3 m height, lives only thirty to fifty years.

Rose

Rosa spp., *Rosa rugosa* 'Pink Robusta'

CHRISTIAN REFERENCE

"No one shall be crowned with roses who has not first been crowned with the thorns of our Lord."[21] Now isn't that a cheery thought from St. Francis de Sales! Though in many representations it's true; the rose in art is associated with more than twenty martyred saints, though it is primarily associated with the Virgin Mary:

> According to ancient legend, before the Fall of Man the rose had no thorns, and the Virgin is called the "rose without thorns" because she was untouched by Original Sin. In keeping with this tradition, the theme [in art] of the "Madonna of the Roses" or the "Madonna of the Arbor" became … widespread. … Also in connection with the Virgin, the flowers usually appear in scenes of the Immaculate Conception, the Assumption — in which roses sprout alongside lilies inside Mary's empty tomb — and the Coronation of the Virgin.[22]

Rosa rugosa 'Pink Robusta'

The rose has been part of our heritage for centuries, being initially portrayed in the Old Testament. The oldest living rose, *Rosa canina* or wild dog rose, is a native climbing rose that grows in Germany against the Hildesheim Cathedral apse. Though the cathedral was bombed in 1945, the roots of the rose survived and bloomed again among the rubble.

There are associated colors for a Rosary garden that can be easily translated to a garden dedicated to the fruits of the Spirit. Check the Supplemental Catholicism (p. 259) section for this information.

Symbolism:

- red for sorrow, also passion (as in a deep love for another)
- white for martyr's death
- peach for modesty, humility, and chastity
- pink for grace, gentleness, joy, and happiness

Prayer Garden Theme:

- divine mercy
- Stations of the Cross
- fruits of the Spirit
- Marian
- Rosary
- saints

CULTURE

With multiple species, hybrids, and cultivars, your rose selection will be based on Zone and personal preference.

The hardiness and features of roses are diverse. In general, roses grow well in Zones 6–9. *Rugosa* roses are a shrub rose hardy in Zones 3–9. Non-grafted roses tend to be hardier in cooler climates. Requiring full sun, some need afternoon shade in warmer climates; need evenly moist and fertile soil that is slightly acidic and well drained. Some cultivars need regular feeding and protection from blights and insects.

Listed here are the basic types of roses and a general description; exceptions exist within any group and are not noted. Be warned — deer eat roses!

Hybrid tea: Blooms all season, single bloom per long stem, doubled or semi-doubled flowers.

Floribunda: Abundance of flowers all season, hybrid tea-type bloom or open-face in sprays of varying size and colors, hardier and more disease resistant than teas.

Grandiflora: A cross between teas and floribundas, tea-type flowers in sprays on long stems all season, tallest of the modern roses, hardier than teas.

Climber: Single-stemmed or clustered sprays of flowers; most have a single bloom period. They are not vines and must be tied to supports, and most require yearly removal of older canes. For mistake-free cane removal, in spring cut oldest canes just above the crown and wait a couple days. It will be obvious by the wilting which canes to prune out.

English rose: A type of shrub rose, very fragrant, and long lived; most are repeat bloomers with large globular flowers.

Shrub (illustrated here): A wide range of blooming periods, blossom types, and fragrances. Sturdy, long-lived plants with broader range of cold tolerance, tall, arching, good for hedges — some growing 7′ / 2.1 m high — and disease resistant.

The *Rosa rugosa* 'Pink Robusta' blooms a flush of flowers in early summer and repeat blooms throughout the season, displaying blooms, buds, and hips at the same time. Hardy in Zones 3–9, tolerant of seaside conditions, and fairly drought tolerant.

Species: Found in the wild and can be invasive in some areas, single open-face flowers, blooms once prolifically in early summer, fragrant, up to 8–9′ / 2.4–2.7 m wide and tall, produces multiple hips to feed wildlife.

Sweetshrub

Calycanthus* spp., *Calycanthus floridus

CHRISTIAN REFERENCE

The genus *Calycanthus* has fragrant leaves that, when crushed, smell like allspice, a combined scent of cinnamon, cloves, and nutmeg. Thus the symbolism for the allspice herb, *Pimenta dioica*, was transferred to *Calycanthus*.

In Central America where the allspice is native, it carries the symbolism of compassion and benevolence from its medicinal uses, which include the ability to reduce inflammation, boost the immune system, increase circulation, and reduce pain. The scent of the sweetshrub calls to mind the "merciful nature" of its eponym.

Mercy is significant in our Christian tradition, as it characterizes God's love for us, and bridges the distance from us to him. Through Saint Faustina, Our Lord reinforced for us the importance of mercy, and of trusting in his compassion. He, through Saint Faustina and Pope St. John Paul II, established devotion to the divine mercy.

In the *Catechism of the Catholic Church*, we read that the theological virtue of charity produces the fruits of joy, peace, and mercy, all fruits of the Holy Spirit (1829). Again the *Catechism* describes the corporal and spiritual works of mercy as "charitable actions by which we come to the aid of our neighbor in his spiritual and bodily necessities" (2447).

Calycanthus floridus

Compassion is one of the earliest lessons God's people needed to learn, as we read in Hosea 6:6: "For it is loyalty that I desire, not sacrifice, / and knowledge of God rather than burnt offerings."[23] This instruction was repeated by Jesus. When sitting in Matthew's house, he reminds the Pharisees of this requirement, saying: "Go and learn the meaning of the words, 'I desire mercy, not sacrifice.' I did not come to call the righteous but sinners" (Mt 9:13).

Being compassionate and kind is a foundational principle taught to us in childhood. We order our life accordingly and encourage the young to blossom through this reciprocal gift, in order to continue sharing the fruits of charity. Our Blessed Mother embodies all of these holy virtues; the sweetshrub would be an excellent addition to any Marian garden.

The flowers of sweetshrub are fragrant, with the intensity and scent varying between cultivars. When its blooms are combined with evergreens in an arrangement, they together symbolize mercy and eternal life.

Symbolism:
- mercy
- compassion
- benevolence

Prayer Garden Theme:
- divine mercy
- fruits of the Spirit
- Marian

CULTURE

Calycanthus floridus is hardy in Zones 4–9, and requires full sun to light shade, especially in hotter climates. It needs average watering and evenly moist, organically rich soil, though it will tolerate clay. This species grows 8–12′ / 2.4–3.7 m spread by 8–12′ / 2.4–3.7 m height.

The fragrant burgundy flowers appear along the stems at nearly every leaf node, and begin opening in late spring. As mentioned above, fragrance intensity and scent vary. They are good cut flowers, but keep in mind proper pruning practices when you prune a branch from the shrub for the vase.

Calycanthus species become leggy when grown in part shade and will need to be pruned to maintain their shape. Pruning should be done immediately after flowering to allow buds to form throughout the summer for next year's blooms.

Mulch is essential to maintain an evenly moist soil. Sweetshrub has a sensitive outer bark and breaks down if it lacks proper air movement at ground level. When laying mulch, give a leeway of about 8″ / 20 cm from the base of the stem to the edge of the mulch.

Trinitarian Flower

***Bougainvillea* spp.**

CHRISTIAN REFERENCE

Bougainvillea is known as the trinitarian flower because of the repeating sets of threes in the flower's structure. The flowering stem has three stalks, from which a grouping of three brightly colored bracts forms. Near the center of each bract, a small tubular flower is supported.

Bougainvillea

We first read of the Holy Trinity in Matthew 3:16–17, at the baptism in the Jordan: "After Jesus was baptized, he came up from the water and behold, the heavens were opened [for him], and he saw the Spirit of God descending like a dove [and] coming upon him. And a voice came from the heavens, saying, 'This is my beloved Son, with whom I am well pleased.'" Those present that day saw the physical presence of both Jesus and the Holy Spirit, and heard the voice of God. A similar manifestation occurred at the Transfiguration to Peter, James, and John.

As Jesus' ministry is about to come to an end, we read the scene of the agony in the garden, where the Trinity is again present (see Lk 22:39–46). At Gethsemane, the Son is praying to the Father, and we can assume that Jesus' divine will was sustained by the Holy Spirit, until eventually Jesus is comforted by an angel.

These two events are presented in the mysteries of the Rosary. In the Luminous Mysteries we meditate first on the Baptism in the Jordan in gratitude for faith, then on the Transfiguration and spiritual courage. In the Sorrowful Mysteries we meditate on the Agony in the Garden and the call for repentance.

The family, made up of husband, wife, and children, reflects the unity of love in the Holy Trinity. Thus we can also use the symbolism of this plant to reflect on the holy family, and on our own immediate family.

There is also a trinity, with a lowercase t, of the person's duty toward God. "Jesus summed up man's duties toward God in this saying: 'You shall love the Lord your God with all your heart, and with all your soul, and with all your mind'" (CCC 2083).

The *Bougainvillea,* with its threefold nature, is a plant worthy of a place in every prayer garden.

Symbolism:

- Holy Trinity

Prayer Garden Theme:

- Holy Spirit
- Rosary

CULTURE

The *Bougainvillea* is wildly diverse. The species includes trees, shrubs, or vines, and varieties and cultivars are numerous considering how easily it hybridizes. In general it is hardy in Zones 9–11, requiring full sun and well-drained soil. It has low watering needs in containers, and is drought tolerant in the landscape.

Its size will depend on the species. Container-grown types average 4–8′ / 1.2–2.4 m spread by 2–3′ / 61–91 cm height. Though the *Bougainvillea* thrives on neglect, container-grown plants require frequent fertilization.

It flowers in six- to eight-week cycles, and in warmer regions blooms all year. A light pruning at the start will increase branching, but beware — this plant has thorns that are hard to see.

Witch Hazel

Hamamelis spp., *Hamamelis* × *intermedia* 'Arnold Promise'

CHRISTIAN REFERENCE

Although the word *hazel* — taken from the Hebrew word *luz* for "nut bearing" — is found in some versions of the Bible,[24] its scriptural use is believed to reference the almond. The name *witch hazel* evolved from words meaning "to bend" (*wych*) and "lively" (*wicke*), referring to being "weak-wooded" — it is not related to the word *wiccian*.

The genus name, *Hamamelis*, comes from a name that Hippocrates applied to the medlar, a small, hawthorn-like fruit. The name combines two Greek root words meaning "fruit" and "together," referring to the plant's habit of producing flowers at the same time as seed dispersal.[25]

The combination of flowering and setting seed is an indicator of a spiritually developed nature, well portrayed throughout Christianity.

Hamamelis has a long history with people. The medicinal properties of witch hazel have been known for centuries, and a Y-shaped branch cut from the shrub was used for finding water, termed "dowsing" — a practice still active today and a point of controversy for thousands of years.

In the stories of saints, Saint Kentigern, also known as Saint Mungo, is prayed to for protection against bullies. He was an illegitimate child born in Scotland and was given the endearing name Mungo (meaning "dear one") by his tutor, Saint Serf. Mungo was gifted and held a special place in the

Hamamelis × *intermedia* 'Arnold Promise'

hearts of his teachers. For this, he was often bullied by his peers at the monastery. At a very young age he began performing miracles. The most popular is the story of his bringing a red bird back to life.

Another incident during his childhood happened when he was left in charge of the fire in the monastery. The boy arose from sleep and found that all the fires in the monastery had gone out through a treacherous act by his peers. Mungo, in his frustration, left the building and went out into the garden to the surrounding witch hazel hedge. He took a branch from the bush and, turning to God, raised the branch, and blessed it with the Sign of the Cross. As he finished his prayer, flames from heaven ignited the witch hazel as he held it in his hand. And so Mungo entered the monastery with his little burning bush and relit the fires.

Symbolism:
- protection
- healing

Prayer Garden Theme:
- saints
- angels

Some cultivars of witch hazel have an impressive movement of colors during autumn pigmentation. The edges of the leaves form bands of red, orange, and yellow, with the center green spotted with purple; eventually the plant fully colors to a vivid red.

CULTURE

Hamamelis × intermedia is a group of hybrids with several cultivars. Here is a fragrant yellow cultivar with an intense autumn color, 'Arnold Promise'.

Hardy in Zones 5–8, it requires full sun but will tolerate light shade. The blooms appear in late winter, often the first color in the Midwest garden in the United States. The flowers are fragrant, with long, strappy petals that on cold days will curl in to protect from freeze damage, and help to extend the four to six week bloom period.

Like most witch hazels, this plant requires average water, with more needed in times of drought to prevent leaf scorch. The soil should be slightly acidic, organically rich, evenly moist, and well drained, though the plant will tolerate some clay.

'Arnold Promise' grows 12–15′ / 3.7–4.6 m spread by 12–15′ / 3.7–4.6 m height.

Gardening Basics

"As we extend the tendrils of our faith above and through the walls of our resistance, our lives become green, verdant, affirming. We are the wild rose basking in the sun. As we cling to our conscious optimism, finding footholds of faith despite opposition, our lives become rooted in the soil of grace. We are nurtured, prospered, and blessed."

— Julia Cameron[1]

This section will be a refresher for the experienced gardener. If you think you have a "black thumb" and fear killing off any attempt to create a garden, be not afraid. With the knowledge in this section, selecting the right plant for the right place becomes easier, and you will slowly grow in confidence.[2]

Most of what is included here is a simplified view of horticulture. Depending on where you live, you can glean detailed information from university extension services, local suppliers, and other gardeners.

Begin by mapping out the area where the garden will be located. You will then assess the site for duration of sun or shade, soil condition, and watering requirements.

1
Creating a Base Map

A base map is like a blueprint of your garden or property and is created in a few steps. First, sketch the property's shape; second, assess the elements of your property; and lastly, refine your information on a base map.

1. **Sketch**: Roughly draw the shape of your property and include all the features: house, walkways, shrubs, pond, etc. You will need to measure everything and add these measurements to your draft to be refined later. Be sure to mark which way is north. This will help determine shaded areas as you plan your garden.

2. **Assessment**: Look at what you have drawn and see if any of these things can be changed, if you want to change them. Hard structures such as buildings and drives, fences, and utilities are permanent; as are mature trees or shrubs you want to keep — if they are still in good condition and a pleasing shape. Look at existing service areas like air conditioners, garbage containers, or utility meters and areas where water pools. Draw a dashed circle indicating their location.

3. **Base Map**: Using your measurements, draw to scale what you have indicated in your sketch. For a small garden sketch, use a 1:1 scale with ¼″ / 1 cm graph paper, where 1′ / 30 cm equals one ¼″ / 1 cm square. For a base map of a large area you'll want to use a five- or six-foot (1.5–1.8 m) scale, depending on your property size; then draw with each graph square as 5:1 or 6:1. Make a copy of your map and, using tracing paper laid over the copy, draw the features and plants you want to add to your yard.

2
Evaluating the Site

The site evaluation involves gathering information on the physical nature of your chosen garden area. You are working with a very small portion of your landscape, so your evaluation will be narrow and focused, and will directly affect the plant selection for your garden.

If you already have a garden in place and are only sectioning off a portion of it as a prayer area, then this will provide you with an overview. Do make notes of your existing garden; you may be inclined to adjust the existing plantings to match your new awareness of a sacred space and symbolic plants.

HARDINESS ZONE

First, you will need to know what Hardiness Zone you live in. This will tell you what plants will survive in your area (Zone). There are both cold and heat considerations for hardiness, as well as overall climate, such as humid or arid — in this book I address cold hardiness. A Hardiness Zone, whether addressing heat or cold, tells you that a plant grown in that area can endure a 50 percent kill off of its root because of temperature and still survive.

Following are cold Hardiness Zone maps of North American and European continents, and a Climate Zone Map for the Australian continent. The global cold Hardiness Zone designation is included here. Australia follows a more logical classification for gardening, one that considers metorological factors and not just temperatures. Also check gardening resources in your area to get more accurate information.

You can create what is termed a micro-climate to slightly adjust a small portion of your garden to allow plants grown at the edge of their Zone to survive. For example, to create a micro-climate in my Zone 5 garden, for a plant hardy in Zone 6, I would grow it near the foundation of the house (warmer soil) on the leeward side (east and south) protected from winds and winter storms, and mulch heavily during the winter.

North America Hardiness Zone Map

European Hardiness Zone Map

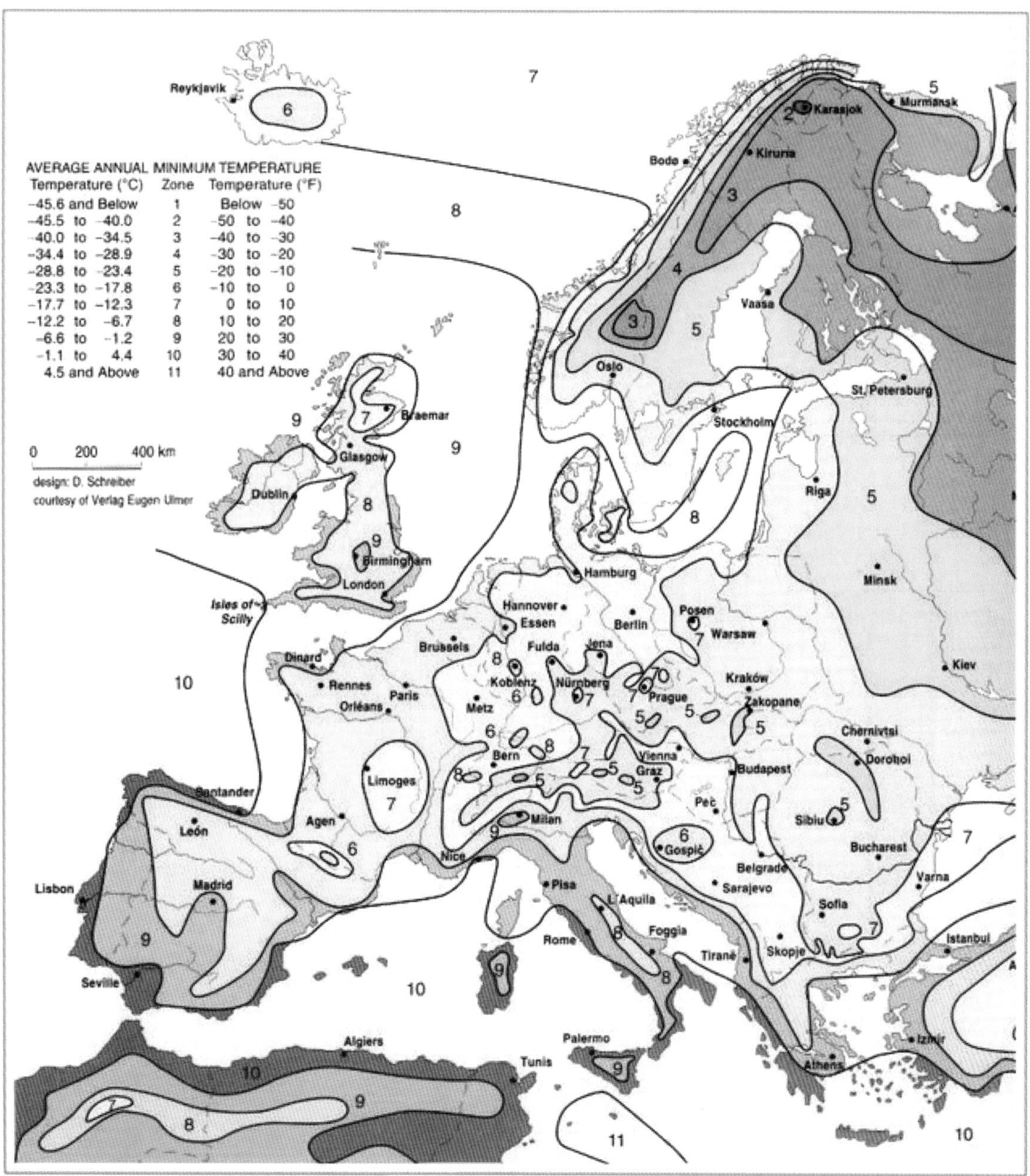

Map of Climate Zones of Australia

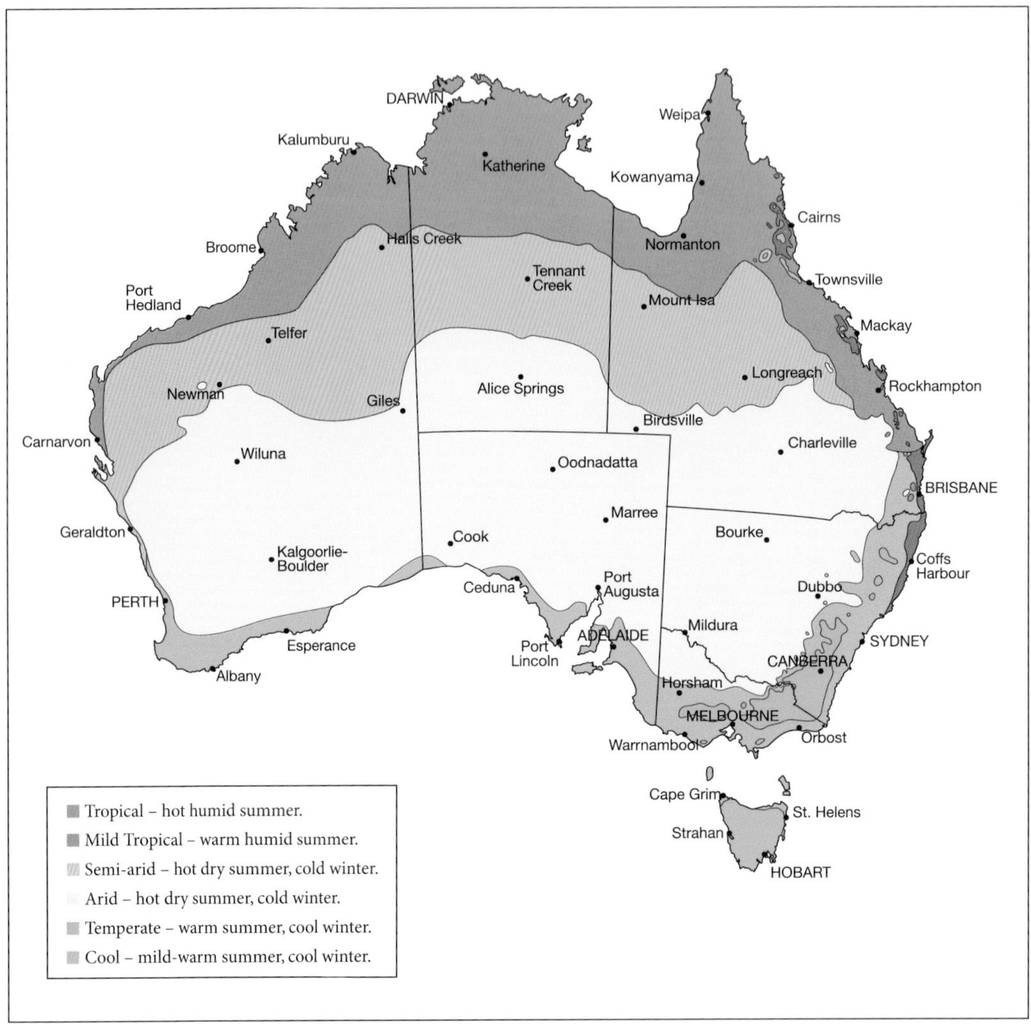

SUNLIGHT AND SHADE

Defining the quantity and quality of light in an area is the next essential step to creating a garden. You will want to know how many hours during the day that direct sunlight rests on your location. Generally defined, full sun equals six or more hours; light shade equals four to six hours; partial shade equals about two to four hours; and full or dense shade either receives no direct sunlight or only up to two hours. Check your location at different times throughout the day to determine sunlight and shade durations.

Notice the term "direct sunlight"; this is unobstructed and uninterrupted sunlight directly resting on a plant's leaves. Shade is altered or diffused sunlight. Often a garden has more than one kind of shade. Types of shade are defined as follows.

Woodland or Heavy Shade: This is an area where sunlight is blocked, covered by trees or structures all day. Heavy shade gardens are the most challenging and rewarding to develop. Classified as full shade.

Light, Dappled, or High Shade: In this environment the sun is filtered through high branches all day. Most of us have this type of shade, especially if we live in a suburban area. Classified as part to full shade.

Afternoon Shade: Is an area that has gentle morning sun and light to heavy shade all afternoon. This is the easiest light condition in which to develop a shade garden. Classified as part shade.

Morning Shade: Here an area has light to heavy shade in the morning, and full, hard sun all afternoon. Most shade plants will not tolerate this type of an environment; the afternoon sun is too harsh. Classified as full sun.

Sunny Area: Here there is full sun from dawn to sunset, more than six hours. Classified as full sun.

Dry Shade: Very specific plants are required for dry shade, whatever shade category you are working with. These areas exist between buildings that block rainfall, shaded slopes, or some heavily wooded areas. A small area of dry shade may be improved by creating a raised bed or amending the area to hold more moisture by adding peat or compost. Do not raise the soil around tree trunks! Piling soil or mulch around the trunk will cause decay to rot the bark and kill the tree. For larger areas, use the right plant in the right place.

Moist and Well-Drained Shade: This is a more common environment in yards. It is rich in organic matter and has a nice soil composition that holds moisture without becoming heavy. This offers the broadest range of plantings, especially when the shade is not heavy and dense.

SOIL

Dirt is what you sweep up off the floor; soil is what you grow plants in. Now that that distinction is clear, the soil of your garden can be anything from seaside sandy loam to nutrient-rich dense clay. Soil provides a habitat for what I've termed earth-works: bacteria, fungi, insects, and other necessary organisms. It also provides nutrients, water, and oxygen; moderates temperature; and anchors a plant.

For many home gardeners, this topic causes the overwhelmed brain-freeze response. Here are some general guidelines to ease you into understanding and help you to identify your soil type.

Start by looking around your site and seeing what plants grow and their overall conditions. Use any regional plant guides, either online or in print, to gain a better knowledge of the area in which they grow. Weeds are also a good indicator of soil. A few weeds in an area mean little, but when growing in mass they are clear indicators of soil types — and a good farmer knows well the weed. Well-groomed lawns are not a good indicator of soil type, because they are often watered and fertilized instead of being self-supporting. Also, look at the general condition of plants growing in the surrounding area beyond your property, and note which ones are thriving and which are spindly.

For a definitive analysis of your garden soil's chemical composition, you will need to take samples to be tested at an agricultural service in your area. Contact them for specifics on how to proceed with the test, and make an appointment to have someone explain what the test results mean and how to amend the soil if needed. The following three characteristics indicate the condition of the soil, though not the chemical makeup.

1. **Texture**: Soil texture is determined by the relative portions of sand, silt, and clay. Texture is inherent to the soil of the area you live in. Texture influences the soil's properties, such as drainage — you've read many times "evenly moist, well drained." With a little effort, the texture of a *small* area of soil can be altered and improved with amendments such as peat, sand, or compost.
2. **Tilth:** The physical condition of the soil as it relates to ease of seeding, emergence, and root penetration. Essentially, this is the soil's ability to support plants. You can improve the tilth of soil by improving its texture.
3. **Compaction:** This means that the soil particles have been mechanically pressed together to the point of nearly eliminating the spaces for air and water movement. This creates a condition known as hard pan. Think of a dirt road or driveway … no amount of tilling will return this hard, compacted soil to a cultivatable condition. It has lost its tilth.

You can do a simple check of the soil texture at your site by digging a six-inch-deep hole, picking up a handful of the soil, and lightly squeezing it. You are looking for the amount of moisture being retained. Obviously, if it has just rained, wait a couple of days for the soil to drain before doing this test.

When you squeeze the soil, is it dry and crumbly (sandy)? Is it cool and slightly damp while holding together (loam)? Or is it heavy, clumping, and somewhat sticky (clay)?

To further assess soil texture, the quick and well-known method described in the next section uses a tall quart / 1 L jar, water, and soil. As the particles of soil separate, they will naturally sort themselves out by weight and will create layers: Heavy sand will be at the bottom of the jar, medium-weight silt will be in the middle, and smaller clay particles at the top (sometimes if clay is very fine and light it may float, making the water appear cloudy). The relative proportions of these layers help you see what type of soil you have.

An ideal combination of sand, silt, and clay particles is called loam and is considered the best garden soil. Knowing how close (or far) you are from loam will help you decide what amendments to add to the soil.

The Quart Jar Soil Test

1. Take a soil sample from a few 6″ / 15 cm deep holes dug at the site location. You can use soil from different sections of the garden for an overall view, or make a test for each divergent garden area. Remove debris, and mix together and break up any lumps. Then measure out one cup (~250 ml) of soil.
2. Use a clear, clean, empty quart/liter jar with a tight lid.
3. Fill the jar about half full of garden soil.
4. Fill the jar to 1″ / 2.5 cm from the top with water.
5. Tighten the lid and shake the jar for a minute so that all the particles are in suspension.
6. Set your quart jar soil test aside in a location where it can remain undisturbed for twenty-four hours so the particles have a chance to settle, though you will begin measurements after a minute. The soil particles will separate into sand, silt, and clay layers.
7. Get a ruler and hold it against the side of the jar. Begin measuring the sediments.
8. After one minute, measure and record the number of inches/centimeters of the settled particles of sand.
9. After an hour, measure and record the depth of the next layer, subtracting the level of sand recorded. This is silt.
10. After 24 hours, measure the level and subtract the two previous numbers. This is the clay.
11. Calculate the percentage: Divide the depth of each layer by the total depth of soil particles in the jar, and then multiply by 100.[3]

Reading the Results of Your Quart Jar Soil Test

If your jar test is 20% clay, 40% silt, and 40% sand, you have the perfect combination of loam. The other types of soil are:

30% clay, 60% silt, 10% sand = Silty Clay Loam
15% clay, 20% silt, 65% sand = Sandy Loam
15% clay, 65% silt, 20% sand = Silty Loam

If you choose to amend a small portion of a garden area, common amendments include:

- Composted yard trimmings
- Leaves from deciduous trees
- Crop residues
- Composted manures

The color of the soil gives a clue to its character — light colors usually have less organic content than dark soils, and dark soil warms faster in the spring.

Loam and sandy loam (where you have a bit more sand than silt in your jar) are usually the best types for gardening. If you have a noticeable amount of clay, don't fret. There are plants that do well in partial clay (clay tolerant), and other plants that are called "clay busters," whose roots permeate and help loosen the clay.

A small caveat here: Just because your soil structure is hard and doesn't drain does not necessarily mean it is dense clay. Compacted soil that has lost its tilth will not separate out into three layers. In either situation — heavy clay or compaction — planting a garden in that location is not an option and you will need to give way to using containers.

3
Watering

A garden hose that can be dragged to your area is probably the most you will have to consider. Of course, if you plan on locating your prayer space at the back of forty acres, watering will be an issue.

Be sure to consider how long the area remains wet or dry after a rain or soaking. The lack of water on a dry site will be a factor in how much time you will need to set aside to attend to the garden. If you have located your space in a sandy area, at the top of a slope, under the eaves of the house or under a grove of trees, you can be sure that the area will most likely be dry. To accommodate this type of soil, you could select drought-tolerant plants, amend the soil, use mulch to help hold more moisture, or plan to water regularly.

A yard that is in a low-lying area or one with a high water table may have drainage issues. The wet area may be a condition of the environment; in that case, select the appropriate plants to create a bog garden. If the area remains temporarily damp for a long period after a rainfall, it could be pooling of runoff. Here, a rain garden would be the best option if you can't reroute the source of the water. For a simple fix, look where the nearby downspouts are located, and determine how to reroute them.

Let's begin with basic watering techniques. Drip irrigation using a soaker hose is best, though above-ground irrigation with sprinklers (or hand watering) is more frequently used. Watering early in the day is ideal, especially when the dew is still on the leaves. Midday watering loses too much to evaporation. Late afternoon is second best, when the leaves can dry before evening. You'll want to avoid wet leaves at sunset — the dark dampness through the night encourages a variety of diseases. There will be times when the only spare moment you have to water is in the evening — don't fret. An occasional evening watering is better than not watering, especially during a particularly dry spell.

A simple way to test the depth of watering requires a long screwdriver or longer piece of rebar. After watering for an hour, push the smooth metal probe into the soil. Your first indicator of depth will be when you feel resistance; soil when wet is easier to penetrate than when dry. Pinch your finger around the shaft at ground level, and pull the probe from the earth: This is the depth to which the water has permeated. With trees and shrubs, take this measurement at the outer edge — the drip line — of the branches.

I've found that an old rusty piece of rebar, if left in the soil for a minute or two, will discolor from the moisture and give another indication of depth.

With this measurement as it relates to an hour of watering, you can estimate how long to water to achieve the needed depth.

A specific plant's watering needs depend not only on soil retention, but also on its root zone and size; average watering for a tree is very different than average watering for herbaceous plants. A general guide for depth of watering, using a rule of three, is to water smaller herbaceous plants to 1′ (30 cm), shrubs to 2′ (61 cm), and trees to a depth of 3′ (91 cm).

A rain gauge is essential for a gardener; you need to know how much water per week has been received whether by rainfall or sprinkling. Average watering for a flower or vegetable garden — having shallow roots — is an inch / 2–3 cm per week. Depending on soil conditions, temperature, ground covers, and other environmental factors including the Zone designation, you may need to adjust.

In hot and dryer climates, or if you choose a garden requiring minimal water, xeriscaping should be considered. Follow the Landscape Symbols in this book for plants that are drought tolerant. Heavy clay soils absorb water more slowly and hold water longer, so they will also need less watering. Sandy and porous soil drains more quickly and will require additional watering.

It is better to drench the garden, watering deeply and less often, than to water often and shallowly. Shallow watering causes roots to develop at the surface, which decreases plant stability and prevents the proper root depth needed to endure dry spells.

Keep the soil cooler by using organic mulch. This is not only good for roots and amends the soil; it will also conserve water. Around trees and shrubs, mulch should never come in contact with their bark! Spread the mulch and keep a two-finger distance from the base of shrubs — if the plant is multi-branching, measure from the outermost stems. For trees, pull mulch away from the trunk by measuring a two-fist width, about 10–12″ (25–30 cm). Mulching under trees close to the trunk is more for weed control, since most fine roots for water uptake are located nearer the drip line.

In summary: Water deeply early in the day to the appropriate depth, at an average of 1–2″ (2.5–5 cm) of water per week. Group plants with similar watering needs together. Water new plantings and seedlings more often until established — return to average watering after a couple of weeks. Water trees and larger shrubs at the drip line where finer root capillaries will absorb water more efficiently.

4
Fertilizing

To ensure the health of your plants, begin with a basic and complete fertilizer on a schedule beginning in spring, and follow the instructions on the label of the product for amounts and frequency. Below is a chart of the different types of fertilizers and amendments that you can add to your soil.

Before adding a lot of fertilizers or nutrients, have a soil analysis done, which will tell you what supplements to add. Remember, using more is *not* better when it comes to fertilizing! Too much will kill the plant.

Soil pH (level of acidity) is crucial to nutrient uptake in plants. Most plants prefer a soil pH between 6.0–7.0. If the pH is outside this range, plants cannot absorb the necessary nutrients.

Here is a little ditty that I created and use as a handout in the programs I present. Participants who are not experienced gardeners commented that they found it helpful in remembering the codes for fertilizers.

N= Nitrogen = **N**ice Leaves
P= **Ph**osphorous = **ph**lowers & **ph**ruit
K= Potassium[4] = that which you **k**eep covered, as in the roots

When you look at the analysis on the package of a fertilizer you will have a better understanding of what each number means in relation to your plants.

FERTILIZER & AMENDMENT CHART[5]				
Name	**Form**	**Type**	**Main Nutrients**	**Additional Nutrients**
Bat guano	Powder, Granule	Organic	Nitrogen, Phosphorus	Macro and micronutrients
Blood meal	Powder	Organic	Nitrogen	
Bone meal	Powder	Organic	Phosphorous	Nitrogen
Bulb food	Powder	Inorganic	Phosphorous	Nitrogen, potassium
Dolomite lime	Powder	Inorganic	Calcium	Magnesium, also raises pH
Fish emulsion	Liquid	Organic	Nitrogen	Phosphorus, potassium
Greensand	Powder Granule	Organic	Potassium	Magnesium, micronutrients
Liquid seaweed	Liquid	Organic	Potassium	Nitrogen, micronutrients, trace elements
Magnesium sulfate	Powder	Inorganic	Sulfur, magnesium	
Mushroom compost	Granule	Organic		Macro- and micronutrients, trace elements
Rock phosphate	Powder	Organic	Phosphorus	Micronutrients, calcium
Super phosphate	Powder	Inorganic	Phosphorus	Sulfur
Worm castings	Powder, Granule	Organic	Nitrogen	Calcium, micronutrients

5
Reading Plant Tags

Reading a plant tag is essential when choosing a plant for your garden. Though tags may be slightly different — seed or bedding plants versus trees and shrubs — they all contain the basic and necessary information about the plant. I encourage you to keep the plant tag in a garden journal along with a few notes on the plant's location in the garden.

Besides a picture of the plant, which can be called a glamour shot of the most perfect representation, you will find the following:

Botanical name which will include genus, species, cultivar, hybrid, or variety.

Common name which can be a bit tricky, but is usually the one most frequently used in the region of sale.

Perennial, annual, or biennial which all indicate a reproductive pattern in the herbaceous plant.

Hardiness Zone places the plant at the edge of its growing zone. Remember, hardiness is based on a plant's ability to recover after it has experienced a 50 percent kill off. If I plan to use the plant in a winter-exposed site, I often choose plants one Hardiness Zone lower than where I live, buying Zone 4 for a Zone 5 garden.

Bloom period is when the flowers begin until they've ended, and this applies not only to herbaceous plants; the bloom period is an important factor for pollination companion planting for fruiting trees.

Light requirement is designated as sun to full shade (see Evaluating Your Site: Sunlight and Shade on page 239).

Water needs will be expressed as low, average, bog garden, etc. You will group together plants with similar watering needs.

Size and **growth habit** are the spread and height, and general characteristics such as upright, sprawling, or groundcover.

Spacing is how far apart to place the plants. I reduce that distance by about a third when planting annuals late in the season, to cover bare spots.

Use and **attributes** will include information such as "good for containers," "securing hillsides," or "pollinator attractant."

Pruning or **divisional needs** are often included on premium tags and indicate when and how to perform these maintenance functions.

On the next page is an image from MasterTag of a perennial, *Helleborus*.

Harmful if eaten/skin irritant
Dañino si se come/irritante de la piel

Bloom Time / Temporado de florecimiento
Late winter to early spring
Invierno tardío a temprano en primavera

Light / Luz
Part Shade to Shade
De Sombra Parcial a Sombra

Height / Altura
20-24" (50-60cm)

Space / Espacio
28-32" (70-80cm)

Water / Riego
Allow soil to dry between thorough waterings.
Deje secar ligeramente la tierra entre un riego y otro.

Hardiness Zone: 5-9 (-20°F/-29°C)

Perennial / Perenne

6
Calculating Plants

To know how many plants you will need to purchase for your garden, based on the size given on the plant tag, you first need to figure out how many square feet there are in the garden area. If your area is closer to a square or a rectangle, measure the length and the width of your space. Multiply the two together. If your area is more of a circle, stretch a tape measure across the widest part of the circle, and then multiply that number by 3.14.

Once you know how many square feet you will be planting, and have chosen specific plants, you can figure how many plants will fit in that area. The spacing information will be on each plant's tag and tells you how far apart to plant each one. By using the chart below, you will know how many plants to buy for each square foot you've calculated.

This may seem excessive for a small garden when you are able to visually determine that you only need three or four plants. But for those of you working on larger, new, or public prayer gardens, the spacing multiplier is invaluable.

SPACING MULTIPLIER

This is a very simple procedure: Take the square feet that you calculated and multiply that by the number in the second column, based on the spacing information for the plant in the first column.

Spacing between plants	Spacing Multiplier; how many plants needed per sq. ft.
4″/10 cm	9.0
5″/13 cm	5.76
6″/15 cm	4.0
7″/18 cm	2.94
8″/20 cm	2.25
9″/23 cm	1.78
10″/25 cm	1.45
11″/28 cm	1.19
12″/30 cm	1.0
15″/38 cm	0.64
18″/46 cm	0.44
24″/61 cm	0.25

7
Planting Hardwoods or Herbaceous Plants

FROM A POT TO GARDEN

The first rule of thumb for all potted plants is that the level of soil around the plant in the garden should be the same level as the soil in the pot. Planting something too high will expose its roots to air. It will also dry out the root ball more quickly. Plant too deeply and the stem, crown (the base of a perennial plant where the stems emerge), or trunk of the plant can rot from lack of air and sunlight.

The process for transplanting starts the night before with watering. Plants take up and hold the largest percentage of water during the night. Your plants will be better able to withstand root disturbances that inhibit water intake during the day when the cells of the plant are turgid (already full of water). If you plan on planting them later in the day after the harshest sun has passed, then set the watered pots in a shaded location until then.

There is only a slight difference between planting herbaceous plants like perennials and annuals and planting hardwoods such as trees and shrubs. Research has shown that larger hardwoods need to have the same soil that was dug out reused to backfill the hole and should not have the soil altered by amendments. Adding mycorrhizae inoculants to enhance root development is fine. Mycorrhizae inoculants are good fungi that help increase beneficial microorganisms at the root level of plants. Adding the inoculants increases root growth and allows the plant to better utilize nutrients in the soil by improving uptake.

The reason for not enhancing the soil is because the root system is less likely to expand beyond the amended soil into harder, less nutrient-rich soil. This causes the roots to form a circular mass that will eventually fill the space — eliminating the necessary proportion of soil to root mass, and create a potential for girdling, causing the roots to literally strangle themselves and ultimately kill the plant. It is always best to select the right plant for the site with its existing soil condition.

These are the steps for planting either herbaceous or hardwood plants:

1. Dig the hole twice as wide and one-and-a-half times as deep as the container or root ball. Fill it with water and allow to drain.
2. For herbaceous plants only, amend the soil with compost.
3. Use enough soil to raise the bottom of the hole to the same height as the container or root ball. Remember, you want the soil level of the container or pot to be the same height as the hole when you're finished. For root-balled trees and shrubs, use a straight narrow

piece of wood that stretches fully the width of the hole to determine appropriate height.

4. Add to the bottom of the hole some of the removed soil premixed with mychorrizae inoculants to enhance root development.
5. Remove plants from their container or root ball wrap (yes, remove the burlap and wire it was shipped in), and carefully loosen their roots. If the roots are severely entangled, or root-bound, you may need to make three or four minor cuts into the sides of the root mass near the bottom in order to be able to gently pull them apart and allow new roots to develop.
6. Place the plant in the hole, spreading the roots evenly and adding a little water. Use a dilute liquid transplant fertilizer, organic or commercial, at this point of watering. Again, be sure the plant will be at the same soil level.
7. Backfill the hole with soil, making sure to avoid air pockets. Pack it slightly with your hands as you go. Don't compact soil by pressing it down really hard or stomping on it!
8. Build up the soil away from the central stem or crown. This forms a moat around the plant that will help contain the water.
9. Water thoroughly. If you have transplanted a very large tree and the root ball seemed dry, leave the hose to drip water near the trunk for three or four hours to saturate the root ball.
10. For trees, stake the trunk to prevent the tree from tipping during the first year while the root system expands. Follow the image below as a guide. Run heavy gauge wire or UV resistant rope through sections of old hose. Rest the hose against the trunk and secure each end of the wire to your stakes. Do not pull the wires too tight! You want to stabilize the tree, not choke it. Throughout the growing season check the supports and loosen as needed if the tree increases in size.
11. Mulch the area up to the ridge of the moat. After your plant is established, you can level the moat and cover this area with mulch as well. Herbaceous plants are usually established in a few weeks. Hardwoods, especially larger trees, may take several months to a year.

HOW TO STAKE A TRUNK

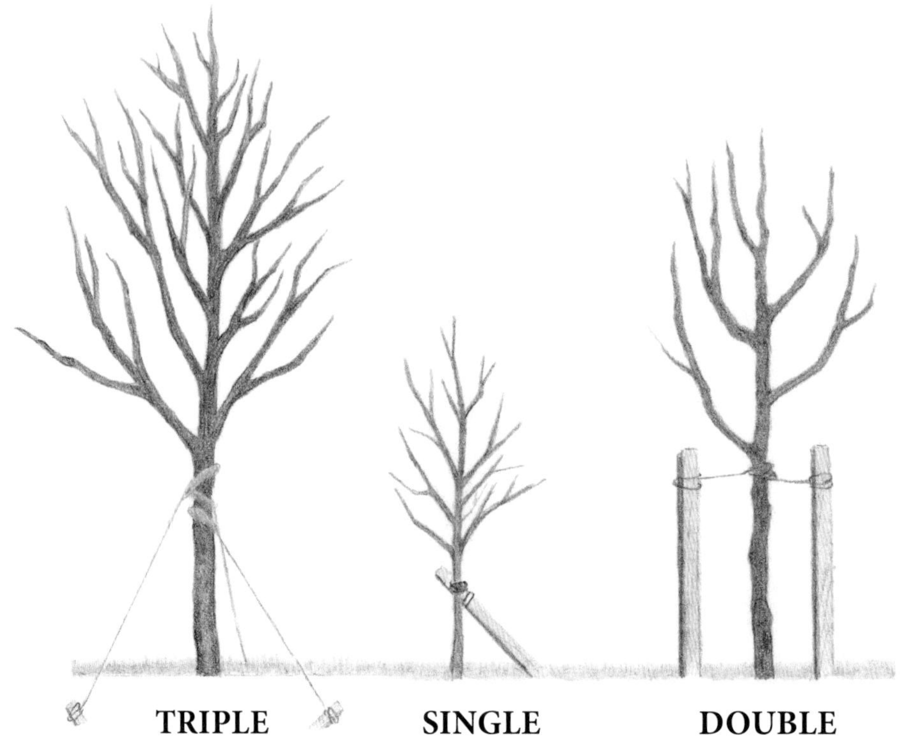

TRANSPLANTING

Transplanting is best done in the spring or, for trees and shrubs, early autumn as they enter into dormancy. If you find that you will be transplanting during the summer, anticipate the need to protect your plants from excessive sunlight, heat, and wind until they are established enough to take up the necessary water (about ten to fourteen days for herbaceous plants).

A method I use involves rigging shade from discarded white material such as pillowcases and sheets. The white fabric diffuses direct sunlight without creating excessive shade. For taller plants, drive posts into the ground so they will be about a third higher than the plant on the sides where the sun and wind come from. Attach the fabric to the posts to form a wall. For plants that are very short, gently place a single layer of white fabric on top before the hottest part of the day, and secure with handfuls of mulch or small rocks. Be sure to pull back the material in late afternoon to allow the plants to breathe during the night and early morning hours.

PLANTING UNDER TREES

First you may need to improve the soil. If you do, take care not to harm the tree's roots or trunk.

The procedure of improving the soil will take two or three years before you can make your final planting. Use containers until time lets you plant your garden around the tree.

Remember that trees are heavy feeders and big drinkers. Even with soil conditioning, your garden under their limbs will need special consideration with regard to planning and maintenance, plant selection, water, and fertilizing.

You can enrich the soil with thoroughly composted organic matter and leaves. Gather the leaves and chop them into small pieces. Combine the organic matter and leaves and spread it under the tree at no more than four inches deep per season. Be sure to stay about six to eight inches away from the trunk. Sprinkle with a little compost activator, or use finely chopped yarrow (*Achillea millefolium*) clippings, and water the area. Keep this area moist, but not waterlogged, until winter.

Mow down any weeds that may take root during the following summer, being careful not to damage any of the roots exposed on the surface. Pile on the next round of chopped leaves the following autumn.

Repeat this procedure one more time, adding enough compost to create a raised area eight to ten inches at the outer edge to less than one inch near the trunk. Again, do not build up compost around the tree trunk. The skirt at the base of the tree, that section at ground level that flares out from the vertical trunk, should be exposed to air movement. By the third or fourth summer you should have a nice, soft, friable soil, and it will be possible to plant your shade garden under the boughs of your beautiful tree.

DEADHEADING

Most gardeners like a lot of flowers all season. Searching for the few perennials that bloom all summer is one way to accomplish this. Another way to extend flowering is by deadheading.

Deadheading is the maintenance practice of removing spent flowers. By deadheading you keep the plants looking tidy, redirect the plant's energy from seed production to roots and top growth, minimize reseeding, and prolong the flowering period by several weeks for many perennials.

Extending a blooming period is different than remontant blooming, where a cultivar is designed to "remount" with blossoms a second time in the season without our intervention.

Deadheading can be a daily activity or done every couple of weeks, depending on seasonal temperatures, rainfall, and the genus and species.

Your cue will be the overall appearance of the plant as flowers decline. But don't wait too long to deadhead, unless you are saving seeds. When spent flowers become seed heads, chemical changes occur that can halt further flower production.

There are several flowering plants that produce flowers along their stems and on a spike, known as lateral blooming. To deadhead, cut just below the spent flower to just above the first set of leaves or next bud.

The other types of spike are those that flower from the bottom up on single or multi-branching spikes. The single-flowering spike should be deadheaded when about three quarters of the stem has finished blooming; cut it off at the same junction as mentioned above. In the case of multi-branching spikes with large flowers, each individual flower head and its stem can be removed to the central spike.

Deadheading flowers of one-time bloomers keeps them looking good but does not prolong the flowering. Some of the more recognizable single-season bloomers are bleeding heart (*Dicentra*), most daylilies (*Hemerocallis*), iris, and lamb's ear (*Stachys*). Daylilies and iris can be groomed daily, but you will also need to remove the spent flowering stalks.

Another method of deadheading is shearing. This is done when masses of flowers die back all at once. With one hand gather up the spent blooms, and with the other clip off the stems and part of the upper leaf cover using garden shears. This method looks messy at first but will look fine in a few days.

PINCHING BACK

The practice will increase the number of tips for plants that are terminal bloomers — meaning they only flower at the end of their branches. Pinching back is done twice — first when the plant has developed about 25 percent new growth, and again about thirty days later.

Pinch back the tips of new growth by about a third to a set of leaves (the node). After about thirty days, repeat pinching back a third of that new growth. For plants with dense branching, as is the case with *chrysanthemum*, shearing by a third is appropriate.

COLLECTING AND SAVING SEEDS

Collecting and saving seeds from one season to the next is simple and allows you to keep growing the plants you love best. Here are a few tips and techniques to guide you.[6]

1. First of all you'll need to have planted open-pollinated varieties. They'll come back true to the cultivar, whereas hybrids won't. Hybrid seeds can't be saved; the majority of seeds turn out to be infertile with a less than 20 percent germination rate, and those that do germinate rarely grow well or true to the parent plant.
2. To gather seeds of a flowering plant, first allow blooms to dry on the stem. Deadhead into a small paper bag. Write the name of the plant on the bag with a permanent marker. Gently crush the flower head with your fingers to release the seeds and discard the chaff. For vegetables, let fruit fully ripen, harvest, wash produce, then remove seeds from flesh.
3. Spread the seeds on newspaper (black ink only), a parchment-cov-

ered baking sheet, paper towel, or paper bag and let them air dry for about a week. Write seed names on the drying paper so there's no mix-up. To save space, place sheets of seeds on large wire cooling racks stacked one atop another and secured with twist ties — before laying seeds on paper to dry, cut the paper to the size of the rack.

4. You can dry vegetable seeds on unprinted paper towels, but they'll stick to the towels when dry. The benefit is that you can roll them up right in the towel to store them. When you're ready to plant, unfurl and tear off bits of the towel, a few seeds at a time, and plant seed and towel into the soil.
5. Gather dried seeds into envelopes, or you can make your own envelopes by copying the pattern I've included here. Once labeled, place seeds in the largest area, and fold over the biggest flap (with leaf pattern). Use a glue stick on edges of smaller flaps; fold over and press to seal.
6. Use clean storage containers that will be airtight. Place seed packets in plastic food storage bags, glass jars with tight-fitting lids (wide-mouth quart / 1 L canning jars work great), or glass canisters with gasket under lids.
7. To keep seeds dry, wrap 2 heaping tablespoons / 35 ml of powdered milk in four layers of plain, untreated, semi-porous tissue (such as facial tissue), fold over and tape corner. Put the powdered milk packet inside the storage container with the seed packets. Replace milk packet every six months if you keep the seeds past the next planting season. You could use a silica gel packet instead.
8. Humidity and warmth shorten a seed's shelf life, so think cool, dark, and dry, but keep seeds from freezing. The refrigerator is generally the best place to store seeds. When it's time to plant, remove seed containers from the fridge — keep them closed until the seeds warm to room temperature. Otherwise, moisture in the air will condense on the seeds.
9. Keep each year's seed harvest together by date. Most seeds last about three seasons — some only two. A glance at the dates will tell you if the seeds are past their prime for planting.
10. When planting season comes, test a small group of seeds for germination rate. Even with careful collecting and storage, a certain number of seeds will not germinate. By checking first, you'll know how many seeds to sow to get the number of plants you'll want in the garden.

God has placed within the seed all it needs for its future. We need only to gather and grow.

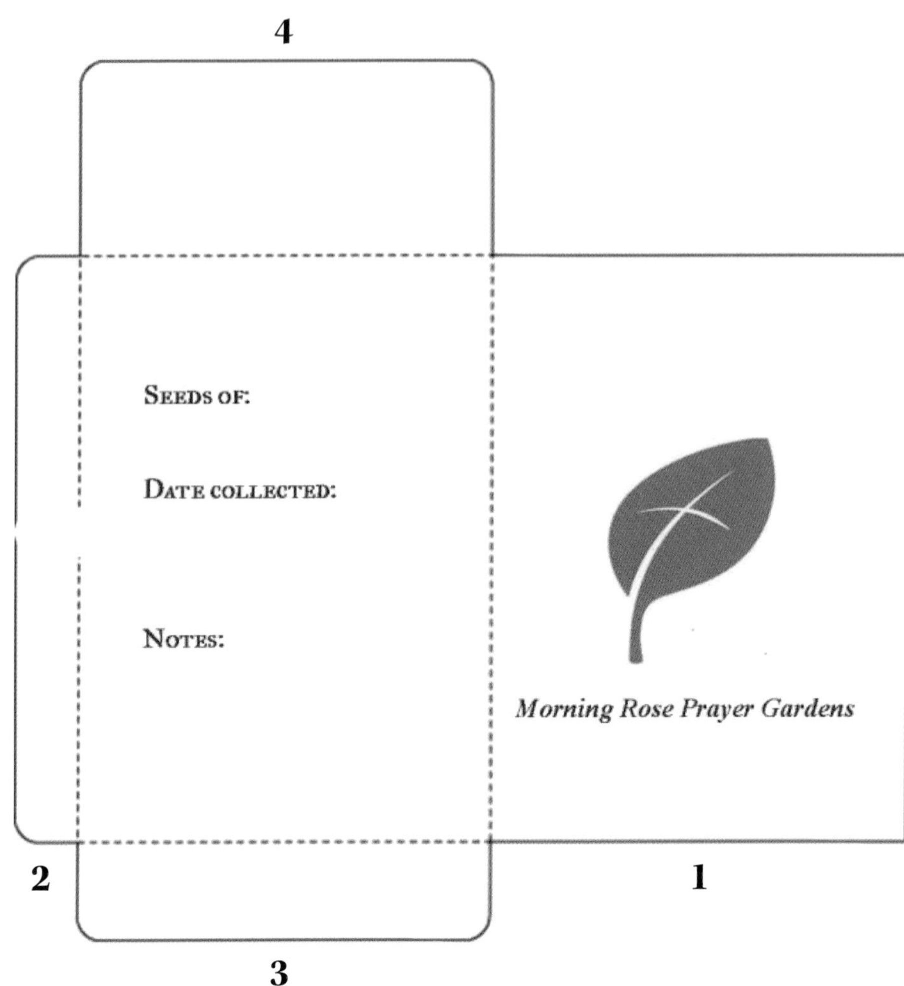
4
Seeds of:
Date collected:
Notes:
Morning Rose Prayer Gardens
2
1
3

8
Clematis Pruning

With its broad range of colors and types, and its Christian symbolism, the clematis is a wonderful vine for any prayer garden. To keep this vine healthy and flowering properly, it needs pruning. When and how to do that is specific to the type of *Clematis* species being grown.

There are three types, easily identified by bloom period.

Type 1: early spring blooming, it sets its buds on old wood. This clematis only needs to have damaged canes removed and the occasional thinning every three or four years. Prune immediately after it is done flowering.

Type 2: blooms on both old and new wood in late spring to early summer. For this group, pruning is done late winter or early spring. Look for the buds that are forming and prune just above them, about 0.5″ / 1.27 cm.

Type 3: blooms only on new wood in mid to late summer. Easiest to prune, cut this group nearly to the ground in early spring.

Supplemental Catholicism

"All we are trying to do is be one with Jesus, to reproduce his life in our own ... to let him rule and live in us."

— Blessed Charles de Foucauld

The purpose of this section is to refresh you on a few traditional observances of our Church, and to share about other Catholic themes.[1]

There are resources beyond this book that inform about the traditions of constructing Stations of the Cross or Rosary gardens. Of course, for the Stations, the sequence of events is either linear or circular within your garden Way. A Rosary garden is a bit more flexible; a garden set in five sections by color for each mystery, pater and mater prayers designated by small gazing balls or stepping stones, or choosing a single mystery as the garden's theme. Included here is information on developing a labyrinth within the Catholic tradition, as well as how to create a small shrine.

As Catholics, many of us have blessed items, such as crosses or statues, and some may have become unsightly and worn over time. You will read how to dispose of sacramentals in a way that honors them as holy objects.

There are many possible garden environments to create for spiritual growth or healing. I hope this chapter inspires you to consider which is best for you.

1
Labyrinths

Although some have co-opted labyrinths for New Age spirituality, they have been around for centuries. The word *labrys* is a term for a symmetrical double-headed ax, a tool still used in forestry. If you look at a single-circuit labyrinth of the neo-medieval period, you can see the resemblance to the ax. The cathedral-style labyrinths, such as that in Chartres Cathedral, are multi-circuits, usually having four divisions.

Early and medieval Christians took Greek and Roman customs and made them their own, and the labyrinth is no exception. During the Middle Ages, people viewed the labyrinth as a symbol of redemption. It was not then used as a form of pilgrimage as it is today.

In time the labyrinth came to be seen very differently:

> During the Crusades when Christians couldn't make visits to the Holy Land, and in the same manner that the Way of the Cross devotion developed as a sort of substitute "pilgrimage" to the Holy City, labyrinths came to be used as substitute "Chemins de Jerusalem" [road to Jerusalem]. Christians, barred from earthly Zion, would walk the labyrinths, often on their knees in penance, meditating on the Passion of Our Lord Jesus Christ.[2]

Labyrinths are designed in such a way that if you follow the path without veering off, you will reach the other end, in the center, an achievement that is seen as the symbol for heaven. What a beautiful way to meditate on the way of Christ — there is only one way in or out; it is narrow; and there is only one path toward our God or away from him. "Though direct, that path, as in following Him as 'The Way,' is a winding road, full of turns and suffering and hardship. … But always, the Heavenly Jerusalem … is in sight from any place in the labyrinth, and one knows that if one remains on that path, he will find himself where he wants to be."[3]

Not everyone is comfortable with this type of meditative prayer. Many Catholics are concerned about the paganistic or New Age associations of the labyrinth. If you desire to walk a labyrinth that is not your own creation, never walk a labyrinth that is not in a Christian holy place or building.

To pray within a labyrinth is a personal endeavor. You could meditate on the mysteries of the Rosary, Stations of the Cross, or any traditions within the Catholic Church such as the seven last words or Mary's sorrows. It is also a wonderful way to work through personal challenges by talking with Our Lord as you walk.

With that said, there are many ways to incorporate a labyrinth into your garden. There are several sources for purchasing anything from small handheld labyrinths to full pattern sheets placed on the ground to guide construction.

If you are inclined to construct a small labyrinth in your yard, choose a simple shape of the neo-medieval period that has seven or fourteen circuits or folds. Seven is always known to be a meaningful number throughout the Bible, and fourteen is the number of Stations of the Cross.

I have always liked the look and feel of a lawn labyrinth. The pattern is trenched out so that the path is the grass, set off with low-set fieldstones or narrow pavers. Setting the stones and pavers low enough allows you to easily pass a mower over the top for easier maintenance.

This arrangement is particularly easy to do at home because the outer edge of the circle can be surrounded by gardens. You can place benches at the starting point and in the center. Your labyrinth could also have a large tree in the middle with a circular bench around the trunk.

2
Creating a Religious Shrine

I've always loved the surprise of coming across a little wooden shrine alongside a path. Sometimes I have left a tiny, folded paper of prayer tucked behind its mounting frame.

Creating a shrine to display in your garden is an easy craft. You can use an outdoor, rectangular, clear-glass lantern with a door, a wooden shrine kit, or, as described below, a birdhouse.

Some shrines are decorated with found objects surrounding a small statue inside; others have an icon of a holy face, or Sacred or Immaculate Heart. Whatever you choose to place inside the shrine, cover it with an outdoor sealant. If using an icon or other prayer card image, larger images work best. The technique of affixing it inside the shrine is the same.

Here is a process to create a holy shrine using a large birdhouse.

1. Remove the front of the birdhouse. Using outdoor caulk seal the interior seams, and paint the inside white, or any other light color.
2. Put outdoor caulk at the four corners on the reverse side of a laminated or exterior varnished image and affix to the back inside wall of the birdhouse.
3. A small real or battery-operated tea light can be set inside a taller birdhouse, and adds a nice touch.
4. Locate your newly created shadow box near where you will sit to pray in your garden, mounted on a post or tree.

3
Types of Garden Environments

Spiritually dedicated gardens offer us a place where both plants and people can grow. By creating a sacred space, we allow our interior landscape — the heart of our faith — to be revealed.

A sanctuary is a place of refuge or protection and can be a building or a garden. It is a haven that we can return to that allows us to pray, to rejuvenate, and to remember. Below are some definitions of types of emotionally, physically, and spiritually dedicated gardens.

GARDEN TYPES

Therapeutic gardens are part of a rehabilitation process that can support both mental and physical healing. Participants actively encounter or work in the garden to recover what they can of a lost skill. A horticultural therapist makes use of a garden of this type to address a medical concern and incorporate a recovery regimen. Most therapeutic gardens that are part of a medical or rehabilitation facility are public spaces with restricted access.

Healing gardens are very similar to therapeutic gardens with one key difference: The visitor to such a garden is not actively working with the physical environment. Healing gardens are more of an outdoor contemplative space. They are designed to lower physical and emotional stress and assist in personal renewal. This type of garden nurtures the spirit while the body is healing. Many healing gardens are part of a medical or care facility, and are usually public spaces, but can be private gardens. Just a small note — some herbal-centered medicinal or aromatherapy gardens are sometimes called healing gardens.

Meditative or prayer gardens are often used for spiritual centering, discernment, and renewal. A garden of this nature may reflect the religion or philosophical belief system of the designer or visitors. Often sacramental elements are present in the designs of these gardens. It is not uncommon for religious elements of prayer gardens to be incorporated into healing gardens as well. Prayer gardens can be both public and private spaces.

Memorial gardens are garden spaces specifically constructed to reflect or honor an individual, group, or issue. Memorial gardens are meditative simply by their very purpose in focusing our attention on a particular issue. Again, these gardens can be both public and private spaces.

As you have probably figured out from the definitions above, garden types easily overlap. Many of the concepts and most of the procedures addressed in this book can be applied to both public and private gardens. The type of garden you intend to create is loosely defined by how you intend to use it.

When conceptualizing your space, keep in mind whether it is to be a public garden being created for an organization, or a private space for you or your family and friends. Your private garden will reflect what brings you, personally, to centering and holy peace. A public garden will be created for others, their desires, and how they will use the space. When creating a public space, you should adhere to regional and community codes. So do your homework and learn what these are before starting the installation.

4
Disposing of Sacramentals and Consecrated Materials

We as Catholics often have items blessed. Things such as rosaries, religious books, statues, and water are called sacramentals once a priest bestows a blessing upon them. As the *Catechism* explains, "Sacramentals do not confer the grace of the Holy Spirit in the way that the sacraments do, but by the Church's prayer, they prepare us to receive grace and dispose us to cooperate with it" (CCC 1670).

To prevent desecration of the material — that is, to avoid dishonoring it — a sacramental that is no longer usable or functional should be returned to the earth. The manner of disposal depends on the nature of the item. But in all cases, the item must be respectfully returned to the elements.

Contaminated holy water should be poured into a hole dug in the earth in a spot where no one would walk over it.

Combustible sacramentals such as wooden or paper icons, holy books, and palm fronds should be burned and then the ashes collected and buried, again in a spot where no one will walk over it.

Sometimes our garden statues become weatherworn and begin to crumble. These should be replaced with new ones that honor the holy persons they portray. The worn-out statue should be broken down into smaller, unrecognizable pieces. As with other earthen sacramentals, it too should be buried in a spot without foot traffic.

Objects made of metals should be melted down and used for another purpose. A Catholic jeweler can help you with this.

On June 23, the eve of St. John the Baptist, it is customary to build a bonfire and burn sacramental materials that are no longer usable. These ashes are then removed from the fire pit and buried.

5
Rosary Garden Colors

Listed here are traditional colors, and the modern interpretation for the psychological influence of colors, as related to the mysteries. See page 281 for more on modern color theory. Below you will also find a full listing of the mysteries of the Rosary.

	TRADITIONAL	MODERN
JOYFUL	White	Gold or orange
SORROWFUL	Red	Deep burgundy-red to purple
GLORIOUS	Yellow	Blue
LUMINOUS	Purple or deep burgundy	White and yellow

JOYFUL

1. Annunciation
2. Visitation
3. Nativity of Our Lord
4. Presentation in the Temple
5. Finding of the Child Jesus in the Temple

SORROWFUL

1. The Agony in the Garden
2. The Scourging at the Pillar
3. The Crowning with Thorns
4. The Carrying of the Cross
5. The Crucifixion

LUMINOUS

1. The Baptism in the Jordan
2. The Wedding Feast at Cana
3. The Proclamation of the Kingdom
4. The Transfiguration
5. The Institution of the Eucharist

GLORIOUS

1. The Resurrection
2. The Ascension
3. The Descent of the Holy Spirit
4. The Assumption of Mary into Heaven
5. The Coronation of Mary as Queen of Heaven and Earth

6
Stations of the Cross

When creating a Stations of the Cross garden at home, it can be as simple as roman numerals on blocks of wood or tags, or as formal as purchasing stations with images. You can make notes here next to each station, or in a separate journal, of the plants suitable to your Zone.

First Station: Jesus Is Condemned to Death
Second Station: Jesus Carries His Cross
Third Station: Jesus Falls the First Time
Fourth Station: Jesus Meets His Mother
Fifth Station: Simon of Cyrene Helps Jesus to Carry His Cross
Sixth Station: Veronica Wipes the Face of Jesus
Seventh Station: Jesus Falls the Second Time
Eighth Station: Jesus Meets the Women of Jerusalem
Ninth Station: Jesus Falls a Third Time
Tenth Station: Jesus Is Stripped of His Garments
Eleventh Station: Jesus Is Nailed to the Cross
Twelfth Station: Jesus Dies on the Cross
Thirteenth Station: Jesus' Body Is Taken Down from the Cross
Fourteenth Station: Jesus Is Laid in the Tomb

7
Daily and Monthly Dedications

DAILY DEVOTIONS

Sunday: Blessed Trinity, the Resurrection, Glorious Mysteries
Monday: The Holy Spirit, souls in purgatory, Joyful Mysteries
Tuesday: The angels, Sorrowful Mysteries
Wednesday: Saint Joseph, Glorious Mysteries
Thursday: The institution of the Eucharist, Luminous Mysteries
Friday: The passion of Christ, the Sacred Heart, Sorrowful Mysteries
Saturday: Mary, Queen of Angels, the Immaculate Heart of Mary, Joyful Mysteries

MONTHLY DEVOTIONS

January: The Holy Name and infancy of Jesus
February: The holy family (Historically, this month had been devoted to the passion of Christ.)
March: Saint Joseph
April: The Blessed Sacrament (Historically, this month had been devoted to the Resurrection.)
May: The Virgin Mary
June: The Sacred Heart of Jesus
July: The Precious Blood of Jesus
August: The Immaculate Heart of Mary
September: The seven sorrows of Mary (Historically, this month had been devoted to praying for religious orders.)
October: The Rosary and the holy angels
November: The deceased souls who are in purgatory
December: The Immaculate Conception and the Nativity

8
Flowers of the Shroud of Turin

The Shroud of Turin was wrapped around the body of Jesus after it was taken down from the cross. Experts in the natural sciences began examining the shroud toward the end of the nineteenth century. Botanical experts on the research team found the imprints of plants and grains of pollen that can serve as seasonal and geographic indicators.

Four plants on the shroud are significant because, as researchers Danin and Baruch report, "the assemblage … occurs in only one rather small spot on earth, this being the Judean mountains and the Judean Desert of Israel, in the vicinity of Jerusalem."[4]

These experts succeeded in identifying thirty-six species of plants on the shroud.* They discovered that almost all of the flower images remaining on the cloth, and the highest concentration of pollens, were where the head of the corpus would have been lying; plant parts and pollens were also located throughout the rest of the shroud.[5]

PLANTS FOUND ON THE SHROUD OF TURIN:[6]

Botanical Name	Common Name (English)
Anabasis aphylla	Anabasis
Acacia albida	Acacia
Artemisia herba-alba	White Wormwood
Atraphaxis spinosa	Atraphaxis
Capparis ovata	Caper
Carduus	Carduus Thistle
Cedrus libanoticus	Cedrus
Echinops glaberrimus	Echinops
Fagonia mollis	Fagonia
Gundelia tournefortii	Tumble Thistle
Haplophyllum tuberculatum	Haplophyllum

*More than thirty-six have been found on the shroud but await unequivocal species identification.

Hyoscyamus reticulatus	Henbane
Linum mucronatum	Armenian Flax
Paliurus spina-christi	Jerusalem Thorn, Garland Thorn, or Crown of Thorns
Prosopis farcta	Dwarf Mesquite, Syrian Mesquite
Reaumuria hirtella	Reaumuria
Ricinus communis	Castor Oil Plant
Scabiosa prolifera	Carmel Daisy
Scirpus	Scirpus
Secale	Rye
Suaeda	Seepweed
Tamarix	Salt Cedar

The botanists found several factors of particular interest to those studying, even doubting, the authenticity of the shroud. These are some of their findings:

- All the plants are ones that grow in Israel. Of these, twenty are known to grow in Jerusalem itself, and eight others grow in the vicinity in the Judean desert or the Dead Sea area.
- Although some of these plants are also found in Europe, fourteen of the plants grow only in the Middle East.
- Twenty-seven of the plants bloom in the springtime at the same time as the Jewish Passover.
- *Zygophyllum dumosum* has both pollen as well as an image on the shroud and grows only in Israel, Jordan and the Sinai region.
- *Gundelia tournefortii* (most frequent of the pollens found by the scientist on the shroud, and indicative of season) was the plant material found where the crown of thorns was imprinted around the head on the cloth.

An Introduction to Prayer Gardens

1
Development of Intent

"The ground invites us to soil our hands, knowing full well that we can never harness more than a single moment of its life-giving powers. Yet the gardener, in his way, knows how to fasten that moment to heaven."

— Tom Zampino, poet, 2021

This material is a small portion from one of the books I've written, *A Garden of Visible Prayer: Creating a Personal Sacred Space One Step at a Time.*

Here are several questions to help you focus and put you in the best frame of mind for planning your prayer garden. Although these questions may seem simplistic and obvious, answer them nonetheless. You will need to write your answers down to work through this process.

1. What are the reasons you visit a garden? Is it because you find it calming, you appreciate its aesthetic beauty, you like sharing time with others or God, or you want to reenergize yourself?
2. Why do you want to create a sacred space? Is it to find peace, escape from the din of daily life, or find solitude?
3. Who is the subject of this garden? Is it for you? Is it a public space? Is it in honor of someone who is deceased?
4. How will it be used? Is it to be a memorial, a retreat, a place to meditate? How will it function (i.e., as an outdoor space for public or private worship)?
5. How will you or others occupy this space? Will you sit in it most of the time? Will you walk within it? Will you use it in the morning or at gloaming? Will you welcome others into it?
6. Where will it be located? Behind the garage? Under a stand of pines? In the vacant lot next to the church?

Look at your answers. Do you see a pattern of intent or purpose? Synonymous words should be present in your answers; circle them, rewrite them, pray over them. These intentions are your foundation.

THE LOOK OF SPIRITUALITY

Here you will identify the objects that would help put you in a frame of mind for prayer. In other words, what aspects of a garden induce a sense of spirituality for you, a sense of connection with the Creator? There are obvious Catholic items, such as statues of saints or angels, icons, or Stations of the Cross that you may be considering.

Many years ago I attended a program about the history and creation of a spiritual landscape[1] and came away with many insights. One of the tools from that program that I still use is a form that I adapted and included here. You should begin with this form, too, and here is how to prepare it.

Take a sheet of paper and divide it into three columns. Write these headings across the top of the three columns:

ITEMS	ADJECTIVES	EMOTIONS

Beginning in the *Items* column, list the elements you would likely find in a garden — things such as *water, birds, rocks, yellow flowers, blue gazing ball* … just write down whatever comes to mind. At this early stage avoid listing a Catholic element in your column; focus first on what would be included around that religious item.

In the next column, *Adjectives*, write down characteristics or descriptions of each item you wrote down in the first column. On example would be *rock … solid, still, unmoving; blue gazing ball … reflective, fragile.* Take your time to really think about what words describe the items in the first column.

The last aspect to consider is what emotions are evoked by these items. This column takes a little more time, as well it should. Here you are identifying what feelings you want to nurture in your sacred space. Using the example of *rock … solid, still, unmoving* could evoke positive emotions of being *strong* and *dependable*, or negative ones of being *cold* and *hard*. These emotions will be different for each person. For example, I personally like large boulders in a garden, yet some of my clients had a real aversion to what they would describe as a hunk of stone lying around.

Remember that there is no right or wrong response in your list. No matter what you write in the last column, be honest with yourself. It will do you no good to try to please someone else with your answers. For example, a vivid orange flower might be beautiful to one person, but you really dislike that color. Or, if you are allergic to oranges, your true response would be a negative one!

Example:

ITEMS	ADJECTIVES	EMOTIONS
rock	**solid, still, unmoving**	**strong, secure**
blue gazing ball	**fragile, reflective**	**contemplation**
tall grasses	**flowing, rapid growth, movement**	**openness**

Fragrance is a topic that deserves attention. In your table, draw a horizontal line under what you have previously written or start a new set of columns. You will add a new section and it will be called *Scents.* In the *Items* column, list the scents of plants you like and ones that stir your memory, and how they are evoked. Examples are *lilies by air movement*, *lavender by touch*, *alyssum by heat/air*, and so on.

The *Adjectives* column is often more difficult to fill in with *Scents* because the other senses are not involved. Describing the characteristic of a fragrance is challenging to all but the most gifted of poets. Scent is a personal and very subjective aspect. For example, the highly fragrant lily 'Stargazer', in the Oriental group, can be described as both heavenly and dizzying in its intensity.

Because fragrances or aromas have a more powerful and direct psychological effect than the other senses, filling in the *Emotions* column is much easier. I have a sweet scent-memory of dill, which is activated by touch, of collecting the herb with my grandmother for making pickles — and so "petting" the dill in my garden evokes the emotion of being a beloved child.

Remember also to identify those scents that are not your favorites when considering a fragrance in your garden. A dear friend of mine develops severe headaches at the scent of spring hyacinths (*Hyacinthus orientalis*). Another woman finds that the scent of paper-white narcissus reminds her of her cat's litter box!

What negative associations, if any, do you have with certain fragrances? Make note of them in your table as well. Add the plant with a negative association in the *Items* column and include in the *Emotions* column a red *X*. You will want to avoid inadvertently adding those symbolic plants with distracting scents as your design progresses.

The last portion of your table is about colors. You can jump ahead to the section about Color Theory, but for now, our purpose here is to identify the emotions that certain colors evoke. Again, draw another horizontal line or start a new set of columns labeled *Colors*, and fill in each column accordingly as you work across the chart.

If you had a big box of Crayola® Crayons you may remember that the colors were labeled in very creative ways — names like Carnation Coral, Aztec Gold, and Jungle Green. They definitely inspired a response and often made me smile. Remember that in a garden, green is more than the background. It too is a color, and there are many shades of green to be considered. The subtleties of color will help you discover what inspires you.

FOCUSING YOUR INSPIRATIONS

This concluding step will help narrow your vision on what you need as well as what you want in your garden. Look closely at your tables, especially the *Emotions* column, and circle the responses that point you in the direction of your desired outcome for a prayer space.

Even though when you look at the *Emotions* column you see a lot of feelings, circle only those that best fit the intent of your space as designated in the first part of this section. If you intend to use your space to invigorate your life, words like "moving" or "delight" should be circled. Should your space be designed as a quiet retreat, then your designated words would be "calming" or "reflective."

Travel from right to left in your table, from the *Emotions* that you have circled to the associated *Items*. Here are the basic building blocks for your space. Highlight those items.

You have now completed a crucial step in defining your sacred space. You have identified your intention of how you will use this space, what emotions you want to evoke, and what objects will fulfill those needs.

The next step is to return to the beginning of this book and continue your journey of creating a sacred garden armed with this new self-knowledge. You are now equipped to choose what will surround that statue, wrought iron crucifix, little wooden icon shrine, or other sacramental object.

2
Color Theory

Color is very influential in a prayer space. In many instances, the spiritual associations of color are personal, expansive, and cultural. What matters is that the feelings evoked by a color meet the desired response for your prayer space.

First is an overview of color theory, followed by the impression and spiritual meaning the color evokes. Liturgical colors are ascribed to specific days or seasons in the Church's year — we see them most often in the priest's vestments at Mass, or the tabernacle veil. These colors can be carried into the seating area of the garden, either by container or vase arrangements, colored cloths, or candles.

The color wheel is a circular diagram in which primary and intermediate colors are arranged sequentially so that related colors are next to each other and complementary colors are opposite. Even though this is more of a design issue, it is important to address how groupings of colors affect the emotions in the garden being planned. In the color wheel, the first three colors are the primary ones from which all other colors are created.

PRIMARY COLORS

There are three: yellow, red, and blue. Undiluted primary colors evoke more intense feelings.

SECONDARY COLORS

There are three here also: orange, purple, and green. These colors tend to blend the emotions of the primary colors. An example is where yellow, which is intense and brings excitement, is combined with blue, which is reflective and detached, to create green, which tends to discourage intensity of focus and brings you to a sense of restfulness.

TERTIARY COLORS

There are six resulting from the combination of primary and secondary colors, such as blue-green, red-orange, and so on. These complete the twelve-part color wheel. Like secondary colors, tertiary colors too are a blending of feelings that the combined colors convey.

HARMONIOUS OR ANALOGOUS COLORS

These are any two to four colors that are side by side on a twelve-part color wheel, such as yellow-green, yellow, and yellow-orange. One of the three colors is usually predominating visually, such as the orange of pot marigold (*Calendula officinalis* 'Geisha Girl') and is accented by other harmonious colors such as red-orange daylilies (*Hemerocallis* spp.) and yellow-orange French marigold

(*Tagetes patula* cvs.). Harmonious color combinations often convey a sense of peace — of being in harmony.

COMPLEMENTARY COLORS

These are any two colors directly opposite each other on a color wheel, such as red and green or red-purple and yellow-green. These opposing colors create maximum contrast and stability or balance. They create a sense of excitement, give drama, and add tension.

Take a moment and recall the purpose of your sacred space. Did you want to create a sense of excitement and revitalizing energy (complementary colors) or a sense of release to find calm (harmonious colors)?

MONOCHROMATIC

This is a single color hue in a range of tints (moving toward pastels) and shades (moving toward darker tones.) A garden all in blues would be considered monochromatic. Similar to a harmonious garden, it not only uses the colors next to each other on the color wheel, it also includes lighter and darker hues.

The emotional energy of the garden will depend on the color choice. If you want to feel invigorated in your garden, use red-orange, orange, peach, vivid yellow. If you want to feel calm, use blue, gray, and silver.

It is hard to create a monochromatic garden, but when done well the results can be very elegant. Be careful though: Monochromatic gardens can often be seen as indulgent, fall into the realm of garish when using bright colors, or appear muddied if using darker ones.

POLYCHROMATIC

This includes a riot of colors that creates a festive and party-like feel to a garden. This color scheme is often used in children's gardens and child memorials.

COOL COLORS

These are at the green-blue-violet end of the spectrum and are more soothing and calming than reds and yellows. Cool colors appear to blend and seem to disappear when seen at a distance and so should be used for viewing up close.

WARM COLORS

These are at the yellow-orange-red end of the spectrum and are more invigorating and exciting than cool colors. These give an impression of warmth and stand out when looked at from a distance.

PASTELS

These are lighter tones (tints of white) and impart a softening and calming of the main color. Pastels, like most warm colors, will help draw light into deeply shaded areas.

SATURATED/VIBRANT

More saturated colors are also considered bold or vibrant and tied to stronger emotions, while unsaturated ones are softer and less striking. Strong sunlight can visually wash out softer colors. Highly saturated and intense colors, including richer greens, work best in full-sun gardens viewed during midday.

GREEN

The most abundant color in the garden. The virtue of hope is symbolized by green and represents growth, fertility, renewal, harmony, tranquility, restfulness, and balance. It is an alluring and enticing color in that it can make us pause and mentally "breathe" before we are even conscious that we need to do so.

Liturgical: Ordinary Time, from Epiphany until Lent and the time after Pentecost. Symbolizes hope, fertility, nature, bountifulness, and freedom from bondage.

BLUE

Leads us to the eternal world beyond. Blue is contemplative and cooling. It represents sky and water. It directs our perspective outward — a looking beyond. Blue is used to calm and relax and encourages openness, communication, and prayer. It is the color most often associated with the Blessed Mother.

PURPLE

Is a meditative color, a color of purpose. It combines the calmness, coolness, and expansiveness of blue with the focus and energy of red. It is a creative color we associate with inspiration.

Liturgical: Season of Advent, season of Lent. (In some areas, a blue-violet is used in Advent, and a richer, deep purple in Lent.) Can be used for requiem Masses (black can also be used for requiems). Symbolizes preparation, penitence, sorrow, and mourning.

RED

Is the warmest of all colors and symbolizes energy, intensity, and fiery passion. It is extroverted activity, vitality, strength, and prosperity. Dark burgundy reds represent mystery. It is the opposite of blue in the emotive spectrum. Because of the amount of energy in the color red, use it very sparingly in a contemplative garden.

Liturgical: Feasts of the Lord's passion (i.e., Passion Sunday, Good Friday), feasts of the martyrs, Pentecost. Symbolizes sacrifice (literally the blood of life), charity, fire, zeal, and the Holy Spirit. Used for a cardinal's non-liturgical garb. On Gaudete Sunday in Advent and Laetare Sunday in Lent, purple may be replaced with rose to symbolize rejoicing.

ORANGE

A primary characteristic of this color is to enhance curiosity and exploration. It is indicative of change, a dynamic of thoughtful change rather than the explosive nature of red, and suggests increased creativity and energy.

YELLOW

Is pure, bright, and the easiest of all colors to see. It is full of intellectual energy, symbolizing wisdom, joy, happiness, attentiveness, and illumination. It brings awareness and clarity to the mind.

WHITE

Is the color of the Holy Spirit, of truth and sanctity. It represents purity, innocence, and kindness. I read somewhere that white teaches us about relationships because, in our perceptions of colors, it tints how we see. White is in itself not a color but the complete revealed energy (manifestation) of all the colors. A very nice explanation of the completeness of the Holy Spirit! Use 10 percent white in your garden to make other colors stand out.

Liturgical: Season of Christmas, season of Easter; feasts of the Lord, Mary, the angels, and non-martyred saints; All Saints Day; nuptial masses, requiem masses. Symbolizes purity, innocence, virginity, joy, virtue, and victory. White is the color of the pope's non-liturgical dress. Silver or gold often accompany or replace white.

BLACK

Perceived as mysterious, suggesting possibility. In metaphoric or Gestalt psychology, black is the void that is full of hidden potential. Like white, it is in itself not a color, but the absorption of all colors. It conceals them. It usually does not work well in shaded areas. Use black sparingly, as an accent, and plant this color — which is actually a saturated deep purple — up close for viewing.

GRAY

The color of emptiness, a lack of movement and emotion. It conveys restfulness, maturity and security. It will stabilize other, more vibrant colors. Gray or silver-leaved plants give the eye a place to rest in the garden.

3
Create Your Own Stepping Stones

Stepping stones are a creative way to decorate your garden. Add your own personal touch using cement stains and found objects. Whenever I've offered a class, the most popular sets of stones are those featuring one of the four mysteries of the Rosary. One ambitious student, after learning the technique, made fourteen stones for a home Stations of the Cross.

Begin by gathering the items you want to embed into your stepping stone. Shells, glass cabochons, stained glass pieces or broken pottery for mosaics, small rocks, metal objects … the list is endless. The objects need to be weatherproof and sturdy enough that they will not break when stepped upon.

You can purchase garden stone kits that include forms, and concrete letter stamping sets.

If you prefer to make your own stone from scratch, find a place where you can work with little damage if you spill or soil something. If the outdoor workspace cannot be hosed off, and you do not want cement stains to remain, be sure to cover the work surface with a plastic tablecloth secured in place. Then you can begin work.

An inexpensive way is to create a form using a 12″ / 30 cm pizza box with duct tape wrapped two to three times around the perimeter of the box for added support. You can also make a wood frame, but be sure to line it with plastic up the sides so the cement will not adhere to the wood. A plastic saucer from a large plant container also works well as a starter modeling form, but be sure to line it with plastic or smear it with petroleum jelly so the cement will come out when it is dry. These homemade stepping stones will look more rustic and naturalistic than ones purchased from hobby and craft shops.

You will need a 3 gallon / 1 L bucket or basin for mixing cement; a hose or bucket of water; waterproof gloves to protect your hands from the acid in the cement; something to cover your nose and mouth, and safety glasses. Cement is caustic and always sends powder into the air when it is disturbed, so protect yourself until the cement is well mixed.

As when making a recipe in the kitchen, have all your ingredients ready before you start mixing, including the forms for the stones; objects for embedding; a trowel or screed for smoothing; and a sturdy plant tag, skewer, or similar object for writing. Adding a piece of wire hardware cloth cut slightly smaller than the size of your stone will help reinforce the cement; though this is rarely necessary, I do it as a precaution.

A 10 lb / 0.45 k pail of dry cement, vinyl-reinforced or quick-set mixes, will make about two 12 × 12" / 30 × 30 cm stones and half of another. For a single

12 × 12 / 30 × 30 cm stone, scoop just over a third of the powdered cement into your mixing bucket, and add water a little at a time; I start with one cup / 250 ml of water and add a quarter cup / 60 ml more of it at a time as needed. Mix this with your gloved hands until it is about the consistency of dropped cookie dough. If you squeeze a handful of the cement, it should hold its form when you open your palm and not squish through your fingers (too wet and soupy) or crumble when touched (too dry).

Scoop the wet cement from the mixing pail into the mold and press it into place. Smooth the surface and edges. Add the decorative objects, and be sure to push them into the cement a good inch / 2–3 cm in from the edge, deep enough so that the cement will hold them securely. Set the finished stepping stone in a dry, shaded location to cure for the next one or two days, depending on the thickness of the stone.

When they are hardened, release your stones from their molds. If you have used glass or ceramics, and you find there is a slight film of cement on them, use a non-metal scrubber to remove the excess.

Place your stepping stone in your garden path, at the edge of your flower bed, or at the base of your statue or birdbath. They also make a wonderful gift.

4
Keeping a Prayer Garden Journal

A prayer garden journal is a way to keep track of what is cultivating in your garden, plant-wise and spiritually. It is a nice way to reflect on the developments during the dormant months of inactivity, and possibly look to what to do differently the following season.

A garden journal can be as simple or as detailed as you prefer. You can create your own with a ring binder using some of the suggestions from the list below, or purchase a journaling book or app.

JOURNAL ITEMS

- Garden layout, base map
- Pictures of garden, seasonally
- Plant diary:
  - Name of plant
  - Christian symbolism
  - Type: tree, vegetable, etc.
  - Purchased as seeds, potted, etc.
  - Date purchased (receipt)
  - Date planted
  - When seeds started, when transplanted
  - Size
  - Culture needs
  - Bloom times and duration
  - Harvest times, duration, yield
  - When divided, deadheaded, pruned
- Successes and failures (what not to plant again!)
- Plants you want to add, try
- Sun and shade log
- Weather, temperatures, and rainfall
- Fertilizer used and application dates
- Soil amendments and application dates
- Pest and disease log
  - Plant affected
  - What damaged it
  - Solution
- Daily, weekly, and monthly observations and seasonal summary
- Daily or weekly prayer reflection, quotes, intercessory prayers offered, gratitudes

Prayer Garden Reference Chart

FLOWERS

Name, Common (botanical)	Jesus	Stations	Holy Spirit	Marian	Rosary	St. Joseph	Bible	Saints	Angels
Anemone, *Anemone coronaria* **'Hollandia'**	X	X					X	X	
Begonia, Angel Wing *Begonia coccinea*	X	X		X	X				X
Bleeding Heart, *Lamprocapnos spectabilis*	X	X	X	X	X				
Bluebells, *Scilla bifolia*			X	X	X			X	
Butterfly Weed, *Asclepias tuberosa*		X		X	X			X	
Calla Lily, *Zantedeschia aethiopica* **'Flamingo'**	X	X	X		X				
Canterbury Bells, *Campanula medium*		X		X				X	
Carnation, *Dianthus barbatus*	X	X		X	X			X	
Columbine, *Aquilegia × hybrida* **'Songbird Cardinal'**	X	X	X		X				
Cornflower, *Centaurea montana*	X			X	X				
Crown Imperial, *Fritillaria imperialis* **var.** *rubra-maxima*		X		X	X				
Cyclamen, *Cyclamen hederifolium*				X	X		X		

Name, Common (botanical)	**Jesus**	**Stations**	**Holy Spirit**	**Marian**	**Rosary**	**St. Joseph**	**Bible**	**Saints**	**Angels**
Delphinium, *Delphinium grandiflorum*				X			X		
English Daisy, *Bellis perennis* **'Pomponette'**		X						X	
Fritillaria, *Fritillaria meleagris*		X			X			X	
Geranium, Zonal, *Pelargonium × hortorum*				X					
Gladiolus, *Gladiolus × hortulanus*	X		X		X			X	X
Globe Amaranth, *Gomphrena globosa*	X	X			X				
Hosta, *Hosta sieboldiana* **'Frances Williams'**				X	X				
Iris, *Iris germanica* **'Lovely Senorita'**		X		X	X		X		
Jerusalem Cross, *Silene chalcedonica*	X	X	X	X	X				
Lamb's Ear, *Stachys byzantina*		X	X	X	X				
Lenten Rose, *Helleborus × hybridus* **'Grape Galaxy'**				X	X			X	
Lily of the Valley, *Convallaria majalis* **var.** *rosea*		X		X	X			X	
Lily; *Lilium longiflorum*	X			X	X	X		X	X
Love-in-a-Mist, *Nigella damascena*							X	X	

Name, Common (botanical)	Jesus	Stations	Holy Spirit	Marian	Rosary	St. Joseph	Bible	Saints	Angels
Lungwort, *Pulmonaria saccharata* **'Mrs. Moon'**		X		X	X				
Marigold, *Tagetes patula* **'Red Cherry'**		X		X	X				
Michaelmas Daisy, *Symphyotrichum novae-angliae* **'Andenken an Alma Pötschke'**								X	X
Morning Glory, *Ipomoea purpurea* **'Heavenly Blue'**	X	X		X	X				
Mum, *Chrysanthemum* **'Ruby Mound'**		X		X	X				
Narcissus, *Narcissus poeticus* **'Actaea'**	X	X	X	X	X		X	X	
Oxeye Daisy, *Leucanthemum × superbum* **'Alaska'**	X		X	X					
Peony, *Paeonia lactiflora* **'Bowl of Beauty'**			X	X	X		X		
Persian Buttercup, *Ranunculus asiaticus* **'Tecolote Orange'**				X			X		
Petunia, *Petunia × atkinsiana*		X		X	X				
Poppy, *Papaver orientale*		X			X		X		
Primrose, *Primula vulgaris*				X				X	
Resurrection Lily, *Lycoris squamigera*	X				X		X		

Name, Common (botanical)	**Jesus**	**Stations**	**Holy Spirit**	**Marian**	**Rosary**	**St. Joseph**	**Bible**	**Saints**	**Angels**
Rose Campion, *Lychnis coronaria*				X	X	X		X	
Sea Holly, *Eryngium* spp.		X			X		X		
Snowdrops, *Galanthus nivalis*		X			X				
Solomon's Seal, *Polygonatum odoratum* var. *pluriflorum* **'Variegatum'**				X			X		
Star of Bethlehem, *Ornithogalum umbellatum*			X	X		X	X		
Strawflower, *Xerochrysum bracteatum* cvs.	X	X		X	X				
Sunflower, *Helianthus annuus* **'Ring of Fire'**			X	X				X	
Tulip, *Tulipa* **'Prinses Irene Parkiet'**	X		X	X			X		
Veronica, *Veronica spicata* **'Blue Charm'**		X	X	X	X		X	X	
Violet, *Viola odorata*		X	X	X	X		X	X	
Yarrow, *Achillea millefolium* **'Paprika'**		X			X			X	

HERBS AND EDIBLES

Name, Common (botanical)	Jesus	Stations	Holy Spirit	Marian	Rosary	St. Joseph	Bible	Saints	Angels
Angelica, *Angelica archangelica*			X						X
Apple, *Malus domestica* **'Haralson'**							X	X	
Basil, *Ocimum basilicum*	X	X			X			X	X
Chamomile, German, *Matricaria recutita*	X	X	X	X	X			X	
Cucumber, *Cucumis sativus* **'Straight Eight'**				X			X		
Fig, *Ficus carica* **'Chicago Hardy'**		X	X	X			X		
Gourds, *Lagenaria siceraria*	X						X	X	X
Grapes, *Vitis labrusca* **'Eastern Concord'**	X	X			X		X	X	
Lavender, *Lavandula angustifolia* **'Hidcote'**				X					X
Lemon Tree, *Citrus limon* **'Eureka'**	X	X		X	X		X		
Parsley, *Petroselinum crispum* var. *neapolitanum*		X		X			X		
Peach, *Prunus persica* **'Reliance'**	X	X	X			X		X	
Plum, *Prunus salicina* **'Santa Rosa'**	X		X	X					

Name, Common (botanical)	Jesus	Stations	Holy Spirit	Marian	Rosary	St. Joseph	Bible	Saints	Angels
Pomegranate, *Punica granatum* **'Granada'**		X	X	X			X		
Pot (English) Marigold, *Calendula officinalis* **'Geisha Girl'**		X		X	X				
Rosemary, *Rosmarinus officinalis* **'Tuscan Blue'**		X		X	X				
Saint John's Wort, *Hypericum calycinum*					X		X	X	
Spikenard, Aralia *racemosa*				X		X	X		
Strawberry, *Fragaria × ananassa*		X	X	X					
Tansy, *Tanacetum balsamita*	X	X	X	X				X	
Thistle, *Echinops ritro*		X	X	X	X		X		
Thyme, *Thymus vulgaris*			X	X	X				

GRASSES AND MORE

Name, Common (botanical)	Jesus	Stations	Holy Spirit	Marian	Rosary	St. Joseph	Bible	Saints	Angels
Clematis, *Clematis terniflora*			X	X	X	X			
Grasses, Ornamental, *Pennisetum setaceum* **'Rubrum'**		X	X	X			X		
Ivy, *Hedera helix*			X	X	X				
Jasmine, *Jasminum sambac*			X	X	X				
Maidenhair Fern, *Adiantum capillus-veneris*		X		X			X		
Moss, *Hypnum imponens*		X	X		X			X	
Passion Flower, *Passiflora incarnate* **'Damsel's Delight'**		X		X	X				
Periwinkle, *Vinca minor*	X		X	X					
Rosary Plant, *Crassula rupestris* var. *monticola*		X		X	X				
Royal Fern, *Osmunda regalis* var. *spectabilis*								X	
Shamrock, *Oxalis regnellii* var. *triangularis*			X					X	

TREES AND SHRUBS

Name, Common (botanical)	Jesus	Stations	Holy Spirit	Marian	Rosary	St. Joseph	Bible	Saints	Angels
Almond, *Prunus amygdalus* **'Hall's Hardy'**		X	X		X		X		
Cedar, *Cedrus atlantica*							X		
Dogwood, *Cornus kousa* var. *chinensis*		X	X						
Fir, *Abies concolor*	X		X					X	
Gardenia, *Gardenia jasminoides* **'Crown Jewel'**			X	X					
Hawthorn, *Crataegus laevigata* **'Superba'**	X	X		X				X	
Holly, *Ilex × meserveae*		X							
Juniper, *Juniperus communis*		X	X	X			X		
Lilac, *Syringa vulgaris*			X		X				
Myrtle, *Myrtus communis*			X	X	X		X		
Oak, *Quercus alba*		X	X				X	X	
Oleander, *Nerium oleander* **'Hardy Pink'**						X	X		X
Poplar, *Populus × canadensis* **'Robusta'**							X	X	

Name, Common (botanical)	Jesus	Stations	Holy Spirit	Marian	Rosary	St. Joseph	Bible	Saints	Angels
Rose, *Rosa rugosa* **'Pink Robusta'**	X	X	X	X	X			X	
Sweetshrub, *Calycanthus floridus*	X		X	X					
Trinitarian Flower, *Bougainvillea*			X		X				
Witch Hazel, *Hamamelis × intermedia* **'Arnold Promise'**								X	X

Culture Reference Chart

FLOWERS

Name, Common (botanical)	Deer resistant	Part shade	Full shade	Bog garden	Drought tolerant	Clay tolerant	Black walnut tolerant
Anemone, *Anemone coronaria* **'Hollandia'**	X				X		X
Begonia, Angel Wing *Begonia coccinea*	X	X					X
Bleeding Heart, *Lamprocapnos spectabilis*	X	X	X			X	X
Bluebells, *Scilla bifolia*	X	X					X
Butterfly Weed, *Asclepias tuberosa*	X				X	X	X
Calla Lily, *Zantedeschia aethiopica* **'Flamingo'**	X	X		X			
Canterbury Bells, *Campanula medium*	X						X
Carnation, *Dianthus barbatus*	X						
Columbine, *Aquilegia × hybrida* **'Songbird Cardinal'**	X	X					
Cornflower, *Centaurea montana*					X		
Crown Imperial, *Fritillaria imperialis* var. *rubra-maxima*	X						X
Cyclamen, *Cyclamen hederifolium*	X		X		X		X

Name, Common (botanical)	Deer resistant	Part shade	Full shade	Bog garden	Drought tolerant	Clay tolerant	Black walnut tolerant
Delphinium, *Delphinium grandiflorum*	X						
English Daisy, *Bellis perennis* **'Pomponette'**	X						
Fritillaria, *Fritillaria meleagris*	X	X					X
Geranium, Zonal, *Pelargonium × hortorum*	X						
Gladiolus, *Gladiolus × hortulanus*	X						
Globe Amaranth, *Gomphrena globosa*	X				X	X	
Hosta, *Hosta sieboldiana* **'Frances Williams'**			X			X	X
Iris, *Iris germanica* **'Lovely Senorita'**	X				X		
Jerusalem Cross, *Silene chalcedonica*	X				X		
Lamb's Ear, *Stachys byzantina*	X				X		X
Lenten Rose, *Helleborus × hybridus* **'Grape Galaxy'**	X		X				X
Lily of the Valley, *Convallaria majalis* var. *rosea*	X	X	X			X	
Lily; *Lilium longiflorum*	N/A						
Love-in-a-Mist, *Nigella damascena*	X						

Name, Common (botanical)	Deer resistant	Part shade	Full shade	Bog garden	Drought tolerant	Clay tolerant	Black walnut tolerant
Lungwort, *Pulmonaria saccharata* **'Mrs. Moon'**	X		X				X
Marigold, *Tagetes patula* **'Red Cherry'**	X					X	
Michaelmas Daisy, *Symphyotrichum novae-angliae* **'Andenken an Alma Pötschke'**	X					X	X
Morning Glory, *Ipomoea purpurea* **'Heavenly Blue'**	X					X	X
Mum, *Chrysanthemum* **'Ruby Mound'**	X					X	X
Narcissus, *Narcissus poeticus* **'Actaea'**	X	X			X	X	X
Oxeye Daisy, *Leucanthemum × superbum* **'Alaska'**	X				X	X	X
Peony, *Paeonia lactiflora* **'Bowl of Beauty'**	X					X	
Persian Buttercup, *Ranunculus asiaticus* **'Tecolote Orange'**	X						X
Petunia, *Petunia × atkinsiana*						X	
Poppy, *Papaver orientale*	X					X	
Primrose, *Primula vulgaris*	X	X	X			X	X
Resurrection Lily, *Lycoris squamigera*	X						
Rose Campion, *Lychnis coronaria*	X				X		

Name, Common (botanical)	Deer resistant	Part shade	Full shade	Bog garden	Drought tolerant	Clay tolerant	Black walnut tolerant
Sea Holly, *Eryngium* spp.	X				X		
Snowdrops, *Galanthus nivalis*	X					X	X
Solomon's Seal, *Polygonatum odoratum* var. *pluriflorum* **'Variegatum'**	X		X			X	X
Star of Bethlehem, *Ornithogalum umbellatum*	X	X			X	X	
Strawflower, X*erochrysum bracteatum* cvs.	X				X		
Sunflower, *Helianthus annuus* **'Ring of Fire'**	X						X
Tulip, *Tulipa* **'Prinses Irene Parkiet'**		X				X	X
Veronica, *Veronica spicata* **'Blue Charm'**	X					X	X
Violet, *Viola odorata*		X				X	X
Yarrow, *Achillea millefolium* **'Paprika'**	X				X	X	X

HERBS AND EDIBLES

Name, Common (botanical)	Deer resistant	Part shade	Full shade	Bog garden	Drought tolerant	Clay tolerant	Black walnut tolerant
Angelica, *Angelica archangelica*	X	X		X			
Apple, *Malus domestica* **'Haralson'**	N/A						
Basil, *Ocimum basilicum*	X						
Chamomile, German, *Matricaria recutita*	X						
Cucumber, *Cucumis sativus* **'Straight Eight'**	N/A						
Fig, *Ficus carica* **'Chicago Hardy'**	N/A						
Gourds, *Lagenaria siceraria*							X
Grapes, *Vitis labrusca* **'Eastern Concord'**	N/A						
Lavender, *Lavandula angustifolia* **'Hidcote'**	X				X		
Lemon Tree, *Citrus limon* **'Eureka'**	N/A						
Parsley, *Petroselinum crispum* var. *neapolitanum*	N/A						
Peach, *Prunus persica* **'Reliance'**	N/A						
Plum, *Prunus salicina* **'Santa Rosa'**	N/A						

Name, Common (botanical)	Deer resistant	Part shade	Full shade	Bog garden	Drought tolerant	Clay tolerant	Black walnut tolerant
Pomegranate, *Punica granatum* **'Granada'**	X				X		
Pot (English) Marigold, *Calendula officinalis* **'Geisha Girl'**	X						X
Rosemary, *Rosmarinus officinalis* **'Tuscan Blue'**	X						
Saint John's Wort, *Hypericum calycinum*	X				X		X
Spikenard, *Aralia racemosa*		X			X	X	X
Strawberry, *Fragaria × ananassa*							X
Tansy, *Tanacetum balsamita*	X						
Thistle, *Echinops ritro*	X				X		
Thyme, *Thymus vulgaris*	X				X		

GRASSES AND MORE

Name, Common (botanical)	Deer resistant	Part shade	Full shade	Bog garden	Drought tolerant	Clay tolerant	Black walnut tolerant
Clematis, *Clematis terniflora*	X	X					X
Grasses, Ornamental, *Pennisetum setaceum* **'Rubrum'**	X	X				X	X
Ivy, *Hedera helix*			X		X		
Jasmine, *Jasminum sambac*	X	X					
Maidenhair Fern, *Adiantum capillus-veneris*	X	X	X				
Moss, *Hypnum imponens*		X	X				
Passion Flower, *Passiflora incarnate* **'Damsel's Delight'**		X			X		
Periwinkle, *Vinca minor*	X	X	X		X	X	X
Rosary Plant, *Crassula rupestris* var. *monticola*	X				X		
Royal Fern, *Osmunda regalis* var. *spectabilis*	X		X	X			X
Shamrock, *Oxalis regnellii* var. *triangularis*		X					X

TREES AND SHRUBS

Name, Common (botanical)	Deer resistant	Part shade	Full shade	Bog garden	Drought tolerant	Clay tolerant	Black walnut tolerant
Almond, *Prunus amygdalus* **'Hall's Hardy'**	N/A						
Cedar, *Cedrus atlantica*	X						
Dogwood, *Cornus kousa* var. *chinensis*	X	X					
Fir, *Abies concolor*	X						
Gardenia, *Gardenia jasminoides* **'Crown Jewel'**	X						
Hawthorn, *Crataegus laevigata* **'Superba'**					X		X
Holly, *Ilex × meserveae*	X	X				X	
Juniper, *Juniperus communis*	X				X		X
Lilac, *Syringa vulgaris*	X				X		
Myrtle, *Myrtus communis*	X				X		
Oak, *Quercus alba*					X		X
Oleander, *Nerium oleander* **'Hardy Pink'**	X				X		
Poplar, *Populus × canadensis* **'Robusta'**					X		

Name, Common (botanical)	Deer resistant	Part shade	Full shade	Bog garden	Drought tolerant	Clay tolerant	Black walnut tolerant
Rose, *Rosa rugosa* **'Pink Robusta'**	N/A						
Sweetshrub, *Calycanthus floridus*	X					X	
Trinitarian Flower, *Bougainvillea*					X		
Witch Hazel, *Hamamelis* × *intermedia* **'Arnold Promise'**		X					

Bibliography

Armitage, Allan M., Chris Johnson, and Asha Keys. *Armitage's Manual of Annuals, Biennials, and Half-Hardy Perennials.* Portland, OR: Timber Press, 2002.

Dressendörfer, Werner, Klaus Walter Littger, Harriet Horsfield, Petra Lamers-Schütze, Meujem Niessen, Andrew Mikolajski, Judy Boothroyd, and Basilius Besler, *Florilegium: The Book of Plants — The Complete Plates.* Cologne: Taschen, 2016.

Bloom, Adrian. *Gardening with Conifers.* Buffalo, NY: Firefly Books, 2002.

Bremness, Lesley. *The Complete Book of Herbs: A Practical Guide to Growing & Using Herbs.* New York: Viking Studio Books, 1988.

Bryan, John E., *Bulbs.* Rev. ed. Portland, OR: Timber Press, 2002.

Catechism of the Catholic Church. Liguori, MO: Liguori Publications, 1994.

Catholic Biblical Association of America. *The New American Bible: Saint Joseph Edition.* Wichita, KS: Catholic Book Publishing Co., 1970.

Craig, Claire, ed. *500 Popular Garden Plants for Australian Gardeners.* New South Wales: Random House Australia Pty. Ltd., 2000.

Creasy, Rosalinda. *The Complete Book of Edible Landscaping.* San Francisco: Sierra Club Books, 1982.

Dirr, Michael A. *Dirr's Hardy Trees and Shrubs: An Illustrated Encyclopedia.* Portland, OR: Timber Press, Inc., 1998.

———. *Manual of Woody Landscape Plants: Their Identification, Ornamental Characteristics, Culture, Propagation, and Uses.* 4th ed. Champaign, IL: Stipes Publishing Co., 1990.

Druse, Kenneth. *Planthropology: The Myths, Mysteries, and Miracles of My Garden Favorites.* New York: Clarkson Potter, 2008.

Easton, Matthew George, M.A., D.D. *Easton's Illustrated Bible Dictionary.* 3rd ed. Edinburgh: Thomas Nelson, 1897.

Ellacombe, Henry Nicholson. *The Plant-Lore and Garden-Craft of Shakespeare,* London: Edward Arnold, 1896. Digitally reprinted by HardPress Publishing, 2012.

Ellis, Barbara W. *Covering Ground: Unexpected Ideas for Landscaping with Colorful, Low-Maintenance Ground Covers.* North Adams, MA: Storey Publishing, 2007.

Ferguson, George. *Signs & Symbols in Christian Art.* London: Oxford University Press, 1961.

Fisher, Celia. *The Medieval Flower Book.* London: The British Library, 2013.

Folkard, Richard. *Plant Lore, Legends, and Lyrics: Embracing the Myths, Traditions, Superstitions, and Folk-lore of the Plant Kingdom.* London: Sampson Low, 1884.

Flowers of Mary: Or Devotions for Each Month in the Year. London: Burns and Lambert, 1862.

Forster, Thomas. *The Catholic Yearbook*. London: Keating and Brown, 1833. Digitally reprinted by BiblioLife, Wentworth Press, 2016.

Foster, Steven. "Witch Hazel *Hamamelis Virginiana* Article and Photos." Steven Foster Group, Inc. Accesssed August 4, 2019. http://www.stevenfoster.com/education/monograph/witchhazel.html.

Gabriele di Santa Maria Maddalena, OCD, *Divine Intimacy*. Translated by Discalced Carmelite Nuns of Boston. London: Baronius Press, 2013.

Gemminger, Rev. Louis. *Flowers of Mary: 1858*. 4th ed. Translated by a Benedictine sister. Baltimore: John Murphy, 1894.

Guroian, Vigen. *Inheriting Paradise: Meditations on Gardening*. Grand Rapids, MI: Wm. B. Eerdmans Publishing Co., 1999.

Impelluso, Lucia. *Gardens in Art*. Translated by Stephen Sartarelli. Los Angeles: J. Paul Getty Museum, 2005.

———. *Nature and Its Symbols*. Translated by Stephen Sartarelli. Los Angeles: J. Paul Getty Museum, 2005.

King, Eleanor Anthony. *Bible Plants for American Gardens*. New York: Macmillan, 1941.

Kowalchik, Claire, William H. Hylton, and Anna Carr, eds. *Rodale's Illustrated Encyclopedia of Herbs*. Emmaus, PA: Rodale Press, 1998.

Krymow, Vincenzina. *Mary's Flowers: Gardens, Legends, and Meditations*. Cincinnati: St. Anthony Messenger Press, 2002.

Landsberger, Sylvia. *The Medieval Garden*. New York: Thames and Hudson, 2003.

Malaguzzi, Silvia, and Brian Phillips. *Food and Feasting in Art*. Los Angeles: Getty Trust Publications, 2008.

McGee, Rose Marie Nichols and Maggie Stuckey. *McGee & Stuckey's The Bountiful Container: A Container Garden of Vegetables, Herbs, Fruits, and Edible Flowers*. New York: Workman Publishing, 2002.

Missouri Botanical Gardens. "Plant Finder." http://www.missouribotanicalgarden.org/plantfinder/plantfindersearch.aspx.

Mulholland, Clara, trans. *The Mystical Flora of St. Francis de Sales; Or the Christian Life Under the Emblem of Plants*. Dublin: M. H. Gill and Son, 1891.

Nau, Jim. *Ball Perennial Manual: Propagation and Production*. Batavia, IL: Ball Publishing, 1996.

Gençler Özkan, Ayşe Mine and Çiğdem Gençler Güray. "A Mediterranean: Myrtus communis L. (Myrtle)." In *Plants and Culture: Seeds of the Cultural Heritage of Europe*, ed. Jean-Paul Morel and Anna Maria Mercuri. Edipuglia Bari, Italy: Centro Europeo per I Beni Culturali Ravello, 2009. https://www.academia.edu/15831004/Myrtle

Realy, Obl. OSB, Margaret Rose. *A Catholic Gardener's Spiritual Almanac: Cultivating Your Faith throughout the Year*. Notre Dame: Ave Maria Press, 2015.

———. *A Garden of Visible Prayer: Creating a Personal Sacred Space One Step at a Time*. Denver: Patheos Press, 2014.

Rose, Nancy, Don Selinger and John Whitman. *Growing Shrubs and Small Trees in Cold Climates.* Chicago: NTC/Contemporary Publishing Group Inc., 2001.

Seaton, Beverly. *The Language of Flowers: A History*. Charlottesville, VA: University Press of Virginia, 1995.

Shewell-Cooper, W. E. *Plants, Flowers, and Herbs of the Bible: The Living Legacy of the Third Day of Creation*. New Canaan, CT: Keats Publishing Inc., 1988.

Singleton, Esther. *The Shakespeare Garden*. New York: The Century Co., 1922. Digitally reprinted by Forgotten Books, 2012.

Skinner, Charles M. *Myths and Legends of Flowers, Trees, Fruits, and Plants in All Ages and in All Climes.* Philadelphia: J. B. Lippincott Co., 1911.

Taylor, Gladys Tall. *Saints and Their Flowers*. London: A. R. Mowbray & Co., 1956.

Taylor, Norman. *Taylor's Guide to Gardening Techniques.* Boston: Houghton Mifflin Harcourt, 1991.

———. *Taylor's Guide to Trees*. New York: Chanticleer Press, 1988.

The New American Bible: Saint Joseph Edition. New York: Catholic Book Publishing Company, 1970.

The New Jerusalem Bible. New York: Doubleday & Company Inc., 1985.

Vickery, Roy. *ANew Dictionary of Plant Lore.* Oxford: Oxford University Press, 1995.

Notes

FOREWORD

1. "The Religious Typology: A New Way to Characterize Americans by Religion," Pew Research Center, August 29, 2018, https://www.pewforum.org/2018/08/29/the-religious-typology/.

AUTHOR'S PREFACE

1. Edna St. Vincent Millay, "Renascene," 1917.

2. *Catechism of the Catholic Church* (Ligouri, MO: Ligouri Publications, 1994), 4.

3. Pope Benedict XVI, throughout much of his writings, taught the doctrine of creation and evolution. His earlier homilies, as Cardinal Ratzinger, were compiled into the book *In the Beginning: A Catholic Understanding of the Story of Creation and the Fall.*

4. Teresa of Ávila, *The Book of My Life*: *Part Two, The Four Waters.* There are many translations of this book available.

GETTING STARTED

1. "The Doctrine of Signatures and Healing Plants," Healthy Hildegard, https://www.healthyhildegard.com/doctrine-signatures-healing-plants/.

2. Beverly Seaton, *The Language of Flowers: A History* (Charlottesville, VA: University Press of Virginia, 1995), 2.

FLOWERS

1. Celia Fisher, *The Medieval Flower Book* (London: The British Library, 2013), 19.

2. "Poppy Anemone," Mahmiyat.ps: *Your Guide to Nature in Palestine,* http://www.mahmiyat.ps/en/floraAndFauna/46.

3. Gary Lee Kraut, "The Begonia Conservatory: Without Rochefort There Would Be No Begonias," Touring in the Spirit of France Revisited, September 12, 2017, http://francerevisited.com/2017/09/begonia-conservatory-rochefort/.

4. This poem comes from a prayer card from the mid-twentieth century; author unknown.

5. Some varieties of *Scilla* spp. have more than six stamens. Nature is so diverse!

6. "Saint George," Catholic Saints Info, http://catholicsaints.info/saint-george/.

7. Gladys Tall Taylor, *Saints and Their Flowers* (London: A. R. Mowbray and Co., 1956), 58.

8. Celia Fisher, *The Golden Age of Flowers: Botanical Illustration in the Age of Discovery 1600–1800* (London: The British Library, 2011), 139.

9. Saint Paulinus was a bishop who died in 431; his feast day is June 22. Thomas Forster, *The Catholic Yearbook* (London: Keating and Brown, 1833), 174.

10. Encyclopedia Britannica, s.v. "St. George: Christian Martyr," https://www.britannica.com/biography/Saint-George.

11. Lucia Impelluso, *Nature and Its Symbols,* trans. Stephen Sartarelli (Los Angeles:

J. Paul Getty Trust, 2004), 115.

12. "*Dianthus carthusianorum*," Royal Botanic Gardens, Kew, http://www.plantsoftheworldonline.org/taxon/urn:lsid:ipni.org:names:302053-2.

13. This etymology comes from the Oxford English Dictionary. There is a misinterpretation on community-based encyclopedia sites that the botanical name comes from the Latin word for eagle, *aquila*. I trust the OED.

14. The horticultural terms *variety* and *cultivar* are often inaccurately used interchangeably. Variety is a naturally occurring variation of individual plants within a species. The distinguishing characteristics are that varieties, through seeds, have reproducible offspring; whereas cultivars are plants bred by horticulturalists, and do not produce true-to-seed.

15. "Aquilegia Express: The Columbine Flower," US Forest Service, https://www.fs.fed.us/wildflowers/beauty/columbines/flower.shtml.

16. The species named here is *Centaurea depressa*. Riklef Kandeler and Wolfram R. Ullrich, "Symbolism of Plants: Examples from European-Mediterranean Culture Presented with Biology and History of Art: SEPTEMBER: Cornflower," *Journal of Experimental Botany* 60, no. 12 (August 2009): 3297–3299, https://academic.oup.com/jxb/article/60/12/3297/523968.

17. Margaret Rose Realy, *A Catholic Gardener's Spiritual Almanac: Cultivating Your Faith Throughout the Year* (Notre Dame, IN: Ave Maria Press, 2015), 76.

18. Flower Style, "Larkspur and Delphinium: *Consolida ajacia: Delphinium elatum*," https://www.flower.style/flowers-we-love/delphinium.

19. Please note that here, colloquial designations are being used. The number of crosses, varieties, and hybridization is complex, and beyond the scope of this book. The species readily available to the home gardener is *Delphinium × cultorum*, and comes from the primary parent, *Delphinium × elatum*.

20. Katharine T. Kell, "The Folklore of the Daisy," *The Journal of American Folklore* 69, no. 271 (January–March 1956): 16, https://www.jstor.org/stable/536936.

21. Ibid., 15.

22. Ibid., 16.

23. Fisher, *The Golden Age of Flowers*, 76.

24. Richard Folkard, *Plant Lore, Legends, and Lyrics: Embracing the Myths, Traditions, Superstitions, and Folk-lore of the Plant Kingdom* (London: Sampson Low, 1884), 194. The *Immortelle* referenced here pertains to the *Gnaphalium* sp.

25. Impelluso, *Nature and Its Symbols*, 96.

26. Anca Husti and Maria Cantor, "Sacred Connection of Ornamental Flowers with Religious Symbols," *ProEnvironment Journal*, 8 (2015): 73–79, https://www.semanticscholar.org/paper/Sacred-Connection-of-Ornamental-Flowers-with-Husti-Cantor/9da8abb4e94bc1ca5cc7c75fffb077d50a923406.

27. *-lys/lis* means lily. Some historians hold that it may have been an earlier King Louis's battle.

28. "*Iris pseudacorus*," Flowers of Israel, http://www.flowersinisrael.com/Irispseudacorus_page.htm.

29. "*Iris germanica*," Missouri Botanical Garden, http://www.missouribotanicalgarden.org/PlantFinder/PlantFinderDetails.aspx?kempercode=f471.

30. An umbel is a cluster of flowers that grow on many short stems from the same point, looking like an inverted umbrella (hence the name).

31. Joshua E. Keating, "Who Are the Knights of Malta — And What Do They Want?" *Foreign Policy,* January 19, 2011, https://foreignpolicy.com/2011/01/19/who-are-the-knights-of-malta-and-what-do-they-want/.

32. David Beaulieu, "How to Grow Flower of Bristol Plant," July 26, 2021, https://www.thespruce.com/maltese-cross-plant-information-2132556.

33. Alan Bullion, "The Dragons of St. Leonard's Forest, Sussex," *The Journal of Geomancy* 2, no. 2 (January 1978): 32–33.

34. Harold N. Moldenke, "Flowers of the Madonna," EWTN, https://www.ewtn.com/catholicism/library/flowers-of-the-madonna-5669.

35. Louis Gemminger, *Flowers of Mary* (Baltimore: John Murphy, 1858), 35.

36. "*Nigella arvensis,* Love-in-a-Mist," Flowers of Israel, http://www.flowersinisrael.com/Nigellaarvensis_page.htm.

37. "I heard Allah's Apostle saying 'There is healing in Black Cumin for all diseases except death.'" Narrated Abu Huraira (d. 678), from *The Prophet's Medicine*, quoted in http://www.flowersinisrael.com/Nigellaarvensis_page.htm.

38. "Lungwort," *The Medieval Garden Enclosed*, The Metropolitan Museum of Art, April 26, 2013, https://blog.metmuseum.org/cloistersgardens/2013/04/26/lungwort/.

39. Taylor, *Saints and Their Flowers*, 29.

40. Vincenzina Krymow, *Mary's Flowers: Gardens, Legends and Meditations* (Cincinnati: St. Anthony Messenger Press, 2002), 68.

41. The word *cempasuchitl* is derived from the word *zempoalxochitl* in Nahuatl, the Aztec language, and means twenty flowers: *zempoal*, meaning twenty, and *xochitl*, flower. The number twenty is much like the number seven in Christian tradition and means many times or numerous; here it is indicative of the flower's many petals.

42. Forster, *The Catholic Yearbook*, 273.

43. Realy, *A Catholic Gardener's Spiritual Almanac,* 179–180.

44. Dr. Leonard Perry, "Legends of the Chrysanthemum," University of Vermont Extension, Department of Plant and Soil Science, https://pss.uvm.edu/ppp/articles/mumsleg.html.

45. Impelluso, *Nature and Its Symbols*, 93.

46. The word *daffydowndilly* has multiple spellings, origins, and definitions that fluctuate in different cultures and centuries. I choose not to enter the fray, so I have mentioned only the Christian association.

47. Celia Fisher in her book *The Medieval Flower Book* (London: The British Library, 2013) offers insight into the how and why of several flowers and their symbolisms in religious texts.

48. Fisher, *The Medieval Flower Book*, 47.

49. "Red Showy Flowers or the Floral Glories of Israel," Flowers in Israel, http://www

.flowersinisrael.com/RedShowyFlowers_page.htm.

50. David Yarham, "Wildflowers and Other Flowering Plants," Magog Trust, January 1995, http://www.magogtrust.org.uk/about/flowers_at_the_down/?artid=59&pageNum=0&blk=282.

51. Forster, *The Catholic Year Book*, 36.

52. Gerald Klingaman, "Plant of the Week: Rose Campion," University of Arkansas System Division of Agriculture Research and Extension, May 18, 2012, https://www.uaex.edu/yard-garden/resource-library/plant-week/rose-campion-5-18-12.aspx#.

53. Folkard, *Plant Lore, Legends, and Lyrics*, 423.

54. Ibid., 55.

55. Dr. Pierre Barbet's book, *A Doctor at Calvary* (New York: Doubleday, 1963) provides a forensic surgeon's analysis of the Shroud of Turin, and argues, somewhat graphically, that the level of suffering Jesus endured was beyond human strength alone.

56. Ibid., 329.

57. William Wordsworth, "To a Snowdrop," InternetPoem.com, https://internetpoem.com/william-wordsworth/to-a-snowdrop-poem/.

58. Michael McCarthy, "White Gold: Britain's New Love for Snowdrops," *The Independent*, February 9, 2008, https://www.independent.co.uk/environment/nature/white-gold-britains-new-love-for-snowdrops-780191.html.

59. John E. Bryan, *Bulbs*, rev. ed. (Portland, OR: Timber Press, 2002), 454.

60. Fisher, *The Golden Age of Flowers*, 136.

61. Impelluso, *Nature and Its Symbols*, 82.

62. Online Etymology Dictionary, s.v. "Veronica," https://www.etymonline.com/word/Veronica.

63. *The Annunciation* painted by John William Waterhouse, 1914, depicts violets as well as several other flowers symbolic of Mary's virtues.

64. Krymow, *Mary's Flowers*, 32.

65. Felix Grendon, "The Anglo-Saxon Charms," *The Journal of American Folk Lore* XXII, no. LXXXIV, April–June, 1909): 132, https://www.jstor.org/stable/3713414.

HERBS AND EDIBLES

1. Encyclopedia Britannica Online, s.v. "Angelica Plant," https://www.britannica.com/plant/angelica-plant.

2. Claire Kowalchik, Anna Carr, and William Hylton, eds., *Rodale's Illustrated Encyclopedia of Herbs* (Emmaus, PA: Rodale Press, 1998), 13.

3. W. E. Shewell-Cooper, *Plants, Flowers, and Herbs of the Bible: The Living Legacy of the Third Day of Creation* (New Canaan, CT: Keats Publishing Inc., 1988), 51.

4. Impelluso, *Nature and Its Symbols*, 149.

5. "Saint Abundantia of Spoleto," CatholicSaints.Info, http://catholicsaints.info/saint-abundantia-of-spoleto/.

6. "Apple Tree," National Park Service, https://www.nps.gov/shen/learn/nature/apple_tree.htm.

7. "Seven of the Most Sacred Plants in the World," BBC Radio 4, BBC, https://www.

bbc.co.uk/programmes/articles/1G40z4B6Ydmh8dSqFQSW1pQ/seven-of-the-most-sacred-plants-in-the-world.

8. Benedict XVI, *Deus Caritas Est*, Vatican.va, par. 10.

9. Esther Singleton, *The Shakespeare Garden* (New York: The Century Co., 1922), 245.

10. Missouri Botanical Gardens, "Matricaria recutita."

11. W. J. Rayment, "Excerpt Analysis, Cucumbers in the Bible," http://excerpts.indepthinfo.com/cucumbers-in-the-bible.

12. Impelluso, *Nature and Its Symbols*, 175.

13. Samer Omari et al., "Landraces of Snake Melon, an Ancient Middle East Crop Reveal Extensive Morphological and DNA Diversity for Potential Genetic Improvement," *BCM Genetics* 19, no. 34 (May 23, 2018), https://www.ncbi.nlm.nih.gov/pmc/articles/PMC5966880/.

14. "Cucumbers," Almanac, Yankee Publishing, Inc., https://www.almanac.com/plant/cucumbers.

15. Impelluso, *Nature and Its Symbols*, 182.

16. Logan Kistler et al, "Transoceanic Drift and the Domestication of African Bottle Gourds in the Americas," Proceedings of the National Academy of Sciences of the United States of America, January10, 2014, https://www.pnas.org/content/early/2014/02/06/1318678111.

17. George Ferguson, *Signs & Symbols in Christian Art* (London: Oxford University Press, 1961), 31.

18. Des Traditions Vivantes: Au Rythme des Saisons, Les Climats du vignoble de Bourgogne, https://www.climats-bourgogne.com/fr/traditions-vivantes_11.html.

19. Michela Centinari, Ph.D., and Michael Chen, "Backyard Grape Growing," PennState Extension, College of Agricultural Sciences, The Pennsylvania State University, June 16, 2005, https://extension.psu.edu/backyard-grape-growing.

20. Online Etymological Dictionary, s.v. "Lavender," https://www.etymonline.com/word/lavender#etymonline_v_6598.

21. Sharon F. "The Difference between Spikenard and Lavender Essential Oil," Sedona Aromatics, Aromatics and Blooms, LLC, May 12, 2014, https://sedonaaromatics.com/the-difference-between-spikenard-and-lavender-essential-oil/.

22. "Citrus Medica," ScienceDirect, Elsevier B.V., 2019, https:/www.sciencedirect.com/topics/agricultural-and-biological-sciences/citrus-medica.

23. Judaism 101, "Know Your Etrog," http://www.jewfaq.org/etrog.htm.

24. Impelluso, *Nature and Its Symbols*, 137.

25. "Protoselinum Crispum," ScienceDirect, Elsevier B.V., https:/www.sciencedirect.com/topics/agricultural-and-biological-sciences/petroselinum-crispum.

26. Folkard, *Plant Lore, Legends, and Lyrics*, 487.

27. Easton's Bible Dictionary, s.v. "Bitter Herbs," https://www.biblestudytools.com/encyclopedias/isbe/bitter-herbs.html.

28. Impelluso, *Nature and Its Symbols*, 168.

29. Ibid.

30. El Greco, *The Holy Family with Mary Magdalen*, c. 1590–1595, in The Cleveland Museum of Art, https://www.clevelandart.org/art/1926.247.

31. St. Francis de Sales, *The Mystical Flora of St. Francis de Sales*, trans. Clara Mulholland (Dublin: M. H. Gill and Son, 1891), 47.

32. Hong Jiang, "The Plum Blossom: A Symbol of Strength," *The Epoch Times*, June 12, 2011, https://www.theepochtimes.com/the-plum-blossom-a-symbol-of-strength_1497107.html.

33. de Sales, *The Mystical Flora of St. Francis De Sales*, 106–107.

34. Chill hours are the cumulative number of hours below a set winter temperature, between 32°–45°F / 0°–7.2°C, that many fruit and nut trees require in order to set fruiting buds in spring.

35. Arbor Day Foundation, "The Best Low-Maintenance Fruit Trees," July 11, 2018, https://arbordayblog.org/landscapedesign/the-best-low-maintenance-fruit-trees/.

36. Liz Rueven, "Prosperity Chicken for Your Rosh Hashanah Table," *The Times of Israel*, September 17, 2017, https://www.timesofisrael.com/prosperity-chicken-for-your-rosh-hashanah-table/.

37. Impelluso, *Nature and Its Symbols*, 145.

38. de Sales, *The Mystical Flora of St. Francis de Sales*, 121.

39. Krymow, *Mary's Flowers*, 124.

40. Gemminger, *Flowers of Mary*, 137.

41. Taylor, *Saints and Their Flowers*, 62.

42. Mt 26:7; Mk 14:3; Lk 7:37–38; Jn 12:3.

43. Erasmo Leiva-Merikakis (Father Simeon), "They Looked for Jesus," *Magnificat* 13, no. 1 (April 2011): 221.

44. "Strawberry Varieties," StrawberryPlants.org, https://strawberryplants.org/strawberry-varieties/.

45. Avinoam Danin et al., *Flora of the Shroud of Turin* (St. Louis: Missouri Botanical Garden Press, 1999), 18.

46. Ben Johnson, "The Thistle — National Emblem of Scotland," Historic UK, https://www.historic-uk.com/HistoryUK/HistoryofScotland/The-Thistle-National-Emblem-of-Scotland/.

47. Impelluso, *Nature and Its Symbols*, 134.

48. *Merriam-Webster*, s.v. "Thyme," https://www.merriam-webster.com/dictionary/thyme.

49. Beth Dunn, "The History Channel, A Brief History of Thyme, August 22, 2018," https://www.history.com/news/a-brief-history-of-thyme.

50. de Sales, *The Mystical Flora of St. Francis de Sales*, 49.

GRASSES AND MORE

1. M. G. Easton, "Grass," *Eastons Bible Dictionary*, 3rd ed. (Edinburgh: Thomas Nelson, 1897).

2. Gemminger, *Flowers of Mary*, 24–25.

3. Footnote to Sir 24:23, United States Conference of Catholic Bishops translation,

"Sirach," https://bible.usccb.org/bible/sirach/24.

4. Julia Cameron, *Blessings: Prayers and Declarations for a Heartfelt Life* (New York: TarcherPerigee, 1998), xii.

5. Impelluso, *Nature and Its Symbols,* 101.

6. Fisher, *The Medieval Flower Book*, 70.

7. "Folded Ferns," Answers in Genesis, September 1, 1996, https://answersingenesis.org/geology/catastrophism/folded-ferns/, originally published in *Creation* 18, no. 4 (September 1996). 50–51.

8. "*Adiantum capillus-veneris*," Missouri Botanical Garden, https://www.missouribotanicalgarden.org/PlantFinder/PlantFinderDetails.aspx?taxonid=285802.

9. John Huddlestun, "Was Moses' Name Egyptian?" Bible Odyssey, Society of Biblical Literature, https://www.bibleodyssey.org/en/people/related-articles/was-moses-name-egyptian.aspx.

10. Gemminger, *Flowers of Mary*, 29.

11. Ibid.

12. Janet Belding, "Vinca Minor Varieties," Garden Guides, Leaf Group Ltd., September 21, 2017, https://www.gardenguides.com/118603-vinca-minor-varieties.html.

13. Ronell R. Klopper, "Osmunda regalis," South African National Biodiversity Institute, February 2004, http://pza.sanbi.org/osmunda-regalis.

14. David Hugh Farmer, *Oxford Dictionary of Saints* (Oxford: Oxford University Press, 2004), 401.

15. "Osmunda regalis," Missouri Botanical Garden, https://www.missouribotanicalgarden.org/PlantFinder/PlantFinderDetails.aspx?kempercode=l320.

16. "Osmunda regalis – L," Plants for a Future, 2019, https://pfaf.org/user/Plant.aspx?LatinName=Osmunda+regalis.

17. Patricia Monaghan, *The Encyclopedia of Celtic Mythology and Folklore* (New York: Facts on File, Inc., 2004), 416.

18. Oxford Lexico, s.v. "Shamrock," 2019, https://www.lexico.com/en/definition/shamrock.

TREES AND SHRUBS

1. "Tu B'Shevat: Tikkun Olam and Rosh Hashanah for Trees," Hebrew for Christians, John J. Parsons, https://hebrew4christians.com/Holidays/Winter_Holidays/Tu_B_shevat/tu_b_shevat.html.

2. de Sales, *The Mystical Flora of St. Francis de Sales*, 77.

3. Michael A. Dirr, *Manual of Woody Landscape Plants: Their Identification, Ornamental Characteristics, Culture, Propagation, and Uses,* 4th ed. (Champaign, IL.: Stipes Publishing Co., 1990), 190.

4. Ibid., 188.

5. "Cedrus atlantica: Atlas Cedar," College of Agriculture, Health and Natural Resources, University of Connecticut, http://hort.uconn.edu/detail.php?pid=95.

6. Realy, *A Catholic Gardener's Spiritual Almanac*, 125.

7. The origin of the legend is thought to have originated in the seventeenth century

… a documented assumption, at best.

8. Online Etymology Dictionary, s.v. "Dagger (n.)" and "Dogwood (n.)," https://www.etymonline.com/word/dagger?ref=etymonline_crossreference.

9. "Cornus kousa," Missouri Botanical Garden, https://www.missouribotanicalgarden.org/PlantFinder/PlantFinderDetails.aspx?kempercode=j910.

10. *Abies* spp. are not native to England. More than likely this "fir tree" was in the *Pinus* genus.

11. Saint Boniface was born in Crediton, in what is today England. This quote is taken from their records, https://www.creditonparishchurch.org.uk/.

12. Fr. Gabriele di Santa Maria Maddalena, OCD, *Divine Intimacy,* trans. Discalced Carmelite Nuns of Boston (London: Baronius Press Ltd., 2013), 902.

13. The story has many references; one source is Douglas D. Anderson, "Glastonbury Thorn," The Hymns and Carols of Christmas, https://www.hymnsandcarolsofchristmas.com/Text/Brands/glastonbury_thorn.htm

14. Sylvia Landsberger, *The Medieval Garden* (New York: Thames and Hudson, 2003), 63–65.

15. Ayşe Mine Gençler Özkan and Çiğdem Gençler Güray, "A Mediterranean: Myrtus cummunis L. (Myrtle)," in Plants and Culture: Seeds of the Cultural Heritage of Europe, ed. Jean-Paul Morel and Anna Maria Mercuri (Edipuglia Bari, Italy: Centro Europeo per I Beni Culturali Ravello, 2009), https://www.academia.edu/15831004/Myrtle.

16. Gemminger, *Flowers of Mary,* 117.

17. Ibid., 117.

18. Easton's Bible Dictionary, s.v. "Oak."

19. Michael A. Dirr, *Dirr's Hardy Trees and Shrubs: An Illustrated Encyclopedia* (Portland, OR: Timber Press, 1998), 321.

20. Charles M. Skinner, *Myths and Legends of Flowers, Trees, Fruits, and Plants in All Ages and in All Climes* (Philadelphia: J. B. Lippincott Co., 1911), 201.

21. de Sales, *The Mystical Flora of St. Francis de Sales,* 88.

22. Impelluso, *Nature and Its Symbols,* 118.

23. *The New American Bible* (New York: Catholic Book Publishing, 1970), Hosea 6:6.

24. The word *hazel* is found in Genesis 30:37 in the King James Bible and in Webster's Bible Translation.

25. Steven Foster, "Witch Hazel Hamamelis Virginiana," Steven Foster Group, Inc., http://www.stevenfoster.com/education/monograph/witchhazel.html.

GARDENING BASICS

1. Cameron, *Blessings: Prayers and Declarations for a Heartfelt Life,* xii.

2. Much of this section is a compilation taken from my two previous books, *A Garden of Visible Prayer* and *A Catholic Gardener's Spiritual Almanac.*

3. Norman Taylor, *Taylor's Guide to Gardening Techniques* (Boston: Houghton Mifflin Harcourt, 1991), 47–48.

4. The chemical symbol for potassium, **K**, comes from *kalium,* Latin for potash, derived from the Arabic *qali*, meaning alkali. Potassium is a member of the alkali group of the periodic table.

5. This information was expanded upon from the chart in Rose Marie Nichols McGee and Maggie Stuckey, *McGee & Stuckey's The Bountiful Container: A Container Garden of Vegetables, Herbs, Fruits, and Edible Flowers* (New York: Workman Publishing, 2002), 69.

6. Realy, *A Catholic Gardener's Spiritual Almanac*, 187–189.

SUPPLEMENTAL CATHOLICISM

1. Much of this section is a compilation taken from my two previous books, *A Garden of Visible Prayer* and *A Catholic Gardener's Spiritual Almanac.*

2. "Labyrinths: Symbols of Hell & the Pilgrim's Way," Fish Eaters, https://www.fisheaters.com/labyrinths.html.

3. Ibid.

4. Danin et al., *Flora of the Shroud of Turin*, 18.

5. This material first appeared in my book *A Catholic Gardener's Spiritual Almanac*, 149–151.

6. Danin et al., *Flora of the Shroud of Turin*, 12.

AN INTRODUCTION TO PRAYER GARDENS

1. Dr. Frank Dunbar, "Designing a Spiritual Landscape" (lecture, Hidden Lake Gardens, Tipton, MI, July 9, 2005).

Index

D

E

F

G

J

K

L

M

N

O

P

Q

R

S

T

About the Author

Margaret Rose Realy is a Benedictine oblate, has a master's degree from Michigan State University in communications, has worked/volunteered in the green industry for nearly fifty years, is a Certified Greenhouse Grower, an Advanced Master Gardener, the St. Francis Retreat Center Garden Society Coordinator Emeritus, and has assisted with the Diocese of Lansing bishop's residence and retired priests' community landscapes. She has worked as a greenhouse grower and garden consultant, taught workshops at Michigan State University, and is accredited to teach Master Gardener continuing education hours. She also instructs beginner gardening classes.

Margaret has written homilies and commentaries for the Diocese of Lansing, maintained a blog for five years at Patheos.com, written a biweekly gardening column at the *Jackson Citizen Patriot* newspaper, a division of MLive, and written for *Catholic Digest*. Margaret is a monthly contributor to CatholicMom.com, posts at Aleteia.org, and writes about spirituality and gardening on her blog, *The Catholic Gardener*.

She is the author of three books: *A Garden of Visible Prayer: Creating a Personal Sacred Space One Step at a Time*, *Cultivating God's Garden through Lent*, and *A Catholic Gardener's Spiritual Almanac: Cultivating Your Faith throughout the Year*, the latter of which was released by Ave Maria Press in 2015 and was accepted as a publication for Formed.com. All three books have been granted the Catholic Writers Guild Seal of Approval.

About the Artist

Mary Sprague began crafting her skills by studying art in 1997 at Spring Arbor University in Spring Arbor, Michigan. Her love for the arts involves a wide variety of mediums, which include acrylic paint, encaustic, charcoal, pencil, marker, colored pencil, and making her own paper as art. She has also completed carvings from catalpa wood and alabaster rock. Mary has exhibited her art in the ArtPrize competition in Grand Rapids, Michigan, at the Ella Sharp Museum in Jackson, Michigan, and in numerous art shows. Since 2013, Mary has shared her skills and passion for the arts by teaching a weekly painting class for the community. Her studio is located in Jackson, Michigan.